Wingshooter's Guide to

North Dakota

Upland Birds and Waterfowl

OTHER TITLES AVAILABLE IN THIS SERIES

Wingshooter's Guide to Montana

Wingshooter's Guide to South Dakota

Wingshooter's Guide to Arizona

Wingshooter's Guide to Idaho

UPCOMING TITLES IN THIS SERIES

Wingshooter's Guide to Iowa

Wingshooter's Guide to Kansas

Wingshooter's Guide to

North Dakota

Upland Birds and Waterfowl

Chuck Johnson

Bird Descriptions by

Jason A. Smith

Wilderness Adventures Press

This book was made with an easy opening, lay flat binding.

Published by Wilderness Adventures Press
P.O. Box 627
Gallatin Gateway, MT 59730
800-925-3339

10 9 8 7 6 5 4 3 2 1

Printed in the United States of America

Library of Congress Catalog Card Number: 97-060641

ISBN 1-885106-23-8

To Annie,
A great bird dog and a good companion, who gave us many fine days of bird hunting and three beautiful German wirehaired pointer puppies.
Annie hunted pheasant; bobwhite, Gambel's, Mearns, and scaled quail; chukar and Hungarian partridge; sharp-tailed, sage, blue, ruffed, and spruce grouse; snipe; woodcock; and ducks and geese in Montana, South Dakota, North Dakota, South Carolina, Pennsylvania, Nebraska, Ohio, Tennessee, and Arizona.

HunHaven Annie Oakley
1989–1997

Table of Contents

Introduction

North Dakota is located in one of America's premier waterfowl flyways and hunting is big in the Peace Garden State. There are more Waterfowl Production Areas, National Wildlife Refuges and Ducks Unlimited projects going on in North Dakota than in any other state. The Central flyway flows through central North Dakota and millions of ducks, plus snow and Canada geese, pass through on their southern migration, via that route.

Hunting opportunities for those ducks and geese are almost unbelievable. When I visited in 1996, we watched thousands of geese feeding in the grain fields of central North Dakota. Most of the state's farmers and ranchers welcome waterfowl hunters. Snow geese are actually considered a pest because they inflict great damage on the farmer's crops each year. Current state law allows hunting on any private land that is not posted. Still, I recommend that you ask before you hunt on private land, which helps maintain solid hunter/landowner relationships.

Upland bird hunting in North Dakota is very good. There are excellent populations of pheasants and sharp-tailed grouse in the western, central and southern portions of the state. Hungarian partridge populations have dipped drastically during the past five years, but there is still some good hunting for that crafty bird in western North Dakota.

To help you enjoy North Dakota's bird hunting smorgasbord, there are some good local outfitters who offer hunting opportunities, including combination packages, for both upland birds and waterfowl. Sage grouse are available in the southwest corner of the state during a brief two-day season. Wild turkey, ruffed grouse, and woodcock round out the menu.

A typical hunting day in North Dakota starts with a morning hunt for geese in a stubble field over decoys. At midday you can hunt the CRP fields for upland birds. In the afternoon you can throw out a dozen decoys on one of the thousands of small potholes and catch the evening flight of ducks.

One of North Dakota's big attractions is its plentiful public land. The Little Missouri National Grasslands, alone, provides more than a million acres of excellent, lightly pressured upland bird hunting opportunity. There are also three Indian reservations that allow hunting, however, a hunter must secure the proper permits to hunt them legally.

Because North Dakota is primarily a farming and ranching state, you will find most residents friendly, knowledgeable and receptive to hunters.

My special thanks to the North Dakota Game and Fish Department and to Jerry Kobriger, their upland management supervisor, who drew the game distribution maps for this book. Also, we would like to thank the North Dakota Tourism Department for their help. All of the North Dakota Chambers of Commerce who responded with material for this book are also greatly appreciated.

Tips on Using this Book

- The area code for the entire state of North Dakota is 701. When no area code precedes a phone number, you can assume it is a North Dakota number. You must dial 1 + 701 for all in-state long distance calls.
- Although we have tried to be as accurate as possible, please note that this information is current only for 1997. Ownership of hotels, restaurants, etc., may change, and we cannot guarantee the quality of the services they provide.
- Always check with the Game and Fish Department for the most recent hunting regulations. Prices, season dates, and regulations can change from year to year.
- Private land is open to hunting if not posted.
- Finding a place to hunt: Plan your hunt early. Most of the towns have a list of landowners who allow hunting and also farms that take hunters and provide lodging. We suggest that you write to the towns where you intend to hunt and obtain their lists of places to stay and hunt.

Motel cost key:

$ — less than $30 per night
$$ — between $30–$50 per night
$$$ — between $50 per night & up

North Dakota Facts

68,994 square miles
Ranks 19 in size in the nation
227 miles north to south
384 miles east to west

Population: 634,935
Ranks 47th in nation in population
9.2 people per square mile
Counties: 53
Time zones: Central & Mountain

Attractions
Lake Sakakawea
International Peace Garden
Theodore Roosevelt National Park, North and South Units
Fort Union Trading Post, Medora
Badlands (contains President Roosevelt's Elkhorn Ranch)
Dakota Dinosaur Museum

Nicknames: Peace Garden State
Primary Industries: Agriculture, mining, tourism, manufacturing, oil
Capital: Bismarck
Bird: Western meadowlark
State Flower: Wild prairie rose
Tree: American elm

Major Roads and Rivers of North Dakota

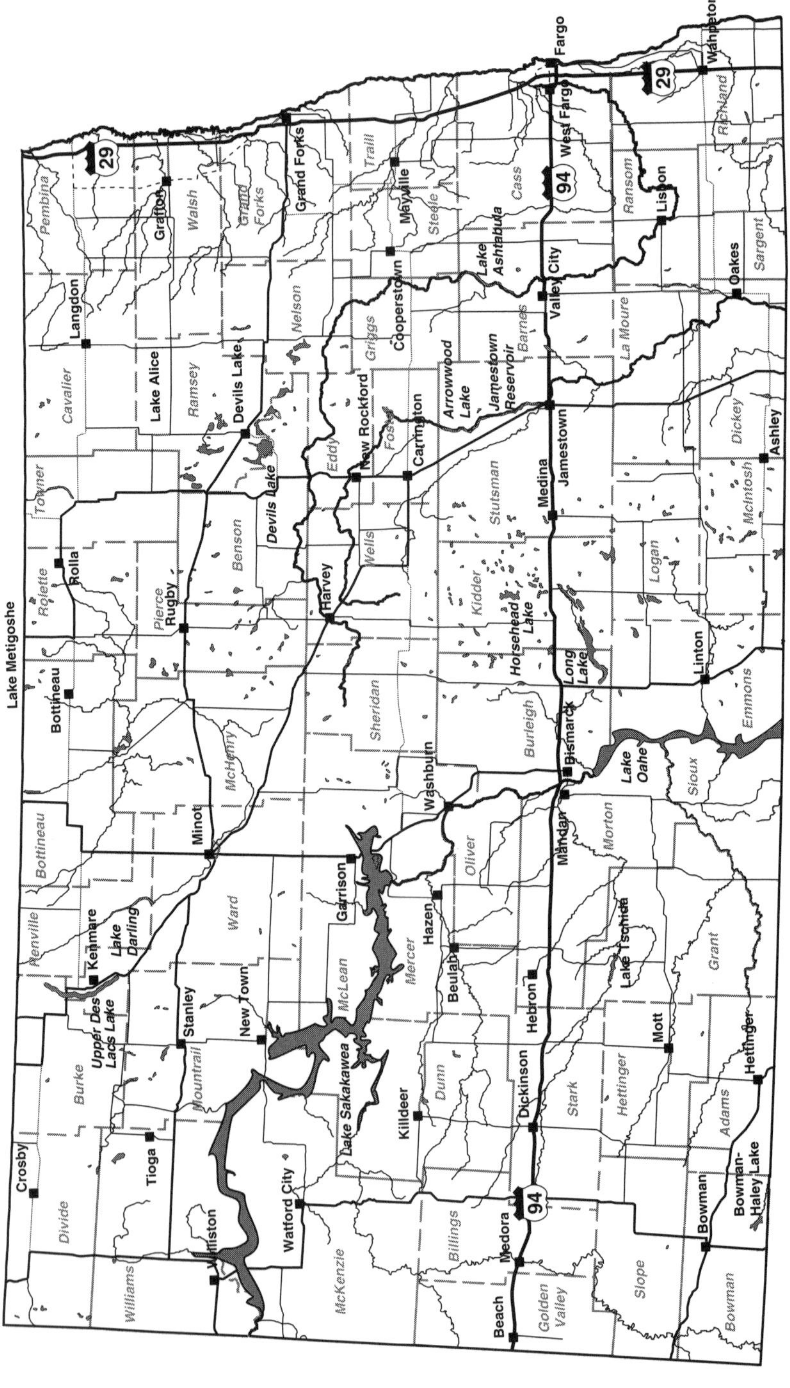

Hunting Regulations

Waterfowl Highlights

Nontoxic Shot

Nontoxic shot is required for hunting ducks, geese, tundra swans, snipe, coot and sandhill crane in North Dakota.

Duck Boats

Boats can be used to transport hunters and equipment to and from shooting grounds. Waterfowl may be hunted from a boat if the boat is beached, resting at anchor, or fastened within or tied immediately alongside a stationary blind.

Goose Regulations

Goose hunting ends at 2 p.m. each day.

Identification

One fully feathered wing, or the fully-feathered head of all waterfowl and snipe must remain attached to the bird during transportation or shipment to final place of storage.

Nonresident Hunting Zones and Licenses

Nonresident waterfowl licenses are good for either 14 consecutive days or two seven-day periods. Nonresidents must choose to hunt in one of three waterfowl zones. Hunters may choose a different zone for each seven-day period. See "Nonresident Waterfowl Zones" map and information on pages 4 and 5.

Note: Nonresidents under age 16 can buy North Dakota hunting licenses at resident prices, if their home state offers the same opportunity (except big game).

Upland Game Highlights

Identification

One leg or foot, or the fully-feathered head or wing of all pheasants, Hungarian partridge and grouse must remain attached to the bird during transportation or shipment to the final place of storage.

Transportation

Each license holder must accompany his/her own game in transportation, and may not transport game for another. However, public carriers may ship birds with receipt of proper bill of lading.

Migratory game birds (sandhill crane, mourning dove) shipped on public carriers must be in a package marked with the name and address of the person to whom the birds are being sent, and the number of each species contained in the package (same rules apply to ducks, geese and swans).

Hunter Education Requirement

Persons born after 1961 must complete a certified hunter education course and present the certificate earned to the license vendor to purchase a hunting license. Certificates from other states or Canada are valid.

Posting and Trespass

It is illegal to hunt on posted land without permission, in unharvested cereal crops and sunflowers without the owner's consent (includes alfalfa, clover, and other grasses grown for seed), or on the premises of another within 440 yards of any occupied building without the consent of the person occupying the building.

Closed or Restricted Areas

State school land is open to public access including hunting unless posted with State Land Department signs. Vehicles are not permitted on state school lands.

Possession Limits

Nonresidents may transport or ship from the state a possession limit of upland game birds.

Vehicle Use

When hunting upland game birds, it is illegal to drive vehicles off established trails.

Guns in Vehicle

North Dakota does not have a cased gun law. As such, uncased guns may be transported inside vehicles, as long as there is not a cartridge or shell in the chamber.

Steel Shot for Upland Game

Nontoxic shot is required for hunting upland bird species on all National Wildlife Refuges. Nontoxic shot is not required for upland game bird hunting on private land, state wildlife management areas or other state or federal lands.

Number of Shells in the Gun

While hunting upland birds, you cannot use a shotgun capable of holding more than three shells. This means the plug must be properly installed in all pump and semiautomatic guns.

Age Restriction

Persons under age 15 afield with firearms must be accompanied by a parent, guardian, or person authorized by the parent or guardian.

North Dakota Tentative Bird Hunting Dates

Species	Season	Daily Limit	Possession Limit
Ducks, geese, tundra swan	Opens October 4	varies season to season	
Mourning dove	September 1 to October 30	15	30
Sharp-tailed grouse	September 13 to January 4	4	12
Hungarian partridge	September 13 to January 4	3	12
Ruffed grouse	September 13 to January 4	1	1
Sage grouse	September 15 to September 17	3	12
Ring-necked pheasant	October 11 to January 4	3	12
Sandhill crane	September 7 to November 3	3	6
Snipe	September 13 to December 1	8	16
Woodcock	September 13 to November 17	5	10

1996–1997 Nonresident License Availability and Fees

License Availability

Nonresident licenses are available at all county auditors' offices in North Dakota, at many license vendors, and at Game and Fish Department headquarters in Bismarck. Nonresident license applications, for use in purchasing licenses through the mail, are available at the Department's Bismarck office:

North Dakota Department of Game and Fish
100 North Bismarck Expressway
Bismarck, ND 58501-5095
701-328-6300

Licenses can also be purchased over the phone with a credit card (see below).

Nonresident Fees

Fishing, Hunting and Furbearer Certificate $2.00

The Fishing, Hunting and Furbearer certificate is the document to which all licenses and stamps are affixed. Only one of these certificates is needed by each licensee. This does NOT allow you to shoot furbearing animals.

Small Game (good for entire season) $75.00
General Game and Habitat (good for entire season) .... $ 6.00
Waterfowl (good for 14 days, or two 7-day periods) $10.00

Nonresidents under age 16 can buy North Dakota hunting licenses at resident prices if their home state offers the same opportunity (except big game).

To hunt ducks, geese, and swans, all the above licenses are needed, plus the state waterfowl license. In addition, hunters age 16 and older need a federal waterfowl stamp.

Licensing by Phone — 1-800-406-6409

If you need a hunting or fishing license in a hurry, the North Dakota Game and Fish Department has a new service that offers residents and nonresidents the option of ordering most licenses over the phone.

For fishing, small game, waterfowl (not including federal duck stamp), sandhill crane, nongame and furbearer licenses, you can be **instantly licensed**.

All you need is your credit card (Visa, MasterCard, or Discover) and hunter safety number (if needed) for hunting licenses.

When using this service, you don't have to wait for your license to arrive to hunt or fish (exceptions are deer and antelope bow licenses). Just keep the license number the agent gives you. With this number a game warden can verify that you are licensed. Paper copies of the license and regulations will also be mailed.

North Dakota Nonresident Waterfowl Zones

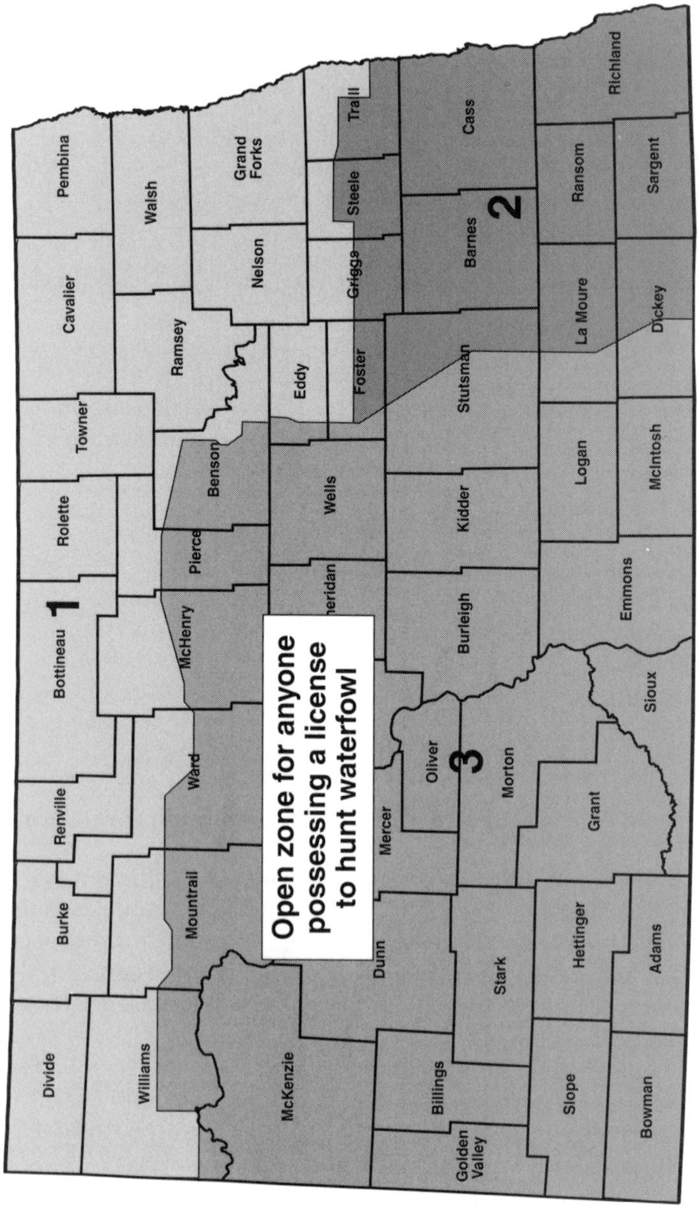

Nonresident Waterfowl Zones

When applying for waterfowl licenses, nonresidents must choose one of three zones in which to hunt for their 14-day license period. A hunter who chooses the two seven-day option may choose a different zone for each seven-day period. Following is some brief information on each zone.

Zone 1

Maximum of 9,000 nonresident licenses available. Most snow goose hunting in North Dakota takes place in Zone 1. The greatest concentrations of snow geese are in the area from Hwy 1 in the east to Hwy 8 in the west. Good duck hunting is available throughout the zone, while Canada geese are generally scattered.

Zone 2

Maximum of 4,500 nonresident licenses. Southern and western portions of Zone 2 offer the best duck hunting opportunities. Canada geese are scattered, but generally more concentrated in the southern one-fourth of the zone. Good snow goose numbers can also be found in the southern quarter, but usually not until late October or early November.

Zone 3

Unlimited number of nonresident licenses available. **Also, nonresidents who choose to hunt in Zones 1 and 2 may also hunt in Zone 3.** The eastern one-third of Zone 3 (east of Missouri River) is some of the state's best duck hunting country. This area is also a primary staging area for lesser Canada geese, with some larger Canada geese mixed in. The extreme northeastern part of Zone 3 generally attracts fair numbers of snow geese. Ducks are scattered throughout the southwestern portion of Zone 3, with some isolated concentrations. The best hunting for large Canada geese is along the Missouri River system.

Guides, Outfitters, and Lodges

North Dakota has plenty of guides, outfitters, and lodges that cater to bird hunters. They offer a variety of services ranging from deluxe facilities to individual guides who offer only guide services. We have listed many of those guides and the services that they offer, based on the information that we received from them. There are many more guides than are listed here, but we only listed people who responded to our questionnaire. Call and talk to the guide service that interests you to find out exactly what services they offer. Also, ask for references. The type of hunt offered varies with each guide. Many guides are looking for large parties and hunt with lots of people, while some guides take only one group at a time. By checking a guide out first, you can determine if the hunts offered fit your plans.

For a complete listing of guides you can write to:

The North Dakota Game and Fish Department
100 North Bismarck Expressway
Bismarck, ND 58501
701-328-6300

Ring-necked Pheasant

Phasianus colchicus

FIELD FACTS

Local Names

Ringneck, rooster

Size

Males have long tail feathers, which can account for two-thirds of the overall length of a pheasant. Excluding the tail, pheasants are a little over a foot long and weigh a bit more than two pounds.

Identification in Flight

Male pheasants cackle when flushed, usually running well ahead of hunters and taking flight when cover has run out. The long barred tail feathers are very obvious, as is the dark bronze body, green head, and red wattles (cheeks). Females can be mistaken for sharp-tailed grouse, especially early in the season, and the hens—not legal game in North Dakota—very often flush underfoot. They may utter faint cackles, but they have shorter tails and a dull brown appearance.

Appearance

Ring-necked pheasants are considered by many the King of the Uplands, and they are perhaps the most sought after—and harvested—upland gamebird in the country. Male pheasants (roosters) are brightly colored with long, flowing tails that can't be missed in flight. The body is bronze with an array of blue, greens, and yellows on the back. The head is an iridescent green with a red wattle surrounding the eye and cheek; a stark white ring around the neck gives the bird its name. Mature males have small ear tufts and a silver cap on top of their heads.

Hen pheasants are a mottled light tan color, and can often be mistaken for sharp-tailed grouse, though hen pheasants are larger and do not show the amount of white that sharptails do. Hens will also have long tails, but not as long as the roosters. It is important to know that only roosters are legal for harvesting.

On the Wing

Roosters are unmistakable in flight. The loud cackle and thunderous wingbeats from the cover are what many hunters live for. The long tail adds to the bird's perceived size, and the white ring around the neck contrasts with the darker body. Hen pheasants will flush closer, and they may give faint cackles upon flushing but will usually stay quiet.

Ring-necked Pheasant Distribution

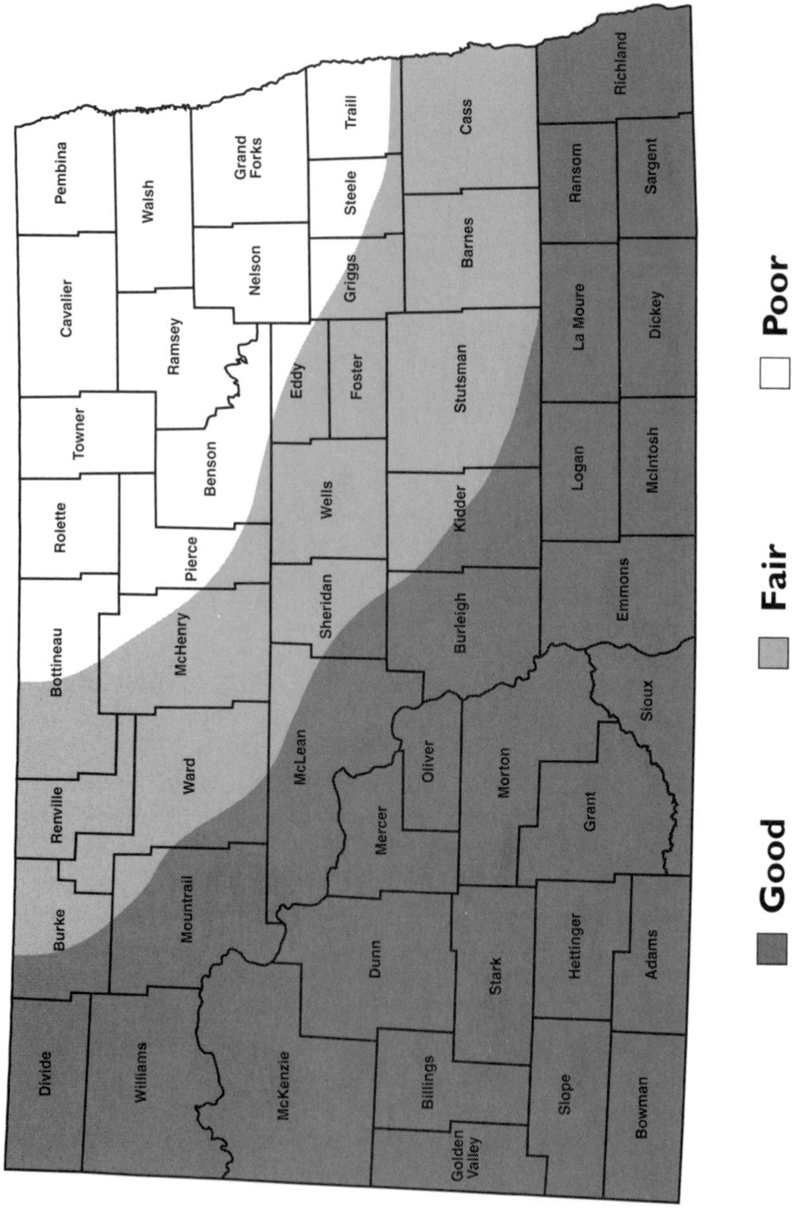

Cock pheasant. (Photo: Craig Bihrle)

Their flight pattern is the same as other prairie birds—one of rapid wingbeats and glides, and they achieve their fastest speeds after flying for a short while. A passing pheasant that has been in the air for several hundred yards may be moving faster than 45 miles per hour. Roosters are notorious for running through cover, preferring to escape on foot instead of in the air. But once cornered—by human or a good dog —or at the end of cover, the bird takes flight.

Daily Habits and Food

Pheasants usually roost in fields close to feeding areas. A good tactic is to hunt early in the morning in thick hayfields before they move into cornfields to eat and then move to water if it's available. During late morning and early afternoon, they will move back into the grass fields to loaf and dust. Then they head back again for more food.

Corn is the food most commonly associated with pheasants, but they will also eat other waste grains, such as barley, wheat, and oats. Both juveniles and adults consume a large variety of insects.

During harsh winters that can pound the Midwest, pheasants congregate in areas where food is easiest to access. In extremely harsh times, when snow and ice cover up their food sources, pheasant populations may nosedive. But these hardy birds will usually bounce back within a couple years of a harsh winter.

Seasonal Patterns

As mentioned before, winter can take a devastating toll on the pheasant population. Pheasants will use snow for roosting, and if storms are especially strong, there could be considerable die-off. This can be either from the snow and ice locking them in their snow roosts, the snow covering their food, or harsh conditions pushing the birds to thinner cover where they can be preyed upon.

In March, a rooster will begin to strut before a female, his wattle greatly engorged, ear tufts raised, and tail fan spread and exposed. After copulation, a nest will be constructed in the grass or weeds, and 10 to 12 eggs are laid. Incubation is a little over three weeks, and the chicks can make short flights after one week.

When fall rolls around, brood dispersal scatters the pheasants, and many birds may join into closely associated flocks. During these times, a hunter may flush a significant number of birds in a small area, especially late in the season when the weather has flattened most of the other available cover.

Preferred Habitat and Cover

No other bird is so closely tied to the cultivation of this country's land as the ring-necked pheasant. Though the mechanization of farming that led to "clean" farms threatened to decimate the population, legislation that brought the 1985 and 1996 Farm Bill and Conservation Reserve Program (CRP) have given the pheasant population in North Dakota a tremendous boost. Today, its numbers are at highs very near those of the 1950s.

The ring-necked pheasant adapted well after its introduction from Asia in the late 1800s. It is a bird of agricultural land; CRP fields of switchgrass and hay; and wooded creek bottoms, draws, and sloughs. Where these grass fields and draws border grain and cornfields, pheasants will most likely be found.

Pheasants find cover during winter in draws and sloughs because more often than not, these are the last places to fill in with snow. Shelterbelts will also provide some winter cover, but those areas are usually thin and fill with snow fairly fast, especially if there is a significant amount of wind. Wherever there is food available during winter, large flocks of pheasants will be seen.

Chris Smith and two beautiful cock pheasants. (Photo: Bob Butz)

Hunting Methods

Pheasant hunting is probably one of the oldest upland hunting traditions in the country, and many hunters were raised pursuing these birds.

There are several ways to hunt pheasants, all equally enjoyable. One is to push through fields, plowing through the most likely looking cover. Hunting the roosting fields near feeding areas early in the morning will prove extremely efficient, and limits can be had in a matter of minutes.

Hunting the open, cultivated cropland for pheasants. (Photo: Blanche Johnson)

Once in standing corn, pheasants can be hard to put up for a close shot, so another method called *blocking and driving* can be effective. More hunters are needed to hunt pheasants in this manner, but it can be extremely effective, especially in the cornfields. Three or four hunters (drivers) push through the corn while the rest of the party (blockers) stands ready at the other end. Caught in this pincer action, the birds will most often run to the end of the corn, and once out of cover—or they see the blockers—will take to the air. Or, if the drivers flush birds while walking through the corn, the blockers may get fast pass shots at the incoming birds. Blocking and driving can also be done in CRP areas, river bottoms, willow- and brush-filled draws.

Once in the air, a rooster pheasant is not a difficult target, but once they get going, these birds can really move! It takes a stout blow to bring one down, though, so be very conscious of not only hitting the bird but hitting him near the head and neck. A crippled pheasant for the dogless hunter almost always ends with a light game bag.

Hunting with Dogs

To deal with cripples, pheasant hunters are almost never seen without a dog. Flushing dogs—Labrador retrievers and springer spaniels—are preferred simply because of their drive to pursue and retrieve downed birds. Because the pheasant is one of the cagiest gamebirds when it comes to running from danger, a hard-working flushing dog will stay hot on its trail.

But pointing dogs also shine on pheasants, especially those dogs that can stick with a running bird and are trained to retrieve. Some of the best pheasant hunts, though, comes with a combination of flushing and pointing dogs, especially if the team has a history of working together. One points, the other goes in and flushes.

Dogs also make the work of pushing through the thick creek bottoms a lot easier, and this may be another case for the flushing dog. The hunter can simply skirt the edges while the dog pushes through. The hunter has to be prepared to take off running after a flushing dog when it hits a scent trail. The pheasant will almost always try running away before flying, so you'll have to keep up if you want a shot when the bird finally decides to flush.

Table Preparations

Pheasants are among the most succulent of all wild game. The white meat of the pheasant's breast and the darker meat of the thighs are a treat to be savored. Pheasants can be tough, though, so any crock pot recipe for turkey or chicken breasts will work for pheasants. If baking, you can stuff the body cavity with onions and coat the meat with salt and pepper and poultry seasoning, or fillet the beast away from the bone, marinade in Italian dressing, and grill topped with pineapple rings. Any recipe you use for chicken will also work for pheasant. You may wish to hang the birds for an evening, but when the birds are warm, skinning them is much easier.

Gun and Shot Suggestions

- **Gauge:** 12 or 16
- **Choke:** Improved and modified for doubles, Modified for single barrels.
- **Shot:** A strong field load of 1⅛ to 1¼ oz. of No. 6 or No. 5 will be your best choice for pheasants. Late in the season, No. 4 is a good choice for long shots.

Sharp-tailed Grouse Distribution

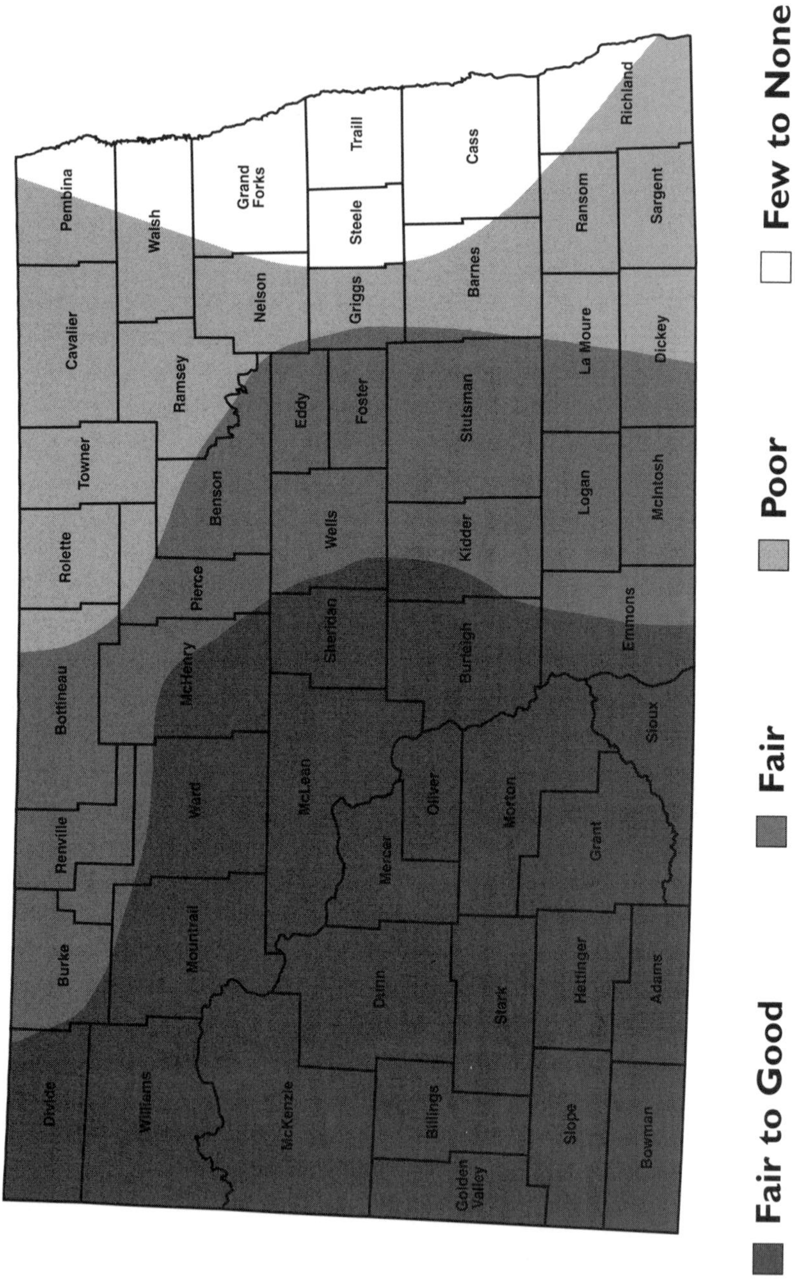

Sharp-tailed Grouse

Tympanuchus phasianellus

FIELD FACTS

Local Names

Blackfoot, pin-tailed grouse, prairie grouse, sharptail

Size

Sharp-tailed grouse closely resemble their woodland cousins the ruffed grouse in size, being close to 17 inches long and around two pounds.

Identification in Flight

The repeated *kuk-kuk-kuk-kuk* call of a flushing sharp-tailed grouse may get confused with a hen pheasant, but sharptails show large amounts of white from their wings, an obvious eye-catcher. In profile, the pointed tail is evident, and their flight is a series of rapid wingbeats and glides.

Appearance

The two long central tail feathers gives this bird its name, and during the gaudy courtship dance of male sharptails, the sharp tail is very evident. Like most prairie birds, sharptails display a pattern of browns, tans, whites, and blacks, which blend them in well with their grassland habitat; and because they are residents throughout the North Dakota winter, they have natural snowshoes like the ruffed grouse. The sexes are almost identical—they can be distinguished by the markings on the tail and crown feathers—in both plumage and size. Though sometimes they can be confused with prairie chicken or hen pheasants, sharptails have much more white on the wings and belly than either the prairie chicken or pheasant, and as opposed to the horizontal brown barring pattern on the chicken, the sharptail has a pattern of brown Vs on the breast.

The wings have white dots along the primary feathers, and on males, even in the fall, a yellow eye comb and purple air sac along the neck will be noticeable is you brush back the feathers. During the courtship dance, the air sac is inflated and very prominent, and the yellow eye comb becomes engorged.

On the Wing

Sharp-tailed grouse will covey up throughout the hunting season, but unlike gray partridge or quail, the covey will flush in staggered ones and twos with a rush of wings and loud *kuk-kuk-kuk-kuk* calls. Early in the season, sharptails—especially if they have not coveyed and you find them alone—can be confused with hen pheasants. But the shorter tail, the call emitted when flushed, and the smaller size will identify them. Flight is composed of a series of rapid wingbeats and glides, and sharptails have been known to fly up to a couple miles, reaching speeds around 30 miles per hour. They can also fly as fast into the wind as they can in calm conditions, an adaptation to prairie wind conditions.

Daily Habits and Food

The daily pattern of sharptails is comparable to that of the gray partridge, which is usually found in the same type of habitat. Sharp-tailed grouse will move to feeding grounds early in the morning, and then to loafing spots for most of the late morning and afternoon. They will feed again before roosting.

Young sharptails will consume insects for about the first three weeks of life, and adults will eat grasshoppers, crickets, and other insects of the prairie. Preferred vegetation consists largely of rose hips and grassland berries (blueberry, snowberry), as well as the leaves of most prairie grasses and legumes. Winter food is composed almost entirely of the buds of aspen and birch trees (although there are few aspen and birch in North Dakota), but will include any prairie grasses that are still accessible through the snow. They feed a great deal in stubble fields, and also like Russian olive trees, and buffaloberry patches.

Seasonal Patterns

The courtship dance of the male sharp-tailed grouse occupies the bird from late March until mid-June. After mating, the females will move within one mile away from the lek—the arena where up to 20 male sharptails will dance and fight—to nest and raise the brood. The nest will have some overhead cover—either a tree branch, log, or thick brush—and the female will lay nine to 13 eggs that hatch after a three and a half week incubation period. Sharptails will begin to make their first flutter-flights close to two weeks after hatching.

In the summer after dispersal and throughout the fall, sharptails form covey groups, and these vary greatly in size. There will be a short display period again in the fall, and the birds will stick together throughout the hunting season. During winter, sharptails will snow roost in burrows or in trees, where they can easily feed on buds.

Preferred Habitat and Cover

Sharp-tailed grouse are birds of the grasslands and prairie, and have made wide use of CRP fields in these areas. However, when hayfields and grasslands become too thick, they will move to another spot, sometimes a great distance away. Periodic burning of the grassland ecosystem will thin the cover and keep birds in the area.

During fall, gray partridge and sharptails can usually be hunted hand-in-hand—be sure to always check brushy draws as well as the grassy sides of exposed knolls and ridges in the open country for a covey of sharptails. There are times when gray partridge and sharptails will flush together, their coveys in proximity to each other.

Open, exposed ground is preferred for the dancing ground location, so the advertising display will be highly visible to females close by. Nesting cover is nothing

Sharp-tailed grouse. (Photo: Craig Bihrle)

more than a scratched-out depression in the grassland setting, usually under a short tree or near the edge of a cluster of trees either in a draw or creek bottom.

Hunting Methods

The nice thing about hunting sharptails is that when the covey begins to flush—even if they're out of range—you've still got a chance. Some birds will hang back—staggered flushes—allowing you to move up and get a closer shot. Keeping that in mind, it may not be the best idea to take a shot at the first birds that get off the ground—they may be out too far. If you can hustle to the spot of the flush, you might find half of the covey still present, where they'll present closer shots.

Hunting sharptails in the open grassland. (Photo: Blanche Johnson)

There are a lot of miles to cover when hunting sharptail, and if hunting without a dog, it can be difficult to get sharptails in the air. They'll often just scamper away—like a pheasant—so if you spot some on the ground, you'll have to run to get them to fly.

Hunting with Dogs

Flushing dogs—Labrador retrievers, springer spaniels, or golden retrievers—work extremely well for sharptails. The covey will usually not flush together, so a flushing dog that will root around in the brush will assure that no birds hunker down and lay low until you pass. If the dog starts busting birds, again, get up there and wait for the birds that are late getting off the ground.

Pointing dogs work equally well, but sharptails like to run. A dog that will relocate and pin a running bird will work nicely on sharptails, and in the wide-open country, a dog—flushing or pointing—will cover a lot more ground than a lone hunter ever could and save walking a lot of extra miles.

This will be hot and dry country for most of the sharptail season, so don't forget a bottle of water—for you and the dog. Short, periodic breaks will be better than one long break in the middle of the day. Keep an eye on the dog for signs of fatigue and heat exhaustion.

Table Preparations

The darker meat of sharptails can be very tender and tasty, especially with early-season birds. Field dressing the birds will cool them down in hot country, and hanging until the evening or next morning will age the meat and add flavor. Soaking the birds in a marinade of red wine, or a mixture of herbs, spices, and vegetable oil overnight before preparing will keep the meat juicy. The breasts can either be grilled, pan-fried, or baked.

Gun and Shot Suggestions

- **Gauge:** 12, 16, or 20
- **Choke:** Improved and modified or modified and full for doubles, modified for single barrels.
- **Shot:** One to 1¼ oz. No. 6 is preferred, but No. 7½ will work well also, especially if gray partridge are present.

Gray Partridge Distribution

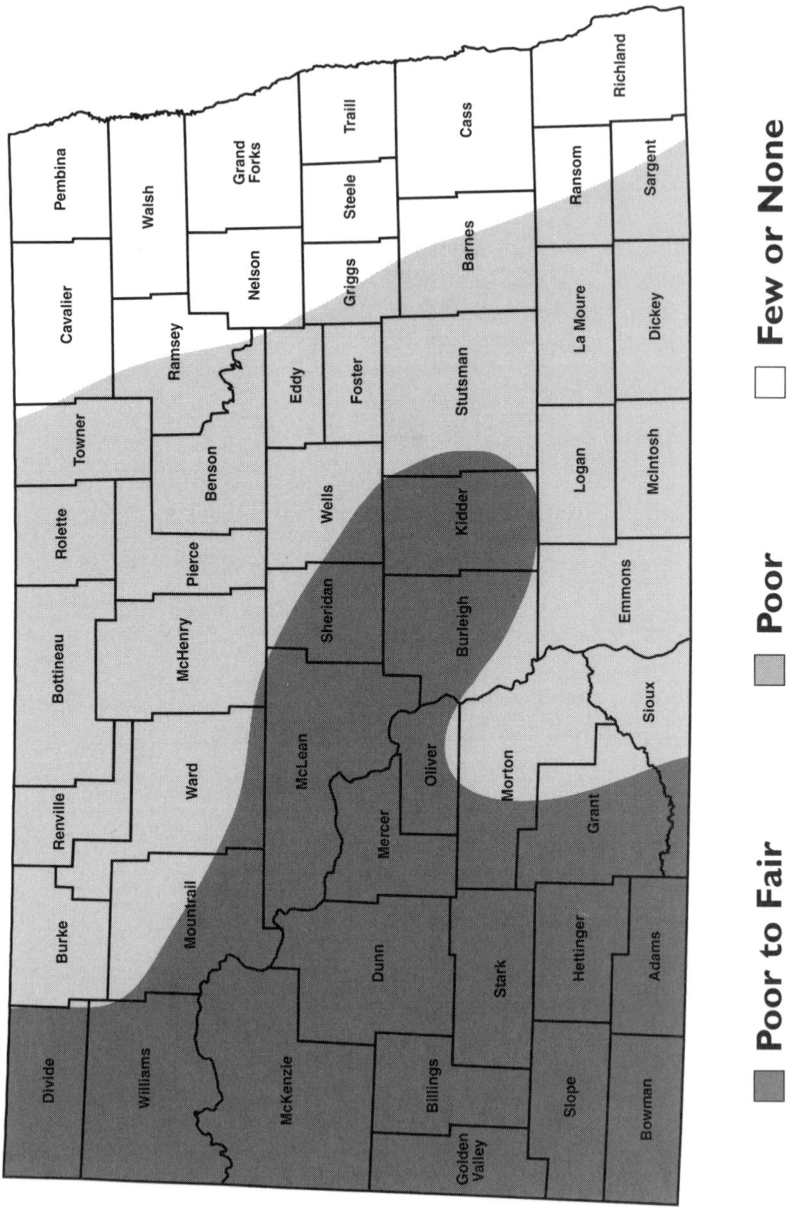

Gray Partridge

Perdix perdix

Field Facts

Local Names

Hungarian partridge, Hun, European partridge

Size

Huns weigh a little less than a pound, with males and females roughly the same size. They are around 12 to 13 inches, bigger than a quail but smaller than a grouse.

Identification in Flight

Coveys of Huns will flush in unison, and the small size, grayish body, and rusty tail are the key identifiers. The covey will usually fly together, beating their wings rapidly and turning together in flight. They do emit a call when flushing that sounds like squeaky door hinges.

Appearance

Huns are beautiful birds, with a brown face and throat, gray breast and flanks, and in males, a large chestnut patch on the belly. The chestnut patch may either be smaller or totally absent in females, but other than that, both sexes are very similar in appearance and size. The back is gray-brown leading down to a rust-colored tail.

On the Wing

Coveys of Huns are hard to approach, especially early in the season; but once flushed, the covey—10 to 20 birds—usually sticks together, and isolated singles are rare. The birds look gray in flight, with the rusty tail flashing as they turn in the air, and their wingbeats are very rapid—they may reach speeds near 30 miles per hour —interrupted by periodic glides. Mixed with the sound of rushing wings from an erupting covey are clucks and other excited vocalizations.

Daily Habits and Food

Huns are up and moving before sunrise, and their day is composed of the same things every bird does: feed, water, rest or loaf, feed again, and then move to a roosting spot. But the fact that they do move before sunrise makes them wary birds early in the morning when you hunt. They may be some of the first birds seen in the morning.

Their diet consists of many types of prairie grasses, grains, and seeds, occasionally picking up an insect or two. Water comes primarily from morning dew. Huns can often be seen walking along dirt roads, gathering grit to aid in the grinding of food, especially seeds. Winter food is in the form of leafy material that is still available, but Huns will dig through the snow to gather some food. Snow also provides a water source for Huns at this time.

Seasonal Patterns

Breeding begins in April, with egg-laying in May. Nests are scratched out in the grassy habitat, and anywhere from 15 to 17 eggs will be laid, hatching about three and a half weeks later, with both parents sticking around through the whole incubation and brood rearing period. As soon as possible, the chicks are moved away from the nest, and when danger approaches, adults may perform a broken-wing act to lead predators away from the nest or chicks.

In the hot months, Huns will be found in the cooler sections of their grassland habitat, inhabiting brushy draws with some overhead cover. The winter will also find them in these places if snow has not filled in the cover. Otherwise, winter cover will be the habitat that remains uncovered by snow the longest.

During fall, Huns congregate in their customary coveys and stay until winter snows drive them to areas that do not have as much snow. Should their fall haunts not be hit too severely with snow, Huns may remain in these areas, coveyed together until pairing begins in March.

Preferred Habitat and Cover

During fall Huns can be located on gently rolling lands of prairie grass, hay, stubble, and grain. CRP fields surrounded by brushy draws and cropped fields serve as excellent habitat during the hunting season. The grassland and hayfield setting is typical of Hun habitat, and lands where there are exposed ridges and grassy knolls will almost always hold a covey on one side of the elevated area.

Winter habitat consists of those areas in this setting that do not fill in with snow as rapidly as other sections. With the approaching spring and pairing of Huns, nests will begin to be formed in the grass and hayfields, hollowed out and lined with surrounding vegetation. The brood and adults will then look for shadier and cooler spots for the summer; coveys will form and inhabit the rolling grasslands and prairie for the fall. During the colder spells at this time, Huns will search out slightly denser cover, moving between these areas and their feeding grounds throughout the day.

Hunting Methods

It has been said that if Huns were birds of the woodlands, they would be outlawed as gamebirds. Simply put, they are strong and fast flyers, and these factors have helped the Hun hold firm in its population status since its introduction from Europe in the early part of the 20th century, not to mention ranking them high on bird hunters' lists of most fun—and frustrating—gamebirds.

Hunting without a dog may be a task, unless hunting through thicker cover where the birds will hold tighter. Because of the open country the birds normally

A covey of Huns rising in open country. (Photo: Blanche Johnson)

inhabit, you should be able to follow an entire covey until it sits down, and you can then follow it up. The covey may—rarely—eventually scatter, in which case hunting the singles will produce closer flushes.

Huns are fast flyers. And the sight of so many birds in one tight flock leads to the problem of picking out just one bird. The only thing that will help you become a better Hun shooter is practice.

Hunting with Dogs

Wide-ranging dogs are extremely useful when hunting Huns, especially if the dog can pin down the birds and keep them from scampering away before you get there. Two or three dogs that will all honor can lead to some breathtaking sights on the prairie, and the more dogs, the more ground can be covered.

Pointing dogs may be preferred in this case because they will hold the birds for you—especially singles—but a flushing dog will do the job just fine as well, though he may flush them a little farther out.

As with other types of bird hunting in the open country, though, there will be times during the season when it will get very hot. Periodic water breaks—for you and the dog—should be a must, and if you make it every 20 minutes or after every covey-

—something that will give you regular breaks—you'll find your hunts and your dog lasting longer.

Table Preparations

The slightly dark meat of Huns can be very tender and juicy, with the right preparations. Field-dressing the birds and cooling them down will preserve them longer, and hanging for a few hours will help to age the meat and add flavor. But getting the meat off the bone as soon as possible and soaking it in a marinade of just about any kind used for other birds will result in the most tender meat. A marinade of Italian dressing or a combination of chicken and poultry seasonings with a little vegetable oil is recommended. While cooking, try not to cut the meat until you're positive it's almost completely done. Piercing the meat early will drain the juices throughout the rest of the cooking time and lead to a dry meal.

Gun and Shot Suggestions

- **Gauge:** 12, 16, or 20
- **Choke:** Improved and modified or modified and full for doubles, or modified for single barrels.
- **Shot:** 1 oz. of No. 7½

Sage Grouse

Centrocercus urophasianus

FIELD FACTS

Local Names

Sage hen, sage cock, spiny-tailed pheasant

Size

Sage grouse are one of the largest upland game birds, with males between 26–30 inches and five to six pounds, and females 19–23 inches and two to three pounds.

Identification in Flight

The sheer size of sage grouse is their best identifier in flight, especially with the noisy takeoff, but once in the air, the underwings flash white, contrasting with the black belly. Both sexes have long pointed tails, and males may have an overall darker appearance.

Appearance

Sage grouse are very large upland birds—the largest of the grouse species—with a patterning of black, white, and brown. Both sexes have a black belly, but males, especially during the mating season, have a large ruff of white feathers with a yellow eye comb. Their tails are a series of pointed feathers, unlike the sharp-tailed grouse that has only two central tail feathers pointed. This lends itself to one of its folk names of "spiny-tailed pheasant."

On the Wing

These large grouse are hard to mistake simply because of size, but also because of the commotion they make getting off the ground, especially the larger males. Once in flight, the white underwings contrast with the grayish body and black belly, and the pointed tail feathers fan out. Males are smooth flyers, but females dip their bodies from side to side while flying. They will fly at speeds from 25 to 30 miles per hour, reaching their maximum speeds after flying for a few moments. Sage grouse cluck and cackle in takeoff and flight. Their vocalizations include many other calls during their spectacular courtship displays.

Daily Habits and Food

The daily habits of sage grouse are still somewhat of a mystery, but they may revolve around the breeding ground, with males not moving too far to roost and feed and the females keeping close tabs on the activity on the dancing ground. Daily habits

Sage Grouse Distribution

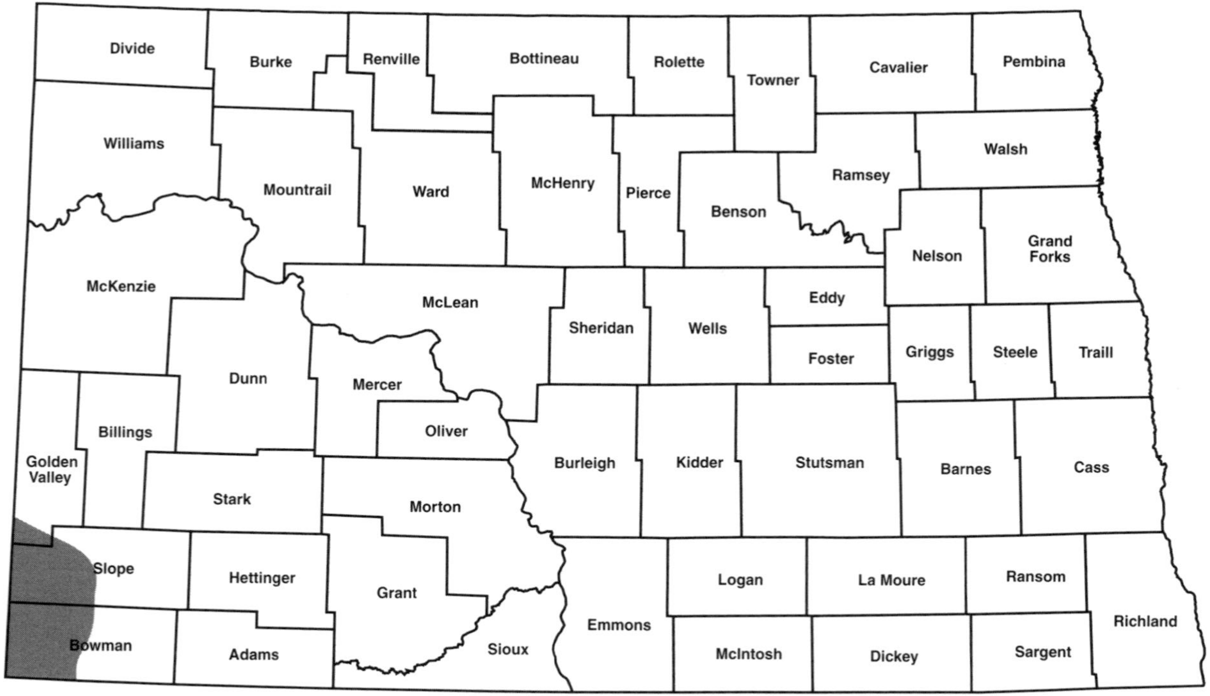

Only Population in State (Fair)

Not overly abundant, sage grouse, the king of Western upland gamebirds, can be hunted in Slope, Bowman, and Golden Valley counties in extreme southwest North Dakota. (Photo: Blanche Johnson)

may consist nothing more than times of feeding, loafing, and roosting, and during the breeding season, intense courtship display or nest preparation and brood rearing.

The diet of sage grouse consists mainly of sagebrush, with some other plains grasses, leaves, and legumes (especially alfalfa and clover) mixed in during the spring and early summer. Young sage grouse—and to a lesser extent adults—will feed primarily on protein-rich insects such as ants, beetles, and grasshoppers in the spring. Winter food is almost entirely sage, with the grouse eating the leaves and shoots of this evergreen plant throughout the season. Sage grouse are unable to digest seeds, so their diet consists entirely of leafy plant matter. Water may be collected at watering holes, dew from in the mornings, and sometimes snow during the winter.

Seasonal Patterns

During the fall hunting season, sage grouse may be found in a gradual movement toward their wintering grounds. Sage grouse do not have a fall display activity, the way some sharp-tailed grouse may begin to dance again or ruffed grouse may

Sage grouse are indelibly tied to mature sagebrush stands. Here, the author admires a sage grouse taken from the cover behind. (Photo: Blanche Johnson)

drum. The winter will find sage grouse spending all of their time in their winter cover, but with the change to spring, a movement toward the dancing ground will begin. This spring cover—sparser than the winter habitat—will serve well to advertise the males, and in the summer, movements may be tied to the dancing ground. Some summer movements may be short distances away from the breeding area, into pockets of thicker habitat, especially in areas where moisture is present.

Females will nest under short sagebrush, laying about eight eggs. After incubation—close to four weeks—the young will hatch and take their early flights between their first and second weeks of life.

Sage grouse have been known to covey up in groups of nearly 100 birds, primarily in late fall and winter, with most of the flock being immature grouse. After brood dispersal in late summer, flocks of closely associated broods will begin to form, and the covey will remain together throughout the winter. In the spring, males will congregate to display and will usually stay coveyed even while not displaying.

Preferred Habitat and Cover

The life of a sage grouse is spent almost entirely in sagebrush. The birds use thick pockets for winter habitat because it provides food and cover, and sparse sagebrush for display areas, especially in places where there may be an exposed ridge, bare spot, or very thin and short (around one or two feet tall) sagebrush. Nests will also be located under sagebrush, and the young are reared in this cover as well, utilizing the insects and succulent plant matter of that habitat.

During the hunting season, focus your efforts on these sagebrush prairies. The grouse will have begun their movements from the sparser vegetation of the spring courtship season to the thicker winter cover. The intermediate cover (with a height of three or four feet) will serve as the perfect fall habitat and should be your first spot to look for the grouse. Pay close attention to those areas that look just a little more green than others—these areas are more moist and will be preferred by the birds. Thick sagebrush draws heading toward some water source are popular hangouts and should be some of the first cover you push through. Fields of thick grasses, especially CRP fields, adjacent to sagebrush will also hold birds during the times of the day when the grouse are feeding.

Hunting Methods

To hunt sage grouse, get yourself a good pair of boots. There is a lot of walking in wide-open country involved in sage grouse hunting.

By observing the lay of the land before you start, you may get an idea of where to focus your hunt. Look for those green areas that contain moisture, especially in the mornings and evenings. In the hot part of the day, be sure to plow through the areas sage grouse may be using for loafing or dusting, usually thicker sagebrush. And another thing about hunting sage grouse—when you find a few, you'll likely find the whole flock.

The edge between CRP fields and sagebrush may hold a covey of grouse, as the birds are feeding in those fields. Always skirt the edges, and don't be afraid of hunting the CRP fields occasionally. If you suspect the grouse are feeding, these areas may be holding birds. Moisture can collect more easily in these places, and a lot of times, where the water is, the birds will be also. If you can find some medium thick sagebrush surrounding a watering hole or irrigation pond or a sagebrush-filled draw leading toward these water sources, you'll spend a fine day shooting sage grouse.

Hunting with Dogs

As with most other bird hunting, dogs always seem to make the hunt more enjoyable. But with sage grouse hunting, this may be one time when you need the dogs to actually make the whole thing more sporting, especially early in the season with young birds. Sage grouse are not all that afraid of people, and in some cases will just walk among the hunters who are trying to flush them. They recognize the four-legged hunters, though, and will flush or run ahead of the dogs. With running sage grouse, be ready to take off much the same way you would after pheasants. Pointing dogs and retrievers work equally well, depending on your fancy. Just remember—these grouse are found in some of the most desolate country, that, in the early part of the season, can get extremely hot and dry. A big burly black Labrador retriever may flush the birds perfectly, but only if he has ample water. Dogs will not last long in the heat without plenty of water.

Table Preparations

Sage grouse have very dark meat, and the taste can be too strong for some people. Younger birds offer a milder taste, and when flushing a covey, try to pick out the smaller birds. Field-dressing the birds will help to cut down on the gamey taste, and it will also help to cool the birds down, important in the early season. Another way to decrease the wild taste is to filet the breasts and marinate them in a favorite mixture overnight. Oily Italian dressing works for just about any game, but a darker marinade of Worcestershire sauce and a bottled herb-and-garlic marinade is tasty on the dark meat. Some people like to hang the birds for several days, but skinning as soon as you get home, preparing them that night, and eating the next day will assure the freshest meat and the best taste.

Gun and Shot Suggestions

- **Gauge:** 12, 16, or 20
- **Choke:** Modified and full for doubles, or modified for single barrels.
- **Shot:** 1-1½ oz. of No. 6 or No. 5.

Ruffed Grouse

Bonasa umbellus

FIELD FACTS

Local Names

Partridge, pat, wood grouse

Size

Ruffed grouse are chicken-like birds of the forest, ranging in weight from one to two pounds, and they measure around 17 inches long.

Identification in Flight

The thunderous flush from thick cover is the best indicator of a ruffed grouse, as well as the large fanned tail with a black bar near the tip that is very evident in flight. In North Dakota, most of the ruffed grouse have a gray appearance, common on birds in the northern tier of states.

Appearance

Ruffed grouse have a spectacular patterning of browns and whites and blacks throughout their body. The ruff, from which the bird got its name, is a black collar of feathers around the neck—large in males and greatly reduced in females—that the male will puff out during displays of courtship or aggression. Besides the ruff, the most characteristic feature of a ruffed grouse is its large fanned tail, a true prize for the bird hunter who bags a grouse. This tail has a black bar near the tip, with white or gray bands on either side of it, and finer dark bands down each tail feather.

Though ruffed grouse have two color phases—red and gray—hunters in North Dakota will more often see the gray phase, and this color in the tail will be very evident. Though many people claim to be able to age or sex ruffed grouse by the tail fan, the most reliable clue as to the sex can be found in the rump feathers at the base of the tail. These feathers will have one white dot for a female, or two white dots for a male.

Ruffed grouse also sport a crest on their head, and in the winter, their feet develop natural snowshoes, with the feathers extending down toward the base of the legs and tiny projections off the toes.

On the Wing

The mighty roar of wings while flushing will signal a ruffed grouse. The tail fan should be very evident in flight—if you can get a good look at the bird—and an overall gray appearance with a lighter belly will show in flight. Ruffed grouse are extremely fast flyers—they can reach speeds up to 40 miles per hour—and in the

Ruffed Grouse

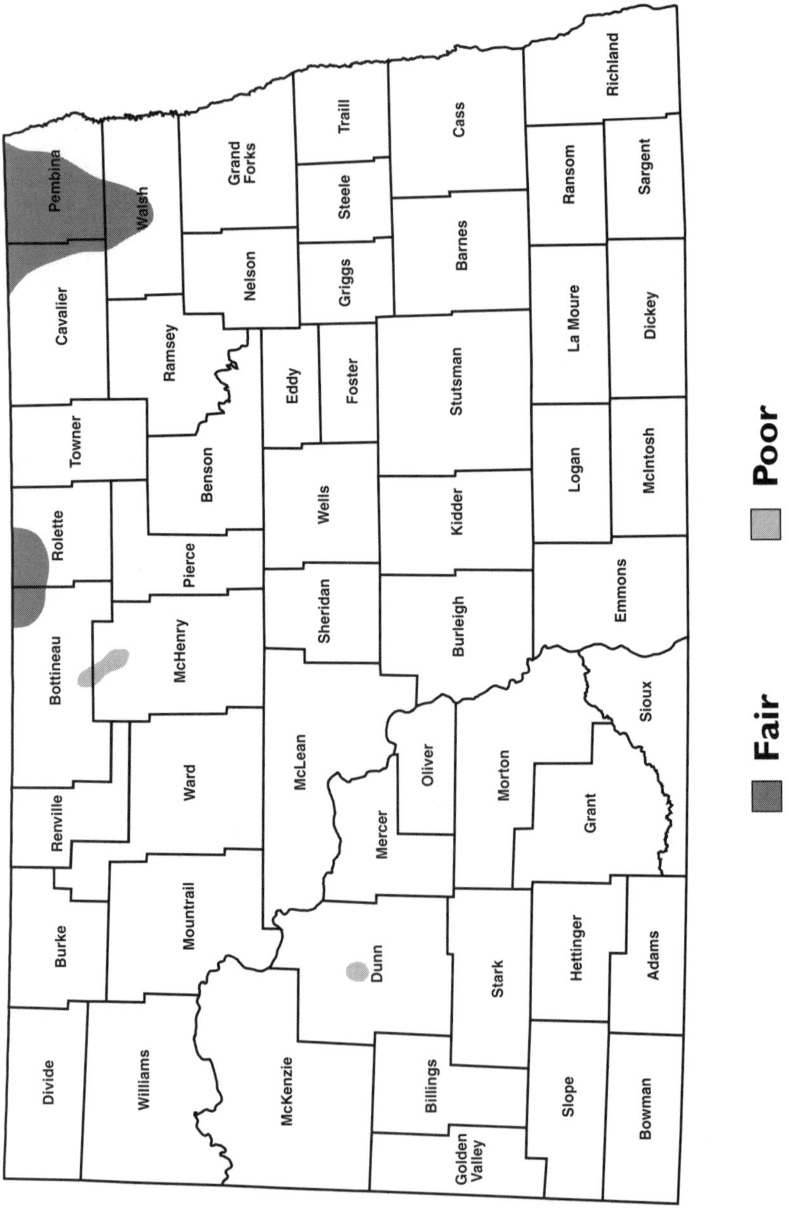

Ruffed grouse. (Photo: Blanche Johnson)

woods, they seem to fly even faster. They are quick to dodge and duck around trees, finding their way through thick forests with ease.

Daily Habits and Food

Depending on the season, male ruffed grouse may spend much of the day "drumming"—an advertising and territorial display in which the male will beat his wings ferociously against his breast—on a fallen log or stump. Drumming is interrupted for dusting, feeding, and roosting.

Ruffed grouse are known for eating a wide variety of food—insects; buds of aspen, birch, willow, and other trees and herbaceous plants; berries of all kinds; and green leaves. Young ruffed grouse will feed almost entirely on insects and then move on to an herbivorous diet, though adult ruffed grouse will still eat insects. Some researchers feel that the population cycle (periods of highs and lows) of ruffed grouse may be tied to a major food source—aspen buds—though there are other theories that are equally plausible.

Seasonal Patterns

The spring season finds the woods filled with the sound of drumming. Males will stake out a territory and advertise their position to females—and other males—with the drumming. The male will then usually strut along his drumming log with his ruff and tail fanned out, and females will approach. The two will copulate, she will lay the eggs, and he will search out more mates.

Nests will usually be located in mature hardwood stands, under low-hanging branches or fallen logs. Between nine and 12 eggs will hatch a little over three weeks after the laying of the last egg. Upon hatching, the young will be whisked away into thicker cover that offers more food in the form of insects, and by an age of one week, the young grouse are making their first flights.

Brood dispersal will follow approximately four months after hatching, with the males off to find suitable cover for future drumming. With the coming fall and the dispersal almost complete, drumming will again take place, usually to advertise that a territory is occupied. Early in the hunting season, though, it isn't uncommon to flush a brood of grouse underfoot.

Winter can be a devastating force on ruffed grouse. If the snow has a lot of crust to it or there are some severe ice storms, the mortality rate on grouse can be very high. Ruffed grouse are "snow roosters" and will burrow into the snow to keep warm and evade predators. The burrows provide excellent insulation for winter protection, staying almost 50 degrees warmer than the outside temperature.

If an ice storm hits while a grouse is in the burrow, the bird may be buried alive or ice can actually clog the nasal passages and the bird can suffocate. While evading predators—namely goshawks and great-horned owls—ruffed grouse will dive into snowbanks to escape. If the snow is crusty, grouse can break their necks while trying to dive, or the crusty snow may just push the grouse into thinner cover where avian predators can hunt more easily.

Preferred Habitat and Cover

The best ruffed grouse habitat is one of stands of aspen of different ages. This mosaic creates edge, and the different age classes of the trees—a second-growth stand about as big around as your forearm; a large, more mature stand; and very young trees growing thick—provide habitat for all of the different seasons. The mature stand offers excellent winter and nesting habitat, the second growth stands provide an abundant supply of food during the fall and summer, and the young stand is excellent cover for raising broods. Places where these ages overlap or are in close proximity to each other will almost always hold ruffed grouse.

When the winter—or late in the hunting season—has seen a hard snowfall or some ice storms, ruffed grouse may move into pine tree stands, seeking shelter and insulation from low-hanging pine boughs. Ruffed grouse can be almost like ghosts in the pines; this type of habitat provides excellent winter cover.

Hunting Methods

Hunting ruffed grouse is considered by many to be the most frustrating yet rewarding form of wingshooting. Ruffed grouse are fast flyers and offer almost entirely snap shots, finding their way behind a tree just as you pull the trigger. Grouse do hold fairly well, and if hunting without a dog, you may get some close flushes, especially early in the season if there are still some broods around. But ruffed grouse cover is thick, and if alone, you'll have to bust through it yourself, and this may only hinder your chances of bagging a grouse even more.

Hunting with Dogs

Pointing dogs are preferred when hunting ruffed grouse. The cover is thick, and with a flushing dog, you may not be entirely ready for a flush. Because the shots are so quick—unlike a prairie bird that can startle you but still give you ample time to calm down and take a shot—ruffed grouse are gone in an instant. Pointing dogs that can pin the birds will allow you to approach and get close flushes, sometimes even pushing the birds in the direction of thinner cover so you can get a better shot.

Those who use flushing dogs, though, find that the dog can bust though the thick cover while the hunter skirts the edges, presenting him with clearer firing lanes.

Keep in mind the time of year when hunting with a dog. Ruffed grouse cover will usually hold some water—either a stream or some low-lying holes that have collected rainwater—and make sure to let your dog take a drink.

Bells or beeper collars are essential when hunting ruffed grouse with dogs. Again, because of the thick cover, it may be hard to keep an eye on your dog all of the time. When the bell falls silent or the beeper collar goes into the point mode, move up and get ready for a quick shot.

Table Preparations

Ruffed grouse offer some of the most excellent upland gamebird meat there is. The white meat of the breasts and thighs can be very tender—especially with young birds early in the season—and a roasting grouse stuffed with apples is hard to beat. You can also fillet the breasts and fix them as you would boneless chicken breasts. If you've hung them for a few hours or a day, you'll get a hint of wild flavor that will add to the meal.

Gun and Shot Suggestions

- **Gauge:** 20, 16, or 12
- **Choke:** Cylinder and improved for doubles, or either choke for single barrels. Later in the season, when the foliage has dropped, you may go to the tighter choke.
- **Shot:** Spreader loads available from various companies are useful. A load of ⅞ to 1 oz. No. 7½ or 8 is recommended.

Hunting the Mixed Bag

In order to have a successful early morning hunt, some late afternoon scouting the day before will help you locate where the waterfowl have been feeding. Around 4 p.m., the birds leave their resting areas and fly to their preferred grainfields to feed.

Blanche and I were hunting in fall 1996 with Jason Brown, guide and owner of Club NorDak operating out of Streeter, North Dakota. Riding the back roads scouting for geese, we spotted a large group of geese and followed them to locate their feeding grounds. By 5 p.m. we had tracked a large group of Canada geese to a harvested wheat field. Pulling in across the road, we parked behind some trees to avoid being seen. We could see three long rows of feeding geese through our binoculars; we quit counting at 1,000 geese. We located the farmhouse to get permission from the owner to hunt the field the next morning.

When we arrived at the field the next morning, we set up our decoy spread in the middle, where goose droppings were plentiful. Being the coldest part of the day, we then stood around drinking hot coffee while we waited for sunrise.

Just before sunrise, four ducks dived into our decoy spread, but before we could grab our guns they were gone. We decided it was time to get into position. Wearing white coveralls, we spread out about 20 yards apart and laid down.

After a tough day goose hunting, Duke takes a break among the dekes. (Photo: Blanche Johnson)

Author hunting upland birds in CRP with his wirehair pups. (Photo: Blanche Johnson)

With Duke laying beside me, I was ready when another pair of ducks came in low. Jason and I rose up to a sitting position, and both of us were able to bring down a bird. By the time Duke had retrieved the ducks, we could hear geese honking on the horizon.

For the next two hours, snow and Canada geese flew over us in wave after wave of huge flocks numbering hundreds of geese. When they paid little

The decoys are set, the hunters are ready, and the birds are on their way; a typical goose hunting scene in North Dakota. (Photo: Blanche Johnson)

A wary pheasant pops out of the tall grass, but the hunter is ready and a shot will quickly follow. (Photo: Blanche Johnson)

attention to our spread of about 100 decoys, we concluded that we needed a smaller group of birds. Finally, about 20 geese circled twice and set their wings for our decoys. When we could see their eyes and the lead goose's feet were almost touching the ground, we sat up and started shooting. After laying on the cold ground for almost two hours, our stiff muscles were not very responsive—it took us six shots to bring down three geese. Duke brought them back and put them in a pile on top of the ducks.

Settling back down again, we watched several more flocks of geese pass over our decoys without coming down. At 10 a.m., we picked up the decoys and headed back to Jason's cabin for a big, home-cooked breakfast.

Our next destination was a nearby ranch where Jason had permission to hunt for upland birds. Most of the ranch was in CRP fields, and there were a number of small ponds and sloughs with heavy grass cover around them, making ideal cover for gamebirds.

Since I wanted our three puppies, Belle, Hershey, and Sprig, to get some real field experience, I let them out and they quickly passed over a low hill. When Blanche and I got to the top of the hill, we looked down and found all three pups on point next to a small pond. After I kicked the grass in front of the pups, two cock pheasants exploded in different directions. Turning to the left, I fired at one of them and missed on the first shot. On my second shot, the pheasant rocked, slowed his flight, and landed, wounded, in a corn stubble field. I called to the pups, and we started searching the cornfield. In minutes the pups were on point, and I flushed the bird and hit it. After chasing the running pheasant, the pups caught the bird. Hershey picked it up and carried it back to me while Belle and Sprig tried to grab the bird from her. We were very pleased with how they performed pointing and retrieving their first pheasant.

We spent the afternoon hunting the CRP with our dogs. Duke and Annie found three groups of sharptails, and we got another pheasant for the conclusion of a great day of hunting both waterfowl and upland birds. The day also proved to us, once again, the value of using versatile gun dogs. Our German wirehairs were able to do it all.

A pack of proud young pups returns with a ring-necked pheasant. (Photo: Blanche Johnson)

Wild Turkey Distribution

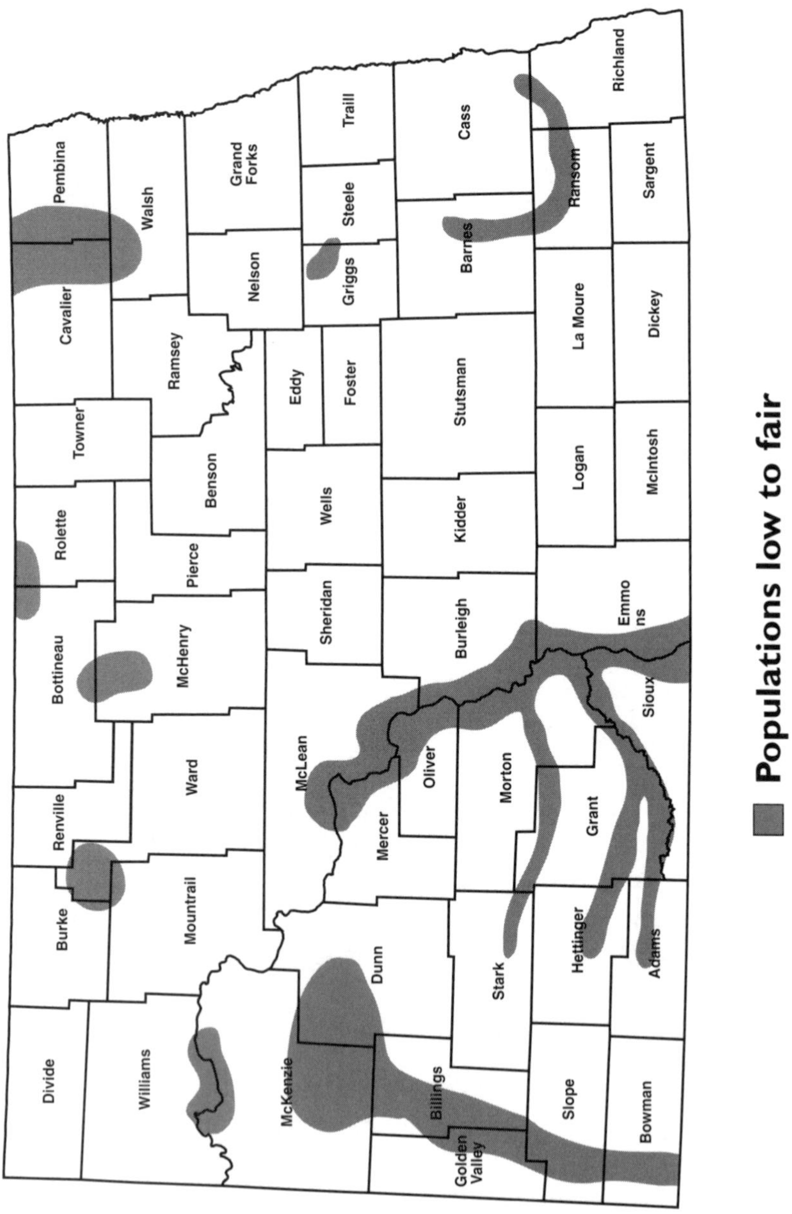

Wild Turkey

Meleagris gallopavo

FIELD FACTS

Local Names

Wood turkey, American turkey, tom, gobbler

Size

These largest of the upland gamebirds are three to four feet in length, and large males can weigh more than 25 pounds.

Identification in Flight

Turkeys are hunted almost exclusively on the ground, so flight identification is rarely needed. On the ground, the bare-skinned, red head of a turkey, combined with a long beard of a mature male, the bronze colored body, and a wide fanned tail are readily identifiable.

Appearance

It is hard to mistake a turkey for anything else. Their breast feathers are an iridescent bronze color tipped in black, the wings are black-and-white barred, and the large tail that fans out in courtship and aggressive displays is tipped in brown with black bars down to the body. And of course, there is the signature bare-skinned red head with a fleshy snood—a projection off the top of the bill—and red wattles.

Big males will have a beard, and this trophy of turkey hunters can extend anywhere from an inch to over 10 inches from the breast. The hens are a little more pale, and their heads are not as bright red. During the spring, the males' (toms') heads have a blue cast.

On the Wing

Despite their size, turkeys do fly up and down from their roosts, usually in a thunderous clatter of wings, appearing to have trouble getting off the ground. Once they get up a good head of steam, though, turkeys can reach speeds near 35 miles per hour. However, turkeys prefer to run, and for this reason, they are hunted almost exclusively on the ground, using big-game, as opposed to traditional bird-hunting methods.

Daily Habits and Food

Turkeys are early risers, flying down from their roosts before dawn. They feed, display, fraternize a bit, dust, and feed some more before returning to their roosts in the evening. Most turkey hunters like to go out the night before to see where the birds are flying in to roost and then set up with a decoy or two near the roost early the next morning.

Turkeys are voracious eaters of just about everything, primarily seeds, acorns, nuts, berries, and various insects and even small amphibians and reptiles. Turkeys will gather small pebbles to use as grit in their powerful gizzards that can grind some of the toughest forage.

Seasonal Patterns

Turkeys are non-migratory birds, and they will make it through the winter in the same type of habitat they occupy the rest of the year. However, they may be found in thicker cover and pine forests, because these areas are less likely to fill up with snow, covering the food supply.

The breeding season is when most turkey hunting takes place, with the large toms being the target during their courtship display of puffed out feathers, fanned tail, strut, and loud gobble. Females will nest near openings in the forest close to some overhead cover. About one dozen eggs are laid, and they are incubated for four weeks. The young—"poults"—stick close to the hen for the first few weeks of life—a time of rapid growth—and once the juveniles are making strong flights up to perches and roosts, the broods will begin to disperse.

Preferred Habitat and Cover

Turkeys will spend a lifetime in hardwood forests bordered by grass, hay, or agricultural fields. With few hardwood or pine forests in North Dakota, the majority of turkey distribution areas feature cottonwoods. Roosting will take place in the larger, more mature trees. Because most of the strutting will occur in open areas, the place to set up a hen decoy is in a field bordering these forests. With the proper calling, a gobbler will race out of the woods for the decoy, presenting a clear shot.

Hunting Methods

The hunting season on turkeys is frequently tied to the breeding season in the spring. This makes it easier to select large, mature toms—adult male turkeys—using decoys and calls of the hen turkey to lure them within range.

The vocabulary of turkeys—and turkey hunters—is comprised of calls such as the *putt, cluck* or *cut, gobble, yelp,* the *kee,* and many others. A hunter needs to be fluent with this language to be a successful turkey hunter.

Locating turkeys before actually hunting them is the best way to prepare, though even this may prove unsuccessful. Turkeys are wary creatures, and if they sense something is amiss, they are quick to flee. Therefore, plenty of accurate camouflage is necessary. It is said that a deer sees a man and thinks it's a stump; a turkey sees a stump and thinks it's a man.

Turkeys should be taken by a shot in the head. A crippled bird can get up and fly or easily outrun you, taking multiple hits in the body. Even if you roll a big bird, move up fast and be ready.

For most hunters, shooting a bird on the ground is something out of the ordinary, but hitting and killing a standing bird is actually a lot harder than it sounds. The head should be visible just above the top of the gun barrel, and the trigger needs to be squeezed, like a rifle. When you hear the gobbler approaching to your calls, mount the gun and prepare. You may be stuck in that position for quite a while, because turkeys can spot the slightest movement with their amazing eyes.

Table Preparations

A large tom can provide a huge meal, and everyone has their own Thanksgiving recipe for domestic turkeys that will work just as well with a wild bird. The nutty flavor of wild turkey, however, surpasses the supermarket bird.

Gun and Shot Suggestions

- **Gauge:** 12
- **Choke:** Full
- **Shot:** Some hunters like a heavy field load of 1⅛ oz. No. 4 or No. 2, but a load of 1⅛ oz. No. 6 or No. 5 will give you more pellets. Remember, you're target is the head—not a very tough part of the bird. Some experienced hunters use No. 6 for the first shot at a standing bird, followed by No. 2 or BB for subsequent shots at a running bird.

Woodcock Distribution

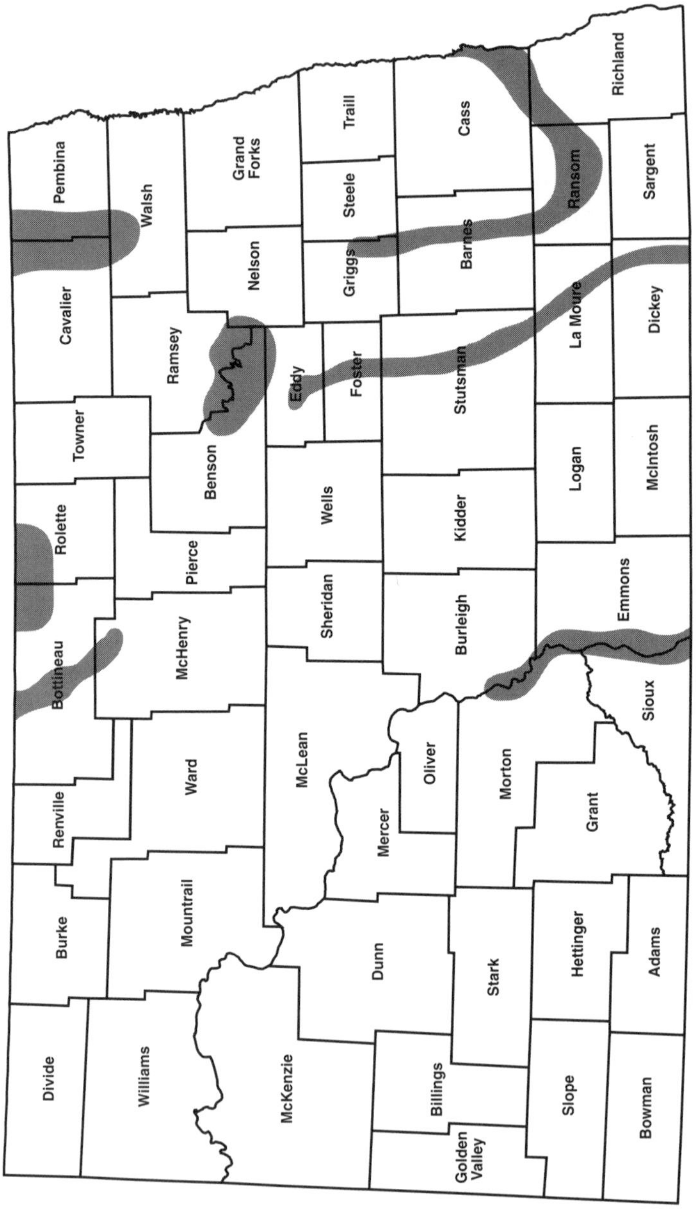

■ Only found in river drainages and wooded areas

Woodcock

Scolopax minor

Field Facts

Local Names

Timberdoodle, becasse, Labrador twister, night partridge, big-headed snipe

Size

Woodcock are stocky migratory upland gamebirds. The females are larger than the males, averaging around eight ounces and six ounces respectively. They are between 10 and 11 inches in length with bills over two inches long.

Identification in Flight

The twittering sound upon being flushed—the sound of air passing through the primary feathers as the bird takes off—and the long bill and plump shape are key indicators of a woodcock. Flight is typically quick through the cover, the bird twisting and dipping into and out of openings.

Appearance

A woodcock is a beautiful mix of browns and blacks, with bold black markings on the head, a long bill, and large black eyes. This stocky bird—which is actually in the sandpiper (shorebird) family but is found in the moist uplands—is closely associated with ruffed grouse, and very often, a hunter will encounter both on the same hunt. Woodcock are well camouflaged with their surroundings of brown leaves, and if they hold tight, they will very often be passed by.

On the Wing

While in the woods after ruffed grouse, you may flush this smaller, plumper bird that will twitter upon taking flight. Woodcock will make sharp twists and turns through the trees, or will head straight to the top of the cover and head for other places once in the clear. They are not fast flyers in the open, under 15 miles per hour, but through the thick cover, they appear quick. During their courtship display in the spring, male woodcock will do a "sky dance," begun by a peenting sound on the ground, followed by a very high spiral flight ending in a warbling song at the top, and terminating in a nosedive back to the original spot the peenting took place from.

Daily Habits and Food

Woodcock will sit tight in the cover during the day when hunters are out, and they'll do their feeding in the evening and after dark. Like the common snipe, they will also eat invertebrates—namely earthworms—and they locate them in the mud with their long probing, prehensile bills. The ears on woodcock are positioned forward of the eyes so that they may hear the movement of the worms, and their large eyes are positioned back in the head, allowing them to watch for predators in all directions while their bills are in the mud. If walking down a dirt trail with puddles in the mud, scout the edges for woodcock tracks, probe holes, and droppings—you may find an indication of a good woodcock covert nearby.

Seasonal Patterns

Woodcock are migrating upland gamebirds, passing through their range in what are called the "flights." Though woodcock do not migrate in flocks, a large number of birds can be found in a very small area at this time, usually very late fall. They will migrate at night, following river courses and using a strong north wind for aid in flight. If the winds calm after a strong blow from the north, they may stick around a while, providing fine hunting.

The courtship display will mark the return of the woodcock in the spring, and after copulation, nests will be laid close to a male's *peenting* ground in a cuplike depression in an alder cut. Four eggs will be laid, with an incubation period of three weeks and the young making their first strong flights between three and four weeks of age.

Preferred Habitat and Cover

The young aspen and alders found in good ruffed grouse cover will be a good spot for woodcock, but a series of medium to tall alders bordering an overgrown pasture or hayfield will provide consistent shooting, especially during the flights. In order to be good woodcock cover, though, there must be water nearby. This will keep the surrounding soil moist so the bird can forage for worms. Ground vegetation can't be too grassy, as it will impede walking because of the bird's long bill. A hillside of alders with a stream at the bottom will be the ideal cover.

Hunting Methods

Walking after woodcock is easier than it is for ruffed grouse, simply because woodcock will not run as far or fast. But holding tight can almost be as bad. Without a dog, expect to walk past most birds.

If you can push through a good covert, especially during the flights, you can move up to 50 birds in a day, even without a dog.

Hunting with Dogs

Pointing dogs are ideal for woodcock hunting, and many fine English setters, shorthairs, Brittanys, and pointers are trained in their first year on woodcock during the flights. The birds will hold well for dogs, allowing the hunter to flush the bird toward a clear shooting area, and a dog that will retrieve will help find the heavily camouflaged bird.

Flushing dogs work well also, but stay close. The thick cover will provide almost entirely snap shots, so if hunting with a flushing dog, you will need to be on its heels to get a shot off. A bell or beeper collar is strongly recommended.

Don't forget to let your dog take a dip and a big drink in that stream you found flowing through the ideal woodcock habitat.

Table Preparations

There is not a lot of meat on woodcock, but they are some of the most delicious birds. Fillet the dark breasts, marinade overnight in Italian dressing, and the next day, place each breast on a wedge of onion, wrap in bacon, secure with a toothpick, and throw them on a hot grill. Place the white thighs on a skewer, brush with barbecue sauce, and put them on the grill as well. It is a very rich meal; served with wild rice, it's one of the finest wild game meals.

Gun and Shot Suggestions

- **Gauge:** 20, 16, or 12
- **Choke:** Cylinder and improved for doubles, or either choke for single barrels.
- **Shot:** A light field load of ⅞ oz. No. 8 or spreader loads of the same size is preferred.

Mourning Dove Distribution

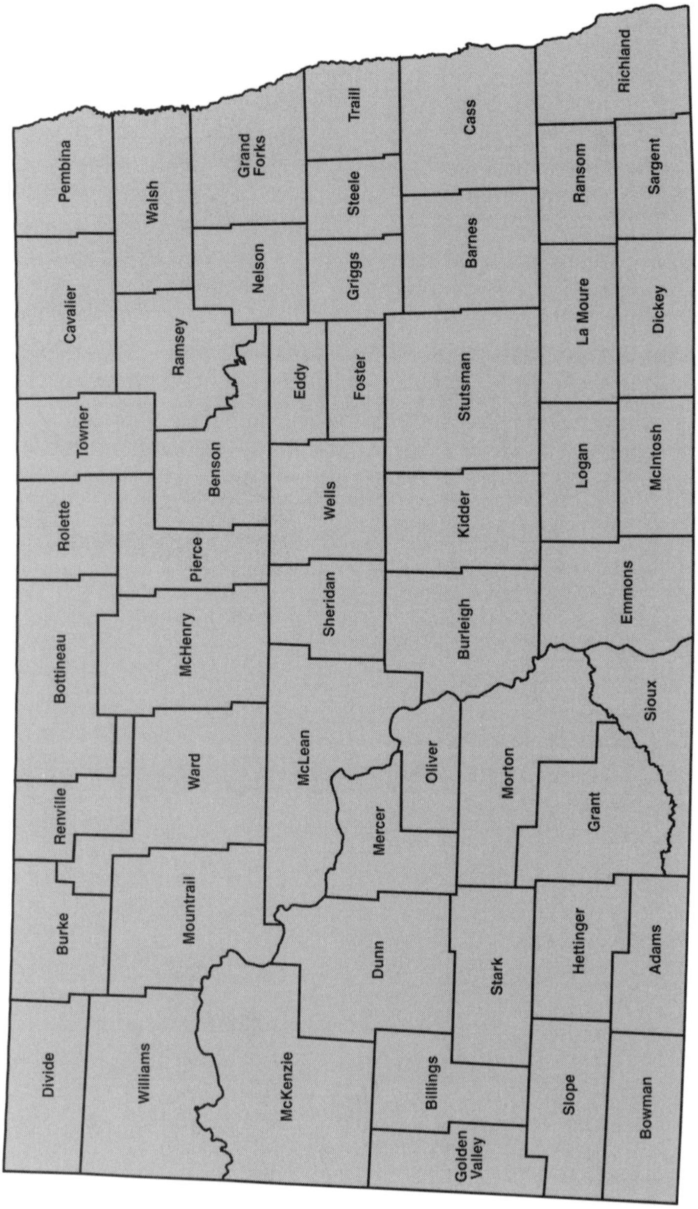

Mourning Dove

Zenaida macroura

FIELD FACTS

Local Names

Turtle dove, moaning dove

Size

Close to a foot long; both sexes similar in size, weighing up to 4 oz.

Identification in Flight

Doves have a streamlined shape, and their long, pointed tail with white outer tail feathers is evident in flight. An overall tan or gray appearance is noticeable, as is a rapid twittering sound while the bird is in flight.

Appearance

Upon close inspection, mourning doves hold a variety of colors, especially in the neck region where there are iridescent red and yellow feathers below a small, black spot. But from a distance, doves appear a drab tan/gray color. There are black spots on the upper wing, and a long, pointed tail is evident both in flight and while the bird is perched. The outer tail feathers are white, contrasting with the tan body and gray back.

On the Wing

Doves are very fast flyers, reaching top speeds of nearly 70 miles per hour. Their flight pattern is twisting, with a wingbeat followed by a glide, except when flushing. Their streamlined shape and pointed tail are telltale signs, as is the twitter of wings while the bird passes by. Look for these birds in large flocks during the shooting season.

Daily Habits and Food

Doves are voracious eaters of all kinds of seeds—sunflower, waste grain, weed seeds, seeds of prairie grasses, and many others. They fly to feeding spots in the morning after roosting on the ground or in trees close by. In the afternoon, they move in flocks to watering holes. After another trip to feeding areas and to collect grit in the late afternoon, doves either head back to water or to their roosting sites.

Seasonal Patterns

Mourning doves are migratory birds, heading for warmer southern climates in early fall. Upon returning in March and April, doves begin to pair, with the male and

Mourning dove. (Photo: Ken Retallic)

female involved in the nest building (in trees), incubation, and brood rearing. A short incubation period of two weeks is needed for the two to three eggs to hatch, and approximately three weeks after hatching, the young are on their own. Because of the short time the young are dependent upon their parents, there is the possibility for a pair of doves to raise up to five broods in one season.

During the hunting season, before migration southward, doves will be found in the same places they use throughout the summer.

Preferred Habitat and Cover

Agricultural landscapes of sunflower fields and other grainfields are the habitat of choice for doves in North Dakota. These areas provide an abundant supply of food, and nearby potholes or ponds provide the necessary water. This open country also usually holds sharp-tailed grouse, gray partridge, and even pheasants. Roosting spots are close by these areas, either on the ground or in trees.

Hunting Methods

Since doves have predictable daily patterns, you should be able to get any type of shooting you want—from walk-up flushes to pass shooting—by following a flock.

Dove hunting has a rich tradition in many states, and for a lot of hunters, doves were the first birds they hunted.

If doves are not legal in the state in which you live, you may be a little hesitant to shoot at the first doves that flush in front of you. In North Dakota, though, doves make up a large portion of the bag of most hunters. Also, because they can most often be found in proximity to other upland gamebirds, the possibility of a mixed bag of three or four species is likely.

Walking up doves is tough, simply from the standpoint that they often flush far ahead. Sitting in cover near water, feed, or under a flight lane between food and water is the best and easiest method to hunt them. It will certainly test your shooting skills. You must get way out in front and keep swinging. The birds move extremely fast.

Hunting with Dogs

While sitting under the flight lane, retrievers are useful in picking up the downed birds. This is hot, dry hunting, so be sure to pack plenty of extra water for both you and your dog. Using dogs while walking after doves may simply push the birds farther ahead, but flushing dogs may be helpful, especially if there is a chance for other gamebirds as well.

Table Preparations

Doves are among the best tasting gamebirds this country has to offer. The dark meat is very tender and can be prepared in any of your favorite gamebird recipes. There isn't a lot of meat, but generous limits on doves can make up for their size.

Gun and Shot Suggestions

Gauge: 12, 16, 20, and 28
Choke: Improved cylinder and modified for doubles, modifed for single barrels.
Shot: A field load of 1 to 1⅛ oz., No. 8 or 7½ is suggested for mourning doves.

Snipe Distribution

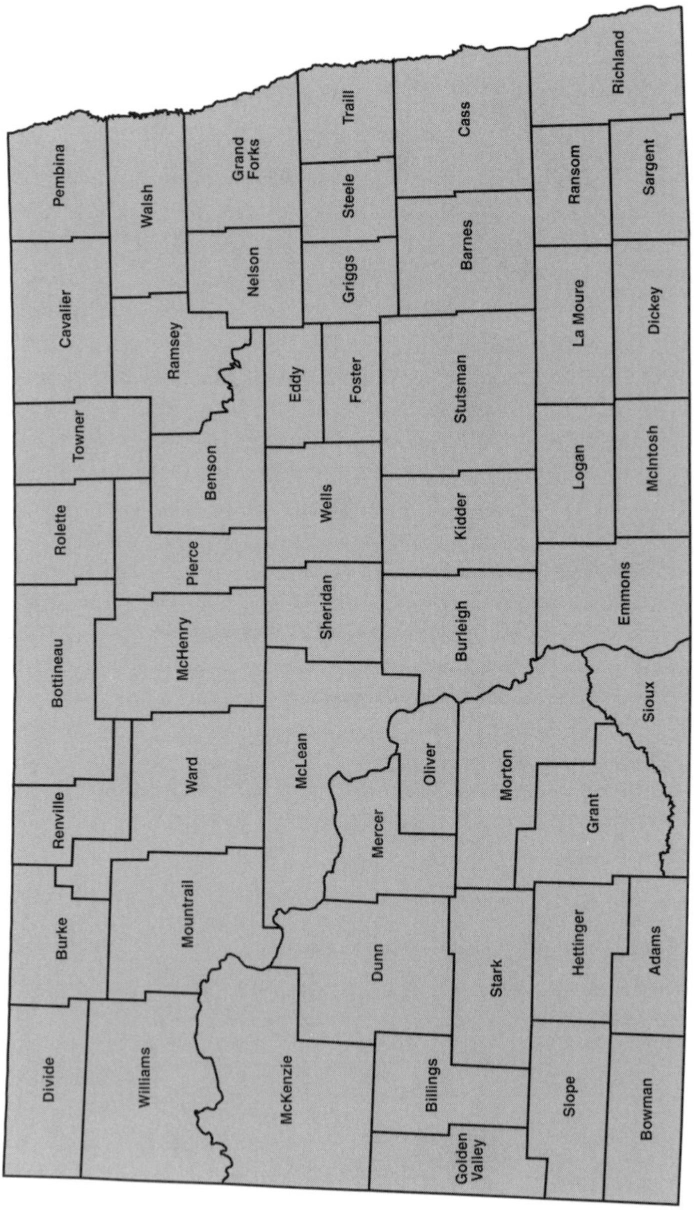

■ Found throughout state

Common Snipe

Gallinago gallinago

FIELD FACTS

Local Names

Jacksnipe, marsh snipe

Size

Though snipe are sometimes confused with the similar sized woodcock, snipe are much more slender, being almost half the weight of a woodcock.

Identification in Flight

The streamlined body of a snipe differs from the similar-looking woodcock, and the open, marshy habitat where snipe are found should also be an indicator. The bird has a gray-brown appearance, and flight is rapid, composed of numerous twists, dives, and streaks. The birds flush with a cry of "scaip," indicating they plan to do just that.

Appearance

Snipe are closely related to woodcock, and many times confused. But snipe are not as stocky, and the bird has more gray to it than the tan color of woodcock. The head is boldly striped over the crown, and the small rusty tail contrasts with the rest of the gray-brown-white body. They have long legs and bills, and like the woodcock, the females are slightly larger.

On the Wing

In the hand, snipe are easy to identify, but because of their fast, zig-zaggy flight, they can be tough to get a good look at in the air; the flight pattern is the best indicator—there are many dips and turns and twists with rapid wingbeats. Snipe take to the air with a flurry of wings, accompanied by a loud shrieking call. Snipe make difficult targets by either divebombing a duck decoy spread or flushing wild in front of a dog, and they can reach tremendous speeds near 40 miles per hour.

Daily Habits and Food

Snipe are crepuscular, flying near dawn and dusk to feed, and they are associated with wetland habitats, making them an addition to a day spent waterfowl hunting. Snipe eat marsh insects and invertebrates almost exclusively, using their long pointed bills to probe through the soft earth and mud near potholes and marsh lands. When the weather turns cold, snipe will generally begin their migration a few weeks earlier than most waterfowl.

Seasonal Patterns

During the hunting season, pay close attention to those groups of small birds that are strafing your duck decoys. While waterfowl hunting, you may find quite a few snipe.

Snipe will usually come back later than the waterfowl, needing the ground to be very soft in order to feed. From April to mid-May is when the snipe begin to return to the North, and they will perform an aerial courtship display that is quite dazzling. The males will make long, steep dives, and the wind rushing over the last two stiff tail feathers on the fanned tail will produce a winnowing sound. Some often think that the bird is calling, but it is actually the vibrating feathers producing the sound.

Snipe will stick around until about mid-October, depending on the weather and availability of food. Usually, they will migrate early along with the smaller ducks.

Nests will be located in dry sections of wet habitat, and it is usually nothing more than a depression in the grass. As is common with members of the sandpiper family, snipe will lay four eggs, and incubation and the first full flights will each take close to three weeks.

Preferred Habitat and Cover

Anywhere you might find waterfowl, if the water is shallow enough, you will probably find snipe. They are found largely around prairie potholes, but swamps, marshes, and flooded fields will often hold a fair number. They have been known to dive in the water to escape danger. If your feet are wet, you will more than likely be in good snipe habitat.

Hunting Methods

If waterfowl hunting, you can take a wander after snipe if you see them flitting around the pothole or marsh, or they may even give your decoy spread a buzz. But a great way to begin a hot early season is to walk after snipe through marshes, around the edges of potholes, or through a damp field that has collected some water. One of the most important things to remember about hunting snipe—and something that most people don't realize—is that you can't shoot lead at snipe. A non-toxic load must be used.

Hunting with Dogs

Snipe hunting will get a flushing dog in shape for the season. The cover will be damp and moist, the dog will stay cooler, and you can get some fine shooting. Pointing dogs are not much use; flushing dogs are the ticket when snipe hunting.

Table Preparations

Snipe are often overlooked as table fare, maybe because there is not a lot of meat on them, but if you like woodcock, you'll like snipe—there is almost exactly the same amount of breast meat, and the taste is almost identical. Follow any recipe for woodcock or dark meat, and snipe will be delicious.

Gun and Shot Suggestions

- **Gauge:** 20, 16, or 12
- **Choke:** Improved and modified, or modified for single barrels.
- **Shot:** A light field load of 1 to 1⅛ oz. of No. 7 steel or bismuth is the ideal load. Tungsten is legal as well, though it may be hard to find light loads.

Sandhill Crane Distribution

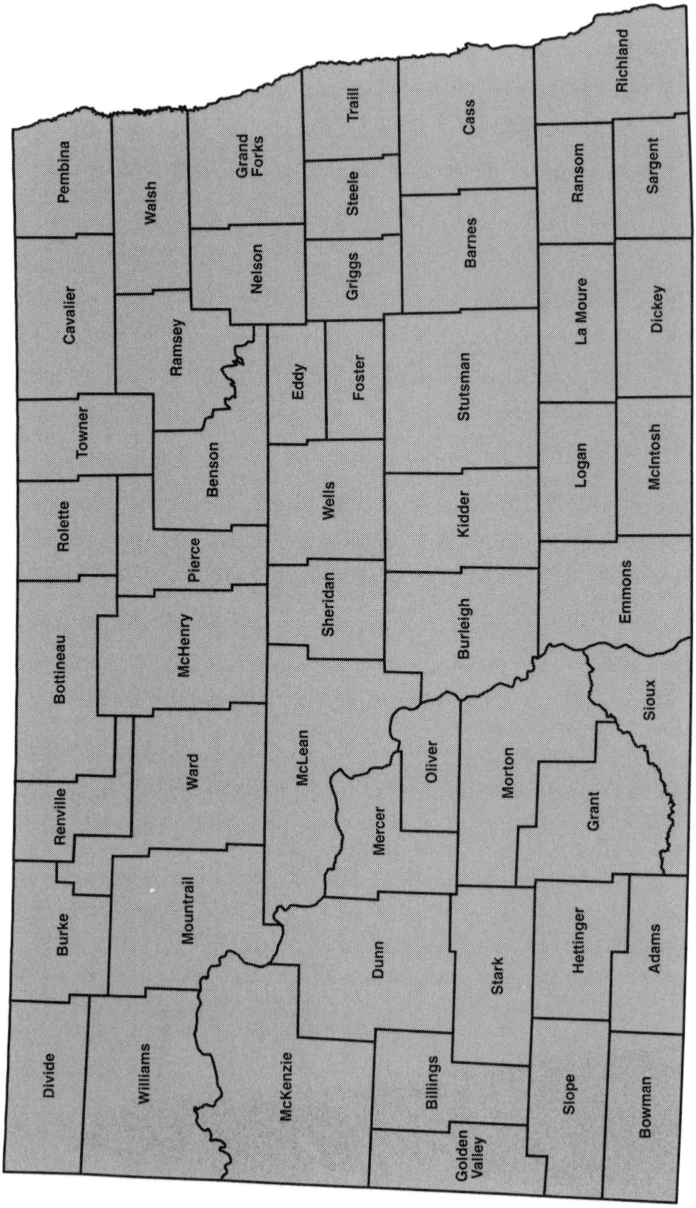

■ Found throughout state but higher density in central areas

Sandhill Crane

Grus canadensis

FIELD FACTS

Local Names

Baldhead, crane, gray crane, upland crane, sandhill, whooper

Size

These big, gliding migrators have a six- to seven-foot wingspan, and may reach three or four feet long. The males are heftier than the females, though this large bird is mostly feathers and legs.

Identification in Flight

The loud, rattling call of the sandhill, audible from almost a mile away, and the long legs trailing behind the bird are hard to mistake for anything other than a sandhill crane.

Appearance

Sandhill cranes stand about four feet tall, with long necks and legs. They have a gray plumage over their entire body, with a white cheek and chin and a red cap. Their long, pointed bills can be deadly weapons against predators.

On the Wing

Sandhills have slow wingbeats, sailing along like hang gliders. These smooth flyers are hard to mistake for geese because of the gangly legs trailing behind as well as the loud rattling call emitted almost constantly while flying. Don't mistake a great blue heron for a sandhill crane, though. Herons will fly with a crook in their necks, and there are heavy fines for shooting one. Cranes fly with straight necks. In addition, herons are usually solitary while sandhills are gregarious. Also, be careful to avoid shooting a whooping crane—its endangered status makes this bird illegal to shoot.

Daily Habits and Food

Cranes leave their roosting grounds of shallow water or marsh land at dawn and fly into cultivated agricultural fields to feed, returning to their roosting grounds in evening flights.

Sandhills will use their long bills to pull out the roots of marsh vegetation, and they will also eat waste grain, seeds, berries, and a variety of small mammals, birds, amphibians, and reptiles.

Seasonal Patterns

In the fall, large flocks of cranes will begin to stage for migration, and it isn't uncommon to see flocks of 500 to 1,000 birds heading south. Returning in the spring, sandhills will perform a courtship dance and will nest on prairie potholes in mounds of marsh grasses and weeds. Usually two eggs are laid, hatching after a four-week incubation period. The young will not be able to fly for about three months.

Flocks of cranes can be scouted during the summer, so when the hunting season rolls around, you may begin to learn their patterns. Early in the fall, watch the flocks of geese closely for small groups of cranes mixed in with the geese.

Preferred Habitat and Cover

Marsh habitat for roosting and loafing, and hayfields, cultivated grain fields, and prairie potholes for feeding are the best sandhill crane habitat types. Cranes will often fly with geese—or at least in the same patterns—and where you might set up for a flock of Canadas or snow geese, you might also get some cranes dropping in.

Hunting Methods

Sandhill crane decoys can be set in fields that the birds are frequenting, and while goose hunting, you may have a few swing close enough for a shot. Not many states offer hunting on sandhill cranes, so hunters visiting North Dakota may want to try their hand at it. Crane hunting is almost identical to goose hunting, except you may need to be a little more cautious about concealing yourself; cranes have very sharp eyes.

There is a lot of air around a crane. The long legs hanging behind—like a rooster pheasant's tail—makes the bird look bigger than it is. Be extremely head conscious when shooting at cranes—placement of the shot will be more important than the type of shot used.

A word of extreme warning: *It is recommended that you not use a dog when hunting cranes.* A crippled crane will wield that long pointed bill like a dagger, and there have even been reports of wounded cranes killing young dogs that tried to retrieve them. If you insist on using a dog, make sure the bird has been completely dispatched before sending the dog for the retrieve.

Table Preparations

Most people think sandhill crane meat is delicious, though they are usually pretty secretive with their recipes. Any recipe used for goose will also work for sandhills.

Gun and Shot Suggestions

- **Gauge:** 12, 10
- **Choke:** Improved and modified for doubles, or modified for single barrels.
- **Shot:** Goose loads will work well for sandhills—1⅛ to 1¼ oz. No. 2, BB, or BBB steel, bismuth, or tungsten. Only steel, bismuth, and tungsten shot are legal for cranes.

The Dabblers

General Characteristics

Dabbling ducks—or "puddle" ducks—are the kind most commonly taken by hunters across the country. These ducks are birds of shallow water—usually no deeper than five or six feet—and they use their forward-positioned feet to tip up to feed. Their powerful wings allow for takeoff straight up off the water. The male dabblers are brilliantly colored, and the wings of dabbling ducks have colorful speculums. The wing's color pattern is a major identification tool, and it is also useful in identifying the bird in flight.

Dabbling ducks are usually hunted in small-water areas—potholes, small streams and rivers, beaver ponds, and small lakes—however, there are some dabblers that will frequent big-water lakes. It is also possible to get excellent dabbler hunting in fields of cultivated grain, which is a major food source for the ducks; their forward-positioned feet make easier walking through fields.

Species and Identification

Mallard

- **Male:** bright green head; chestnut-colored breast; one to three black curls on rump; yellow bill.
- **Female:** overall mottled brown; no curls; orange bill with black spotting.
- **Wing:** large gray wing; purple speculum; white bands bordering both sides of speculum (both sexes).

Black Duck (very rare visitors to North Dakota)

- **Male and Female:** very similar in appearance; size and bill are distinguishing factors; male is bigger with a yellow bill; female bill dull green with black spotting; large dabbler; darker than female mallard with a very dark brown body and buff-colored head; may hybridize with mallards.
- **Wing:** silver underwing contrasts brightly with dark body in flight; purple speculum with no white bands bordering; top of wing is same dark color as body (both sexes).

Gadwall

- **Male and Female:** very similar in appearance; male has darker patterning of gray and white on breast and flanks and dark gray or black bill; female has a brighter brown on breast and flanks with an orange, black-spotted bill.
- **Wing:** white patch in speculum in trailing edge of wing; rust color above the white patch is prominent in males and greatly reduced in females.

A brace of wigeon. (Photo: Christopher Smith)

Wigeon

- **Male:** mature drake is hard to mistake; white streak on forehead; rust-colored breast and flanks; bright white belly; white and black spotted head with a green eye patch that reaches over the eye and extends back behind the head; bill is light blue with black tip.
- **Female:** lack white forehead and green patch; rust color is lighter and back is mottled brown; juvenile males may be confused with females; bill similar to male but duskier.

- **Wing:** white patch on leading edge of wing distinguishes this duck from gadwall; may hold a velvet green color in speculum with long silver and black tertial feathers close to the body; bright white patch is the best identifier in flight; white patch is greatly reduced in females and juveniles.

Northern Pintail
- **Male:** very large duck; long pointed black tail gives the bird its name; white breast extends up into brown head in a thin white line; rest of body is gray, black, and silver; white and black rump; slender light blue bill with black streak down the top; very long neck and long tail evident in flight.
- **Female:** mottled brown; similar to female mallard but with gray legs and longer neck; bill similar to male.
- **Wing:** copper colored speculum with white band on trailing edge of wing; overall gray-brown wing (both sexes).

Green-winged Teal
- **Male:** rust colored head with green eye patch; black spotted breast; gray flanks and brown back.
- **Female:** mottled brown over entire body; white underrump and flanks; both sexes are very small (the smallest dabbler).
- **Wing:** bright green speculum with a white band on trailing edge and a buff colored band on leading edge of speculum (both sexes).

Blue-winged Teal
- **Male:** white crescent streak on a blue head is very evident in flight; rest of body consists of black spots on a brown background.
- **Female:** mottled brown; comparable to female green-winged teal but with a larger bill and more spotting; both sexes are small.
- **Wing:** green speculum with a powder blue patch above that show brightly in flight (both sexes).

Cinnamon Teal
- **Male:** head and body is bright cinnamon colored.
- **Female:** closely resembles female blue-winged teal but with a wider bill and darker brown plumage.
- **Wing:** almost identical to blue-winged teal (both sexes).

Northern Shoveler
- **Male:** mature males have a green head; white breast; rust colored belly and flanks.
- **Female:** mottled brown; closely resembles female mallard but bill is unmistakable for both sexes; large spoon-shaped bill.
- **Wing:** almost identical to blue-winged teal only larger (both sexes).

Pintail drakes. (Photo: John Schafer)

Wood Duck

- **Male:** considered by many to be the most beautiful bird in the world; unmistakable array of all colors; prominent crest tops a green head with a white chin and neck; chestnut breast and light brown flanks.
- **Female:** also has a crest on head, but head is gray with a white eye ring.
- **Wing:** only dabbler wing to have the iridescent purple color of the speculum extend up into the primary feathers; white bar on trailing edge of speculum is straight line in males and in a teardrop pattern in females.

Migration

Much of the continent's Grand Passage—the autumn waterfowl migration—passes right over North Dakota, and because of the abundant breeding population, there is also an astounding number of resident birds in the state when the hunting season begins.

Ducks using the Central and Mississippi Flyways will pass through North Dakota, and the overlap of the two corridors can produce astonishing numbers of ducks near the central portions of the state. The teal will be the first to migrate south; early-season hunts see large numbers of both green-winged and blue-winged teal. Toward the end of the season, expect mostly mallards, though there will also be quite a few wigeon and gadwall.

Habits and Habitat

North Dakota sits right in the middle of one the largest duck-producing portions of the continent: the Prairie Pothole region. This region—representing the Great Plains states and the southern portions of the Canadian provinces—is responsible for nearly half of North America's duck population. Consequently, North Dakota receives tremendous numbers of local and migratory waterfowl passing through the state throughout the hunting season.

The scattered prairie potholes throughout the state provide some of the best duck nesting habitat available, and almost all species of ducks will make use of them (except the cavity-nesting ducks such as wood ducks). These potholes, along with the scattered marshes and rivers across the state and the abundant agricultural land, also provide plenty of food in the form of aquatic vegetation, aquatic invertebrates, and waste grains.

Puddle ducks will begin flying near sunrise, leaving their watery roosting spots for fields to feed. About mid-morning, they will return to loaf. Later in the afternoon, they will return again to the fields, leaving near sunset for their roosts once again. When migration is nearing, fat stores need to be built up at a fast rate because the ducks may leave for the South at any moment. At this time, the birds will feed throughout a clear night, using the early morning to loaf, or if they are stopping over in the state, they may feed all day long to replenish and store energy. By knowing their schedule, you'll know when and where to set up to hunt puddle ducks.

Hunting the Dabblers

Most dabbler hunting in North Dakota takes place either over prairie potholes or in fields. Some puddle ducks may pass by while you're set up for big water divers, but most of the time, puddle ducks will be found in shallow-water habitat.

Dabbling ducks are known for dropping from extreme heights in wide spirals, circling the decoy spread numerous times before committing to land. Pintails will make huge turns, and just when you think they are leaving, they will bank around and circle again. Be patient.

The teals, wood ducks, and to a lesser extent wigeon and gadwalls, will be more apt to buzz the decoy spread, catching you off guard. But once they pass through, they may still bank around and either buzz again, circle, or simply turn around and land.

Dabbling ducks will respond readily to the call, and most puddle ducks can be called in with a mallard call. But a pintail whistle will be helpful for pintails, and it may also coax in wigeon, and green-winged and blue-winged teal.

Puddle ducks make heavy use of the abundant agricultural land in North Dakota for feeding. Cultivated cornfields and other grain fields will be used quite frequently, and hunting ducks over land can present shots at huge flocks of ducks pouring into a field to feed.

Out-of-the-way places such as prairie potholes off the beaten path or hidden sloughs and marshes may provide excellent shooting at puddlers. A small bag of decoys may be all that is needed to get birds in. Also, if you can sit under a flight lane, you can get some excellent pass shooting.

Table Preparations

Dabbler ducks are excellent on the table because most of the birds are vegetarians, unlike some of the fish-eating diver ducks. Hanging the ducks overnight is recommended; however, it may make cleaning them a little more difficult. Either pluck the bird, fillet the breast meat from the bone, or clean the duck whole. There are an almost infinite number of duck recipes, and unless you overcook it, the meat is among the finest the state has to offer.

Gun and Shot Suggestions

- **Gauge:** 12, 10
- **Choke:** Improved and Modified for doubles, or Modified for single barrels.
- **Shot:** A nontoxic load (steel, bismuth, or tungsten) is required for all types of waterfowl hunting. For dabblers, loads of 1⅛ to 1¼ oz. No. 4, 2, BB, or late in the season, BBB will work. A light field load of No. 7 steel or bismuth makes a great load for dispatching cripples.

The Divers

General Characteristics

Diving ducks—ducks that dive to great depths under the water to feed—are common on big water lakes and deep impoundments, but they also frequent prairie potholes and bigger marshes. Their wings are smaller than dabbler duck wings, making it easier for them to move through the water when diving, but requiring the duck to run along the water to get up enough speed for flight. Their feet are set far back on the body, specially designed for propulsion through the water, but making it a task to walk. For this reason, there is no diver duck hunting in dry fields. Male divers may be colorful on parts of their bodies, but the wings of both sexes, as opposed to the dabblers, hold no color. The combination of black, white, and gray makes identification by the wing difficult except in a few instances.

Divers are fast flyers, approaching a decoy spread low over the water. Rarely do they circle before landing—usually they just buzz in and splash down. Late in the season, divers can store an amazing amount of fat, toughening the skin.

Species and Identification

Canvasback

- **Male:** very large duck; deep crimson head and black bill; forehead is sloped, making the head appear triangular in flight; black breast and white belly.
- **Female:** light brown, also has sloping forehead; white eye ring; flanks and breast a light tan.

Redhead

- **Male:** often confused with male canvasback, but redhead is more gray; red head not as sloped as canvasback; blue bill with white ring near the black tip; black breast and gray flanks.
- **Female:** similar to female canvasback and female lesser scaup; rounded head; light gray bill with black tip; overall dark brown.

Lesser Scaup (*Nickname: Bluebill*)

- **Male:** mature males show a dark purple head and sky blue bill; black breast and bright white belly and flanks; back is heavily vermiculated (spotted) in white.
- **Female:** has same blue bill as male, but female is an overall brown; white crescent stripe on head near base of bill; juvenile males may also have faint white crescent, but will show flecks of purple in head or vermiculations on back; vermiculations absent in female.

Ring-necked Duck (*Nickname: Ringbill*)

- **Male:** mature male has distinct white ring around gray bill; deep crimson ring around neck may be unnoticeable; black breast and gray flanks are separated by a

Setting up for divers. (Photo: Blanche Johnson)

white stripe that reaches down to the water on a sitting duck; back is not vermiculated, which distinguishes it from a male lesser scaup.
- **Female:** white ring around bill is duller; brown duck with faint white eye ring; juvenile male ringnecks closely resemble females.

Common Goldeneye
- **Male:** mostly white duck; circular white spot on a green head near base of small bill; bright yellow eyes; stark white wing patch is obvious in flight; will produce a whistling sound in flight; back is black streaked with white stripes.
- **Female:** duller white breast and flanks; brown head and yellow eyes; stubby bill may have a bit of orange near tip; bright white neck is obvious when duck sits with head erect.

Bufflehead
- **Male:** white cap; head is a spectacular array of iridescent green and purple; rest of body is mostly white with some black portions on the back; bright white wing patch is evident in flight.

A flock of redheads. (Photo: John Schafer)

- **Female:** brown duck; white cheek patch; much duller white on breast and flanks than male; both sexes are extremely small.

Ruddy Duck *(stiff-tailed duck but included with divers)*
- **Male:** breeding male has clown-like appearance of very big blue bill, white cheek and chin, rust-colored body, and stiff tail; during the hunting season, bill is more gray, and deep rust color has faded to dull brown; still sports white cheek and chin.
- **Female:** very similar to a male during the fall, but cheek and chin not as white; very small duck; not typically hunted.

Hooded Merganser
- **Male:** spectacular plumage of black, white and brown; large white hood with a black rim stands erect when bird is sitting on water; remainder of head is black; bill is long, serrated, narrow, and used for eating fish; white breast and tan flanks separated by black and white stripes.
- **Female:** brown duck; bill same as male; female is easy to pick out from male.

Common Merganser
- **Male:** very large duck; mostly white; green head; narrow bill is long, serrated, and bright red in both sexes; a fish-eating duck; not recommended table fare.
- **Female:** rust-colored head with a white chin; rest of body is gray.

Migration

The migration of divers through North Dakota is a predominantly lateral migration. Most divers will nest in northwestern portions of Canada, and instead of following a southerly migration route, they head diagonally across the continent toward the eastern shore and Great Lakes.

But those ducks that use the Canadian provinces—Manitoba and Saskatchewan —just north of North Dakota for breeding, and the divers that breed extensively on the prairie potholes within the state, will provide North Dakota hunters with large flocks of divers.

Habits and Habitat

What is a big-water duck doing in a state predominated by agricultural fields? The answer is the vast number of prairie potholes that offer excellent nesting opportunities for divers. Canvasbacks and redheads are the primary species that nest on these bodies of water.

Divers move around a little later in the day than dabblers—some of the best diver hunting is between 9 a.m. and 1 p.m. During the migration, though, small flocks of divers may be in the air constantly. Prairie potholes offer prime resting areas for the flocks that are passing through North Dakota on a lateral migration.

Divers may also use the wide rivers—especially the Missouri—for guides while migrating, resting, and feeding habitat. There are some larger lakes in North Dakota that offer more typical diver habitat—deep water, weed beds, fish, and other aquatic animals for food.

Hunting the Divers

In some of the big-water areas of North Dakota—large rivers, lakes, and potholes —divers can be hunted in traditional ways such as layout shooting or hunting decoying birds over large spreads of blocks. In these areas, an experienced diver hunter from the East will be right at home.

But many times, divers will buzz by while you're hunting a small pothole for dabblers. In these instances, if you wish to lure some more divers in, a spread of a half-dozen to a dozen canvasback, redhead, or scaup decoys in addition to your dabbler decoys will work just fine. Place the diver decoys off to the side and in a small cluster, to simulate feeding birds.

Another way to hunt divers is to get under a flight lane from one pothole to another, or better yet, from a small pothole the ducks may be using to roost to a big-water area they are using to feed and loaf, and try for the birds as they pass by. Also, look for pass-shooting opportunities along rivers. Pass-shooting divers is one of the hardest forms of wingshooting there is, but it is very enjoyable.

Calling to divers is usually of no use, even though you may hear some birds making sounds. Simply giving some quacks on your mallard call—if you have mallard decoys out—may add some realism to the entire setup.

Canvasbacks. (Photo: John Schafer)

Table Preparations

Of all the divers, canvasbacks are the preferred duck when it comes to the table. Their flavor is even better than that of many dabblers, and this was one of the reasons for their sharp decline during this century—market hunting. Because most divers will incorporate some fish and other aquatic animals in their diets, the meat can have a strong wild flavor. But if dressed right away and marinated at least 24 hours, diver meat can be very tender and juicy, tasting much like any other dark-meated gamebird.

Gun and Shot Suggestions

- **Gauge:** 12, 10
- **Choke:** Improved and modified for doubles, modified for single barrels.
- **Shot:** A heavy load of 1⅛ to 1¼ oz. No. 2, 1, BB, or BBB in steel, bismuth, or tungsten is recommended (nontoxic shot is required by federal law). Later in the season, when the birds have built up a tough fat layer, switch to a heavier load.

Nonresident Waterfowl Areas

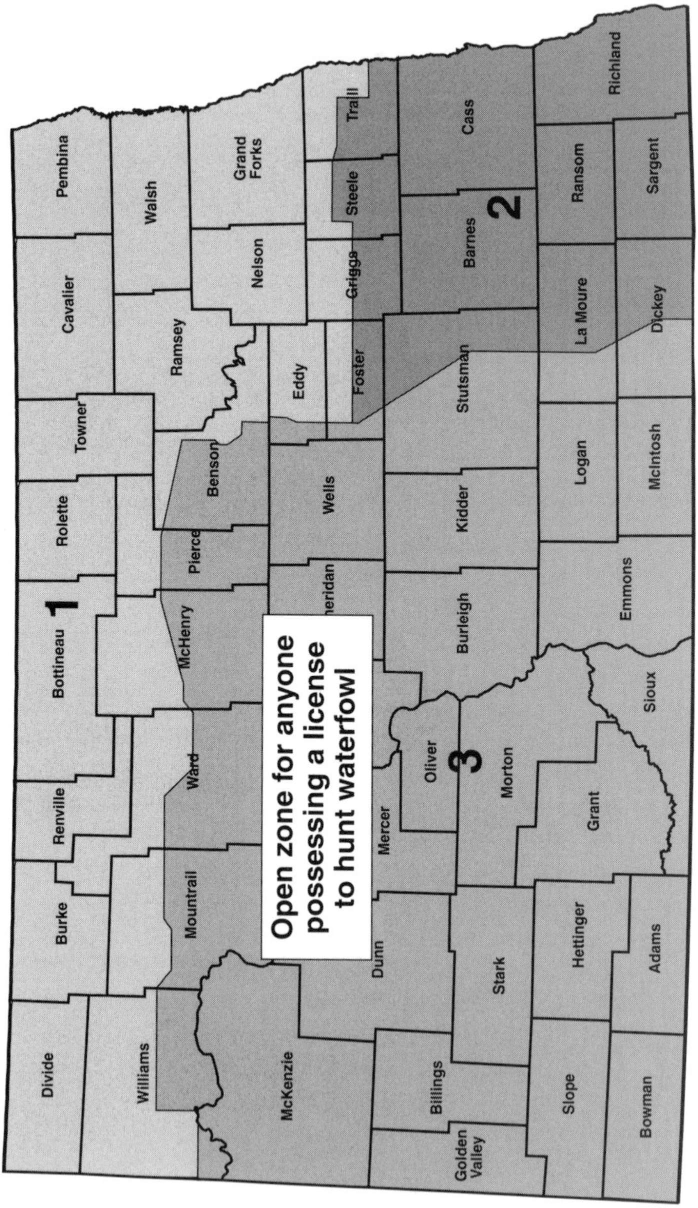

The Geese

General Characteristics

Geese are voracious eaters in agricultural fields, and seldom are they solitary—they flock-up in tremendous numbers, especially during migration. Snow geese are presently at dangerous population highs, and North Dakota is a major stopping point for migrating flocks of snow geese that can number in the hundreds of thousands. Because geese eat a wide variety of grains, the cultivated land of North Dakota provides an abundant supply of food for the large birds.

Geese are constantly chattering to each other, both in the air and on the ground. While feeding on the ground or loafing on the water, there will always be a few birds—sentinels—with their heads erect, on the lookout for danger. They will feed into the wind so they can take off quickly if danger approaches, and early in the season, a flock of birds may be found in smaller, family groups.

Note: Goose hunting ends at 1 or 2 p.m. each day, depending on the season.

Species and Identification

Canada Goose (*Nickname: Honker*)

A dark goose; species of goose most often hunted; distinctive honk in flight and on ground; black head and long black neck; white cheek patch; pale brown breast and flanks; white rump; many subspecies of which size is the best determining factor.

Snow Goose

White goose; flies in tremendously large flocks; hard to hunt because of gregarious nature; high-pitched bark is characteristic; subspecies of lesser and greater snow geese are distinguished by size.

- **White Phase:** goose is completely white; pink bill and legs; black "grin" on bill; black wingtips are obvious in flight.
- **Blue Phase:** often incorrectly thought to be a separate species; white head, pink bill, and same black grin; rest of body is an intricate patterning of black, gun barrel blue, gray, and white; black wingtips not as obvious because the rest of body is also dark.

Ross' Goose

Very similar to snow goose, but smaller; about the size of a large mallard; also has two color phases that are similar to color phases of snow geese; lacks the black grin on bill.

Greater White-fronted Goose (*Nickname: Specklebelly*)

Dark goose; pink bill; name comes from white band around base of bill; some will have black barring on breast feathers making belly appear speckled; distinctive laugh for a call in flight and on the ground; highly desirable on the table.

Greater white-fronted goose (specklebelly). (Photo: Christopher Smith)

Migration

In North Dakota, there is an overlap in the Central and Mississippi Flyways, resulting in large flocks of migrating geese. Canada geese will also use much of North Dakota for nesting and rearing broods. For this reason, there are also large resident populations.

The customary formation for migrating flocks is the V, and on clear days, the flocks may be very high. If the weather keeps them in the area for a while, though, flocks may begin to join in staging areas, leading to fields full of thousands of geese.

Habits and Habitat

The prairie potholes are also used by Canada geese for nesting, but for the most part, the habitat of North Dakota is ideal for feeding and resting the massive migrating flocks of Canadas and snows.

Snow geese in flight. (Photo: Christopher Smith)

Geese will fly to feeding areas early in the morning, and later that morning, will head back to potholes, rivers, or lakes to loaf. Early afternoon will find them again in the fields, and toward sunset, the birds will head to roosting spots. Large migrating flocks may stay through the night in fields to eat and store energy for an upcoming flight.

Hunting Geese

Most goose hunting is done in cultivated grain fields. The habits of the birds make them somewhat predictable as far as finding the fields they will use from day to day, with the exception being snow geese. Scouting a few flocks for a day will give you an idea of where to hunt—not only which field but where in the field.

Hunting Canadas and white-fronted geese is a little easier simply because they do not congregate in such large flocks. Snow geese are nearly impossible to lure in to a spread of a few dozen decoys because a flock may hold thousands of birds. Large numbers of decoys will need to be laid to get a good chance at snow geese.

Geese can also be hunted on prairie potholes or large lakes. The birds will use these areas for loafing, and later in the morning and evenings, they will return here to loaf and roost after feeding in the fields most of the day. Also, if you can sit below a flight lane between a field and a water area being used, you will get excellent pass shooting opportunities.

Because the birds are so large, they can take a lot of shot, especially in the belly. Therefore, your target should be the head and neck. The big body can be an easy target to shoot at, but it may not result in a killing shot. A shot to the head and neck will bring a goose down on the spot; however, there will be times when a dead goose—or a crippled bird—will sail hundreds of yards. If you are consistently hitting geese in the head and neck, this will rarely happen.

Table Preparations

The dark meat on geese can be very strong, especially the snow geese. White-fronted geese, though, is some of the most delectable of all game. Prepare geese any way you would other waterfowl.

Gun and Shot Suggestions

- **Gauge:** 12, 10
- **Choke:** Improved and modified for doubles, or modified for single barrels.
- **Shot:** A stout load will be needed to bring geese down. Again, nontoxic shot is required, and a load of 1¼ oz. No. 1, BB, BBB, T, or F shot is recommended.

Giant Geese

After hearing reports of the fabulous goose hunting in North Dakota, I was really interested in the chance to bag a giant Canada goose, which can weigh up to 16 pounds.

My wife, Blanche, and I scheduled a hunt for late October with Scott Moser, who runs Northland Outfitters out of Medina, North Dakota. Arriving in Medina the evening before our hunt, we stayed at the Chase Inn, a rustic country inn that caters to hunters. They have great accommodations and fine food.

Scott and his father picked us up at 5 a.m. During the night, the temperature dropped to a single digit, and it was a cold 20-minute ride to the fields. We set up our decoys in a large, harvested grain field, with a mixture of snow and Canada goose decoys set up in small family groups. About 30 yards behind our decoy set, we put a dozen giant Canada shell decoys. Scott had provided us with white coveralls, so we didn't bother with a blind, instead laying down in the field.

Blanche was positioned behind us with a camera, and my German wirehair, Duke, was laying down next to me. The first birds to work our decoys were several, small groups of mallards coming in low to the ground like stealth fighters, but it was too early to shoot and impossible to tell the difference between hens and drakes. Soon we could see large flocks of geese coming off the water and circling. It was now legal shooting time.

Author and his German wirehaired pointer, Duke, set up for an early morning goose hunt. (Photo: Blanche Johnson)

The moment of truth: a nice flight of geese locked up and coming in. (Photo: Blanche Johnson)

Author ready for incoming flight. (Photo: Blanche Johnson)

A mature goose is a mouthful for any dog. Here, Duke brings one in. (Photo: Blanche Johnson)

One last pair of mallards dived on our decoys, so Scott and I sat up and fired, each of us nailing a nice bird. As Duke brought in the second duck, the first flock of geese made a pass at our spread. As they set their wings and started in, they spooked and pulled up just before coming within range. With 20 or more flocks in the air, the sky was filled with both snow and Canada geese. While a number of flocks passed over our decoys, it was difficult trying to entice a group down. Just as one group would get interested, another group of geese would fly near and call them away. Finally, after about 20 minutes, one group of eight Canadas set their wings and came straight at us. Waiting until the lead goose was right above us, we sat up and fired. Three geese plummeted out of the sky and hit the ground with a thud.

We had several groups of snow geese look at our spread, too, but were unable to entice any of them close enough for a shot. Snow geese are wary and much more difficult to decoy than Canada geese. Not to worry, it wasn't long before another group of Canada geese set their wings and started to glide into our decoy spread, looking like B-52 bombers ready to drop their bombs.

They came silently and flew very low. We waited until they were only five yards in front and about 25 feet above us before we started shooting. I shot the lead goose as it flew over my head and had to duck to avoid being hit by it. Scott

Dog and hunter team up to control a wounded goose. (Photo: Blanche Johnson)

shot true, as well, and there were three geese on the ground to retrieve. When Duke went to retrieve my goose, he picked it up and then dropped it. His attempts to pick it up and carry it were not working. Finally, he grabbed the goose where the wing joins its body and brought it to me. When Duke got close, I could see why he was having difficulty with the bird—the goose was a monster (the meat packing plant that cleaned our game weighed it at 16 pounds).

While Duke was retrieving the other geese, he found one of them winged. When he got close to the goose, it charged him, and there was a five-minute thrust and parry duel between him and the wounded goose. Every time Duke would try to grab the goose, it would peck and hiss at him. Finally, Duke came back and sat down at my side and looked at me as if to say, "Hey, finish this goose off and then I'll retrieve it."

We had our limit of two geese each by 10 a.m., but the spectacular sight of thousands of honking geese will stay with us forever.

Hunting Waterfowl

There are several ways to hunt waterfowl in North Dakota: over decoys, jump-shooting, or pass-shooting. Dabblers, divers, and geese can all be taken at certain times by each method. If you have a favorite method, then stick with what you have fun doing.

Hunting over decoys is the traditional way to hunt waterfowl, but pass-shooting can provide a nice change of pace and can actually be more relaxing. Little in the way of gear is needed, and you can just sit down and wait for something to pass by. Jump-shooting is nice if time is limited or if you want to get some exercise. Many people compare jump-shooting waterfowl to "wet upland hunting."

Just remember that each method will present different types of shots at the ducks and geese. Decoying shots—whether on water or land—will mostly be incoming shots at the head and neck portion of the bird—the best killing shots. Pass-shooting presents fast crossing or incoming shots, and you'll need to adjust your lead. Jump-shooting offers the least likely killing shot as the bird will get its back and rear toward you very quickly. If jump-shooting, try to take the birds within the first few wingbeats off the water when the head and neck are exposed.

Boats and Blinds

Most waterfowl hunting in North Dakota will require some sort of blind, but perhaps not a boat. Along the large rivers, lakes, and potholes, though, a boat will allow you to get out where the birds are. A boat can be made into a floating blind by a variety of methods, but simply draping a camouflage tarp over the hull and staying low will often do the trick.

A belly-boat—an innertube with a tough nylon covering and a seat in the middle—will allow you to paddle around a deep pothole. If you don't have a dog, this may be the only way to retrieve a downed bird. These tubes are lightweight and can even provide a little concealment. Some belly-boats are made especially for hunting; a hunter can sit in one in the water among the decoys and lower his profile.

When hunting smaller potholes, you can simply stand in the tall weeds and cattails that may line the shore. If the shore is barren, a pop-up blind or fencing woven with brush will provide the necessary concealment. When field-hunting, fencing can be bent into a "coffin," woven with the surrounding vegetation, and pulled over your body as you lay down in the field. Simply throw the fencing off and shoot when the birds are in range.

While pass-shooting, you may just be able to lay low, hold still, and wait. If there are trees surrounding a pothole, lean up against one and try to blend in. More often than not, the ducks and geese know where they're going, and if you are not too much of an eyesore, you won't flare them.

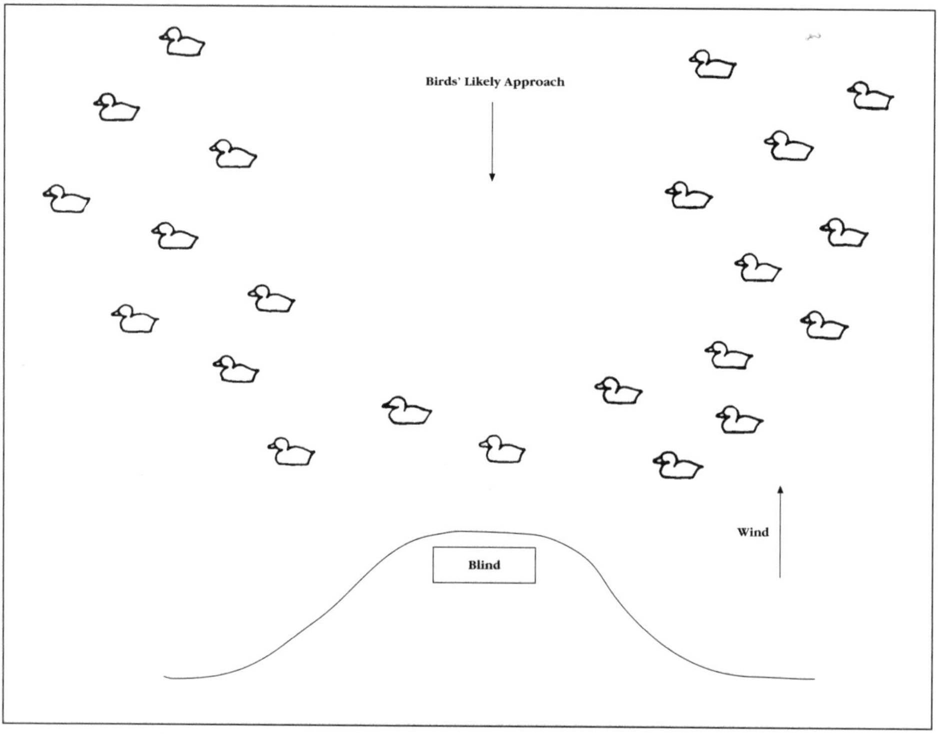

Horseshoe spread: tossing a few decoys away from the main spread adds a touch of realism. (Illustration: Christopher Smith)

Decoys and Decoy Spreads

For ducks, floating decoys are the most useful. They come in a variety of shapes and sizes, but all will work pretty much the same on the potholes, rivers, and lakes. Be sure to have the species of ducks you intend to lure in represented in your decoy spread.

Goose hunting in the fields will require large spreads of decoys, and this is best accomplished through lightweight decoys that can be hauled easily. Silhouettes, shells, foam bodied decoys, or rags will allow you to set up a lot of decoys quickly. There are many ways to set decoy spreads, but a few reliable spreads are illustrated. The horseshoe spread is ideal for dabblers in prairie potholes, but you may also find that simply scattering the decoys around near the blind, leaving an area for the birds to land, works well enough. The open-water setup is a popular spread for hunting divers from a boat blind. This is useful in big lakes or rivers where you are not near the shore. The field spread is well suited for geese.

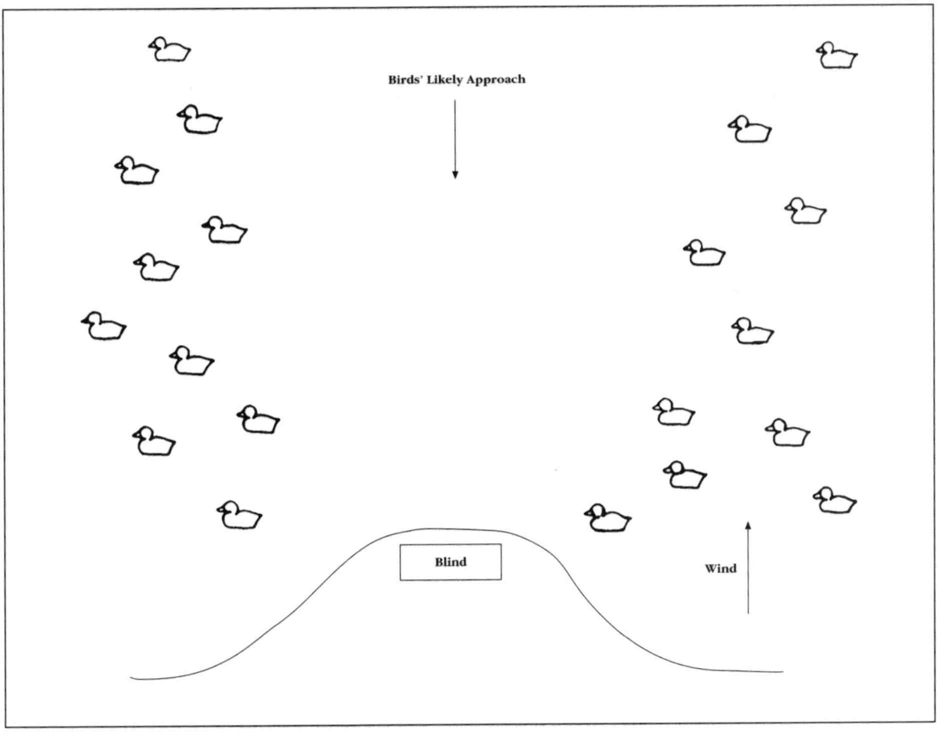

Runway spread decoy pattern. (Illustration: Christopher Smith)

An important factor to remember about setting decoy spreads is to always leave a landing area for the birds within killing range.

Dogs

The retrieving breeds—Labrador retrievers, Chesapeake Bay retrievers, golden retrievers, and springer spaniels—are excellent additions to any duck blind. Some of the versatile breeds such as wirehairs will also perform well, and even some pointing dogs that have been trained to retrieve will work nicely on waterfowl. Their thin coats (compared with retrievers) may restrict them to the early season.

The best way to deal with the possibility of losing crippled birds is to use a well-trained retriever—prairie potholes are often deep in the center, and unless you have a small boat or belly-tube, retrieving dead birds in the middle of the pothole is difficult—and wet. Dogs simply make the process of waterfowling easier by taking care of one end of the whole job. And it's what they live for.

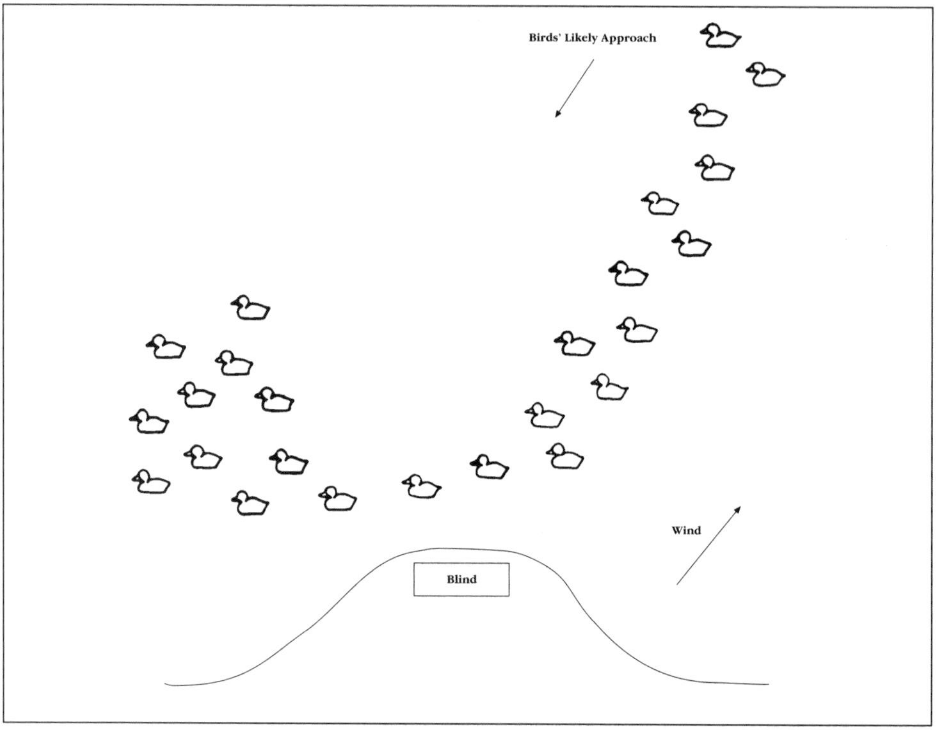

J-hook spread decoy pattern. ((llustration: Christopher Smith)

Paraphernalia

There is probably more gear involved in waterfowling than in most other outdoor pursuits. But some things are essential.

Proper camouflage (plain drab colors work well also), a good flashlight, dependable waders (unless you're hunting in a dry field), durable waterproof and warm jacket and clothing, gloves, and a hat will all make the hunt smoother. In addition, a field bag, camera, and binoculars are handy to have along. A first aid kit should be nearby, and if you're hunting with a dog, don't forget a couple dog bones, a dog vest for older dogs, and a leash if you'll be heading back to the car near a busy road.

A mallard call will be the most useful in a North Dakota duck blind. Nearly all dabbler species—and even some divers—will respond to a mallard call. A pintail whistle is a nice addition, and if geese are a possibility, then of course, pack a goose call.

Dress in layers—you can always take something off if you get too warm. Keep in mind the weather predictions for the day, and play it smart. There will always be more ducks and geese.

The West

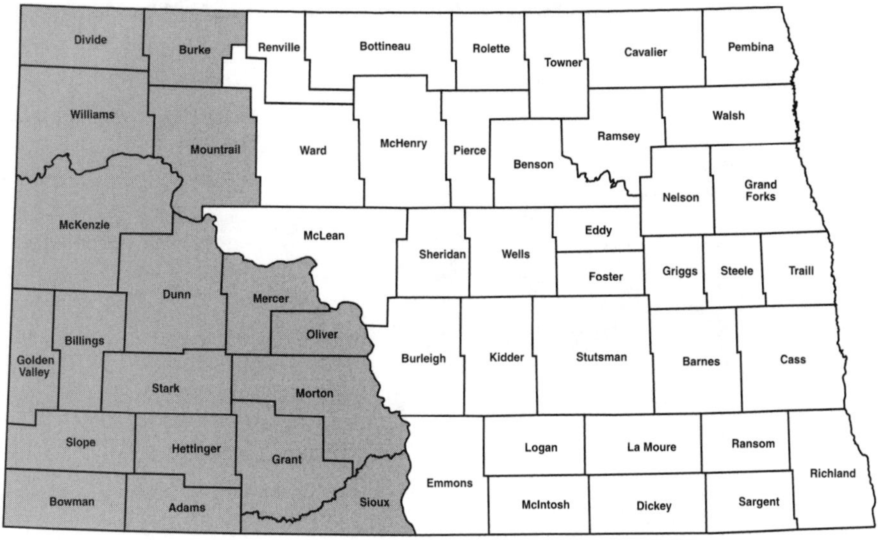

This region begins at the Montana state line and extends over the western third of the state, from its northern border with Canada to the southern border with South Dakota. The Missouri River flows through this region, and it is, perhaps, the focal point for western North Dakota's waterfowlers. Most of this region's terrain consists of rolling hills, vast prairies, and desolate, challenging badlands.

The two largest Indian reservations in North Dakota and the Little Missouri National Grasslands are in this region. The Little Missouri National Grasslands, on its western border, encompasses over a million huntable acres, where sharp-tailed grouse, pheasants, and Hungarian partridge reign.

Due to varied habitat, including the badlands and grasslands, this region offers some of the best upland bird hunting in the state. Southwest North Dakota is considered the heart of pheasant country and also offers the state's only huntable population of sage grouse, which can be found in Bowman, Slope, and Golden Valley Counties.

The upper Missouri River system provides great opportunities for hunting ducks and geese.

Overall, there are no lack of wingshooting opportunities in the West, whether you prefer to pursue pheasants, Huns, and sharptails with your pointer in the grasslands or to sit in a blind on the Missouri River waiting for massive flights of ducks and geese with your favorite retriever. Huns, pheasant, and sharptails are the most abundant upland birds, and the state's greatest concentration of turkeys also reside here. The southwest corner is also the only area open to sage grouse hunting.

This region also offers ample amenities for the visiting hunter, with friendly, small towns that offer nice hotels, motels, and restaurants.

Ring-necked Pheasant Distribution
West Region

■ **Good** ■ **Fair**

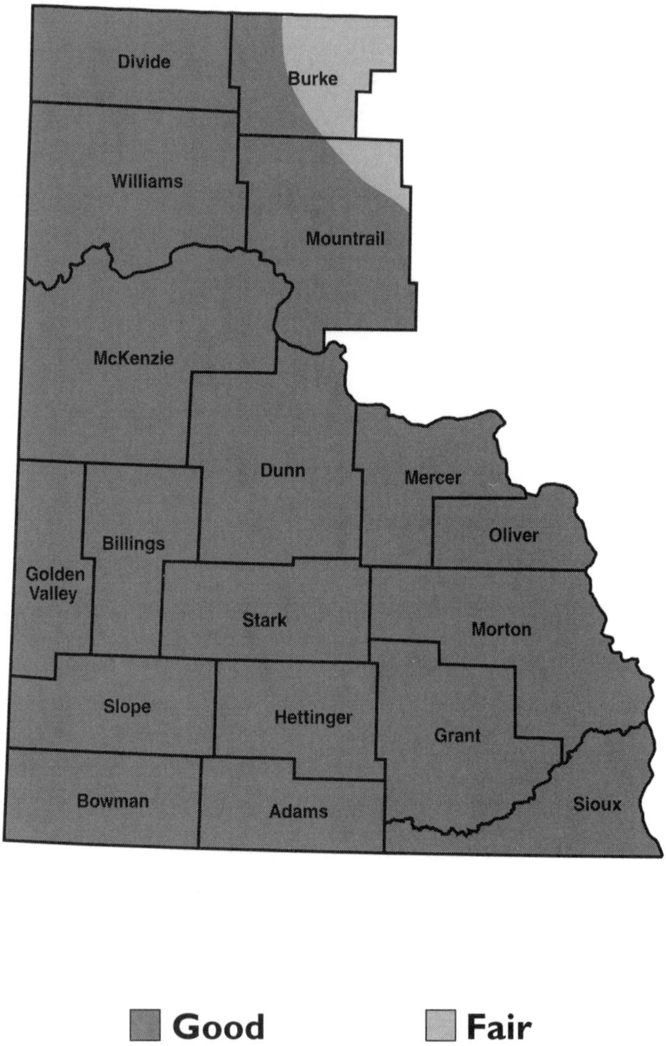

Sharp-tailed Grouse Distribution West Region

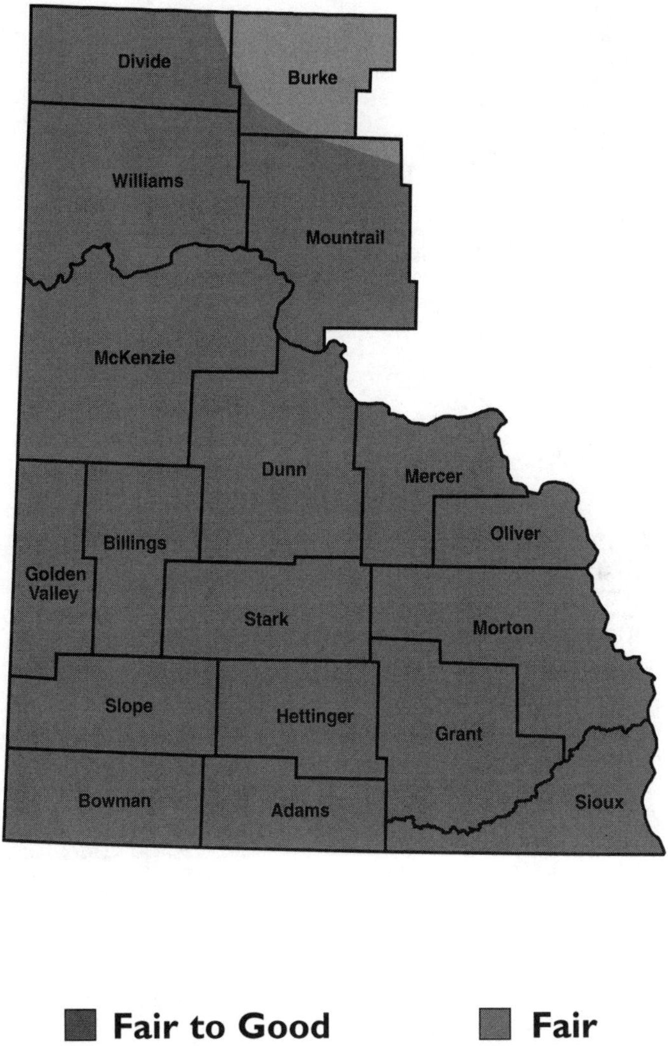

Gray Partridge Distribution
West Region

■ **Poor to Fair** ☐ **Poor**

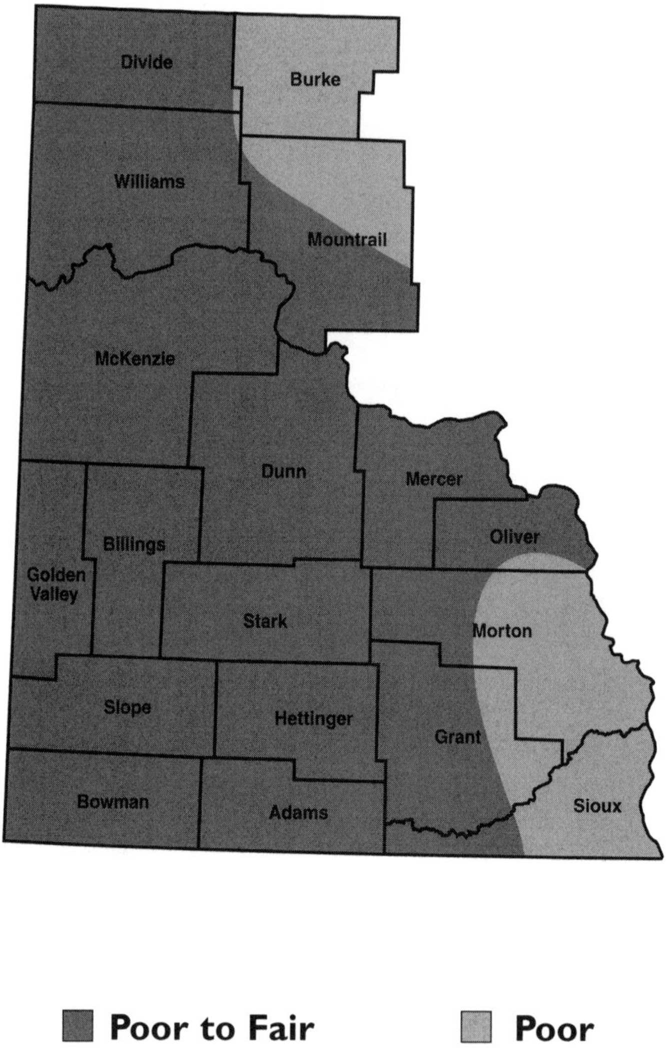

Sage Grouse Distribution
West Region

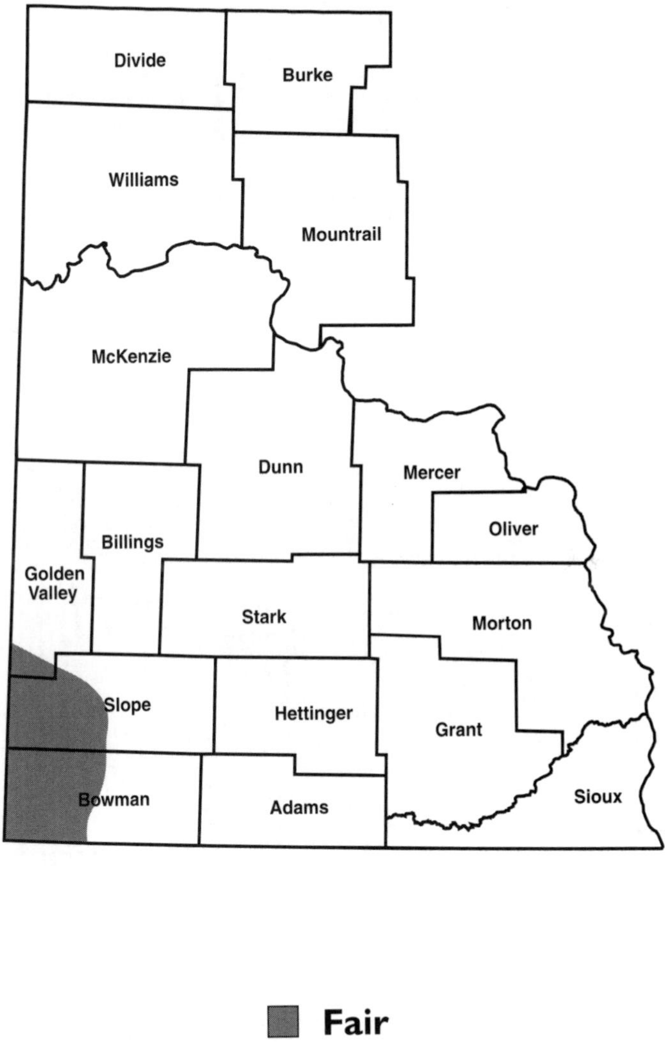

Ruffed Grouse Distribution
West Region

Wild Turkey Distribution West Region

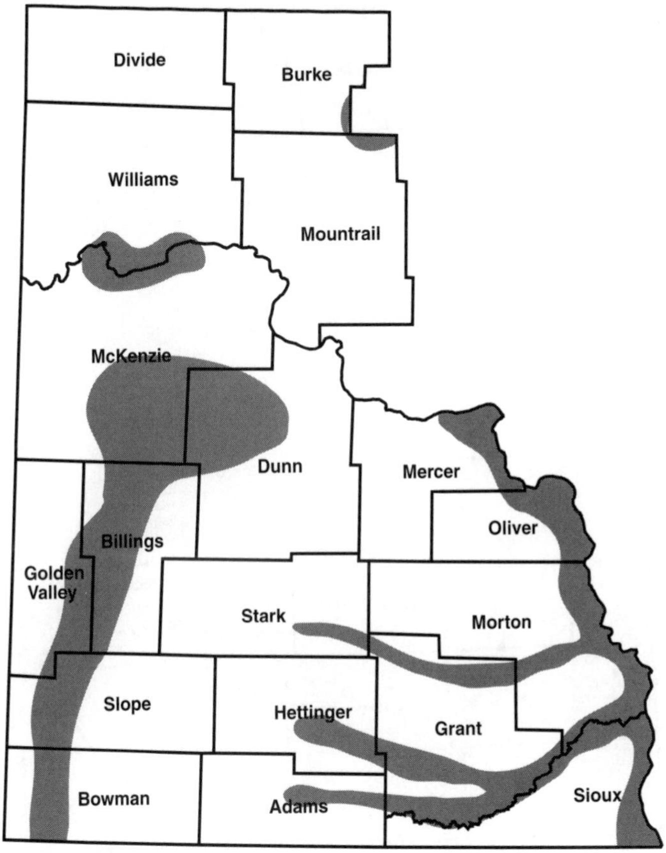

■ **Populations low to fair**

Woodcock Distribution West Region

Mourning Dove Distribution West Region

Found throughout region

Common Snipe Distribution
West Region

Found throughout region

Sandhill Crane Distribution
West Region

Found throughout but denser populations in eastern part of region

Beulah and Mercer County

Population–3,800	Elevation–1,700
County Population–9,808	October Temperature–59°
County Area– 1,044 sq. mi.	Acres in CRP–15,297

Located in western North Dakota, just south of Lake Sakakawea in Mercer County, Beulah is a classic, small town that grew with the railroad. Today, it promotes itself as the lignite (a low-grade coal) capital of the world.

UPLAND BIRDS
Pheasant, Sharptail, Gray Partridge, Turkey, Mourning Dove, Snipe, Sandhill Crane

WATERFOWL
Ducks & Geese

ACCOMMODATIONS

Dakota Farms Inn, Highway 49 North / 40 rooms, six nonsmoking, cable TV, restaurant and lounge / Dogs allowed / 701-873-2242 / $$

Super 8, Highway 49 North / 37 rooms, cable TV / Dogs allowed / 701-873-2850 / $$

CAMPGROUNDS AND RV PARKS

Sun Valley Trailer Court, Highway 21 / RV parking, electrical outlets, week or monthly rates / 701-873-2528

Riverside Park Campground / Limited electrical, plenty of primitive sites / Permit acquired through Parks and Recreation / 701-873-4586

RESTAURANTS

Country Kettle, Main Street / Open 5am to 10pm / Breakfast, lunch, dinner / Beer and wine / 701-873-2233

Southside Diner, Highway 49 South / Open 8am / Breakfast, lunch, dinner / May be closed Saturday and Sunday / 701-873-2930

Subway, Highway 49 & Railroad Avenue / Sandwiches and soup / 701-873-2828

Pizza Hut, Main Street / Pizza and salad, beer and wine / 701-873-5040

VETERINARIANS

Knife River Veterinary, Route 1 Highway 49 South / 701-873-5525

SPORTING GOODS STORES

Coast to Coast, 116 West Main Street / 701-873-4318

Hunting from a boat on the Missouri River. (Photo: John Schafer)

AUTO REPAIR

Downtown Conoco, 202 East Main Street / 701-873-5166

AIR SERVICE

Beulah Municipal Airport, Southwest Beulah

MEDICAL

MedCenter One, 1312 Highway 49 North / 701-873-4445

FOR MORE INFORMATION

Beulah Chamber of Commerce
P.O. Box 730
Beulah, ND 58523
701-878-4586

Bowman and Bowman County

Population–1,500	Elevation–2,850
County Population–3,596	October Temperature–44°
County Area–1,162 sq. mi.	Acres in CRP–711

Bowman is located in southwest North Dakota. Surrounded by the badlands, the rolling grass prairie, and many irrigation reservoirs, Bowman offers numerous amenities for the visiting hunter. Bowman's chief industries are agriculture and cattle ranching.

UPLAND BIRDS
Pheasant, Sharptail, Sage Grouse, Gray Partridge, Turkey, Mourning Dove, Snipe

WATERFOWL
Ducks & Geese

Accommodations

Budget Host 4-U Motel, 704 Highway 12 West / 701-523-3243 / Dogs allowed, must be attended / $
Super 8 Motel, 614 3rd Avenue SW / 701-523-5613 / dogs allowed, no fee / $$

Campgrounds and RV Parks

Twin Butte Campground, RV hookups and tent sites / 701-523-5569

Restaurants

Windy's Bar and Pizza, 408 Main Street South / pizza, pasta, beer / open 9am to 1am / 701-523-3727
Cottonwood Cove Eatery, 208 1st Avenue SW / open 10am / breakfast, lunch, dinner / soup and sandwiches / no cocktails / 701-523-5863
Sharivar Steakhouse & Lounge, 108 1st Avenue SE / steaks, salad, chicken, seafood, cocktails / 701-523-5201

Veterinarians

Bowman Veterinary, RR 1, Box 126 / 701-523-3234

Sporting Goods Stores

Wanners, 104 2nd Avenue SW / 701-523-3171
Coast to Coast Hardware, 23 North Main / 701-523-3240

A stand of tall grass, mixed with brush, is prime North Dakota bird habitat. When you encounter this type of cover, let a dog work it thoroughly and hold that gun at the ready. A pheasant, Hun or sharp-tailed grouse could take flight. (Photo: Blanche Johnson)

AUTO REPAIR

Mann's Automotive, 105 Main Street North / 701-523-3201
Auto Care, Highway 85 & 1st Avenue SW / 701-523-3845

AIR SERVICE

Plains Aviation Airport, 701-523-5606

MEDICAL

St. Luke's Tri-State Hospital, 202 6th Avenue SW / 701-523-5265

FOR MORE INFORMATION

Bowman Chamber of Commerce
Box 1143
Bowman, ND 58623
701-523-5880

Crosby and Divide County

Population–1,250	Elevation–2,000
County Population–2,899	October Temperature–45°
County Area–1,288 sq. mi.	Acres in CRP–97,442

Crosby is located in Divide County, just south of the Canadian border in the northwest corner of the state. With access to prime waterfowl and upland bird hunting on surrounding ranches, this little town grows markedly during the fall hunting season. Book reservations in advance.

UPLAND BIRDS
Pheasants, Sharptails, Gray Partridge, Mourning Dove, Sandhill Crane, Snipe

WATERFOWL
Ducks & Geese

Accommodations
Golden Hub, Highway 5 East / 701-965-6368 / dogs allowed / $$

Campgrounds and RV Parks
Divide County Fair Grounds / 15 hookups, indefinite electrical sites, bathroom and showers / 701-965-6029

Restaurants
Red Rooster, 702 SE 4 / Open 6:30am to 8pm / Breakfast, lunch, dinner / 701-965-6516

Dakota Diner, 104 Main Street / 701-965-4376

Lee's Drive Inn, 501 Main Street / 701-965-4371

Full House Cafe, 104 Main Street / Open 6am to 5pm / Breakfast, lunch, dinner / 701-965-6033

Veterinarians
Western Veterinary Clinic, Hwy 2 & 85 West, Williston / 701-572-7878

Sporting Goods Stores
Coast to Coast, 112 North Main / 701-965-6561

Canam Connection, Junction of Highway 5 & 85 / 701-982-3350

Auto Repair
Bob's Service Center, 109 5th Avenue SE / 701-965-6275

Air Service
Crosby Airport, North of City Hall / 701-965-6722

A solid point on pheasant in the Theodore Roosevelt grasslands.
(Photo: Blanche Johnson)

MEDICAL

St. Luke's Hospital, 702 SW 1st / 701-965-6384
Crosby Clinic, 112 1st Avenue NW / 701-965-6274

FOR MORE INFORMATION

Divide County Jobs Development Authority
P.O. Box 297
Crosby, ND 58730
701-965-6006

Dickinson and Stark County

Population–16,097	Elevation–2,500
County Population–22,832	October Temperature–54°
County Area–1,330 sq. mi.	Acres in CRP–60,849

Dickinson rests in western North Dakota on the east edge of the badlands, a notoriously inhospitable chunk of terra firma that harbors opportunities for ambitious upland hunters and waterfowlers alike. Dickinson itself is an entirely friendly town that offers ample amenities for visiting hunters.

UPLAND BIRDS
Pheasant, Sharptail, Gray Partridge, Turkey, Mourning Dove, Sandhill Crane, Snipe

WATERFOWL
Ducks & Geese

ACCOMMODATIONS

Select Inn, I-94 & ND 22 / Dogs allowed / Country Kitchen restaurant next door / 701-227-1891 / $$

Budget Inn, 529 12th Street West Exit 61 / 701-225-9123 / Air conditioning, cable TV, lounge, restaurant, casino / Dogs allowed, no fee / $$

Comfort Inn, 493 Elks Drive, Exit 61 / 701-264-1132 / 115 units, air conditioning, continental breakfast, cable TV, jacuzzi, indoor pool, restaurant, casino / Dogs allowed, no fee / $$

Queen City Motel, 1108 West Villard, Exit 59 / 701-225-5121 / 33 units, air conditioning, outdoor pool, lounge, casino and restaurant nearby / Dogs allowed, no fee / $

Best Western, 71 Museum Drive, Exit 61 / Open 24 hours / Dogs allowed / Lounge, casino, pool, jacuzzi / 701-25-9510 / $$

CAMPGROUNDS AND RV PARKS

KOA, State Avenue South / 701-225-9600 / campsites along the Heart River, pool

Patterson Lake Recreation Area, Three miles west and one mile south of Dickinson / 701-225-2074 / 24 modern campsites, 40 primitive campsites, coin operated showers

RESTAURANTS

Husky House Cafe, 837 East Villard / Open 8am / Breakfast, lunch, dinner / Home-style food / 701-225-7867

Champs Sports Club, 1125 West Villard / Open 24 hours / Breakfast, lunch, dinner / 701-225-2345

Elks Lodge, 501 Elks Drive / Fine dining for lunch and dinner / 701-264-1137

German Hungarian Lodge, 20 East Broadway / Lunch 11am to 1pm, Dinner 5pm to close / Steaks, seafood, pasta, soup and salad / 701-225-3311

Perkins Family Restaurant, 188 Museum Drive / Open 24 hours / Breakfast, lunch, dinner / 701-227-3001

VETERINARIANS

Dickinson Veterinary Service, 414 25 Avenue East / 701-225-8719

West Dakota Veterinary Clinic, 93 21 Street East / 701-225-0240

Slope Area Veterinary Clinic, SE of City / 701-227-8731

SPORTING GOODS STORES

Coyote's Den, Highway 22 N / 701-225-5773

AUTO REPAIR

Brian's Auto Repair, Highway 22 South / 701-225-8523

Caps Conoco Service, Big Sky Shopping Center / 701-225-3226

DJ's Amoco, 450 12 Street West / 701-225-5724

AIR SERVICE

Dickinson Municipal Airport, Carriers: United Express / 701-225-3822

MEDICAL

St. Joseph's Hospital, 30 West 7th Street / 701-225-7200

Dickinson Clinic, 8938 Second Avenue West / 701-225-5183

FOR MORE INFORMATION

Dickinson Chamber of Commerce
314 Third Avenue. West
Dickinson, ND 58602
701-225-5115

Dickinson Convention and Visitors Bureau
314 Third Avenue West
Dickinson, ND 58602
701-225-4988

Hazen and Mercer County

Population–2,818	Elevation–1,743
County Population–9,808	July Temp.–84°, January Temp.–18°
County Area–1,044 sq. mi.	Acres in CRP–15,397

UPLAND BIRDS
Pheasant, Sharptail, Gray Partridge, Turkey, Mourning Dove, Sandhill Crane, Snipe

WATERFOWL
Ducks & Geese

Accommodations

Roughrider Motor Inn, Highway 200 E / 57 rooms, cable TV, no pets / 701-748-2209 / $-$$

Centennial Log Cabin, HC 2, Box 152, Sanger ND, at Cross Ranch State Park / Historic log cabin rental; overnight use, 1-5 people costs $35; 6-10 costs $45 / Dogs allowed / No electricity or running water / 701-7940-3731

Campgrounds and RV Parks

Moses Park, 7th Street NW / RV park with electrical hookups, no sewage disposal / 701-748-6948

Riverside Park, 1 mile south of Hazen / Tent sites and RV park with electrical hookup / 701-748-6948

Restaurants

The Woodshed, Highway 200 East / Breakfast, lunch, dinner / Cocktail lounge opens at five / 701-748-6989; 701-748-6381

Hot Stuff Pizzeria, 34 Main Street E / Lunch and dinner / Pizza, pasta, bread / No beer, wine, or cocktails / 701-748-2332

Lee's Diner, 47 Main Street / Open 6:30am to 8pm / Breakfast served all day, lunch, dinner / 701-748-5900

Subway, 709 3rd Avenue NW / Sandwiches, soup / 701-748-2626

Veterinarians

Nearest in Beulah

Sporting Goods Stores

Hazen Hardware, 118 West Main / 701-748-6464

Cenex, Highway 200 / 701-748-2511

Highway Express, Highway 200 / 701-748-2950

AUTO REPAIR

B&H Services, 145 West Main / 701-748-6474

AIR SERVICE

Mercer County Regional Airport, P.O. Box 567 / 701-748-5592

MEDICAL

Sakakawea Medical Center, 510 8th Avenue NE / 701-748-2225

FOR MORE INFORMATION

Hazen Community Development
P.O. Box 717
Hazen, ND 58545
701-748-6848

Hebron and Morton County

Population–1,050	Elevation–2,162
County Population–23,700	October Temperature–58°
County Area–1,921 sq. mi.	Acres in CRP–52,262

Hebron is located in southwest North Dakota, just off Interstate 94 in Morton County. With its quick access to I-94 and excellent hunting opportunities in its backyard, the town offers a convenient stopover for traveling hunters or a good base for extended trips in the local area. Pheasant is the primary gamebird.

UPLAND BIRDS
Pheasant, Sharptail, Gray Partridge, Turkey, Mourning Dove, Sandhill Crane, Snipe

WATERFOWL
Ducks & Geese

ACCOMMODATIONS
Brick City Motel, 507 South Avenue / 701-878-4467 / $$
Harry's Service & Motel, 413 Main Avenue / 701-878-4521 / $

RESTAURANTS
Brick City Cafe, 523 Main Avenue / 701-878-4577
Pizza Pantry, 712 Main Avenue / 701-878-459
Wagon Wheel Cafe, 119 Park Street / 701-878-4326

VETERINARIANS
Hebron Vet Clinic, 712 Main Avenue / 701-878-4200

SPORTING GOODS STORES
Hebron Hardware, 619 Main Avenue / 701-878-4504

AUTO REPAIR
Zuroff Repair, 501 Main Avenue / 701-878-4175
Rebels Repair, 803 Main Avenue / 701-878-4763

AIR SERVICE
Hebron Airport (Nearest airport served by a major airline is in Bismarck, which is 65 miles away)

Hunting a field of tall grass near a water source; top upland bird hunting terrain. (Photo: Blanche Johnson)

Medical

Medcenter One, 811 Main Avenue / 701-878-4250

For More Information

City of Hebron
Box V
Hebron, ND 58638
701-878-4600

Hettinger and Adams County

Population–1,750	Elevation–2,705
County Population–3,174	October Temperature–46°
County Area–988 sq. mi.	Acres in CRP–88,699

Hettinger is located in extreme southwest North Dakota, nestled up against the South Dakota line in Adams County. The North Fork Grand River and Shadehill Reservoir twist to the south. With adequate water and irrigated croplands, Hettinger claims to be the pheasant capital of North Dakota. A heavy game bag after a day in the fields here supports that notion.

UPLAND BIRDS
Pheasant, Sharptail, Gray Partridge, Turkey, Mourning Dove, Sandhill Crane, Snipe

WATERFOWL
Ducks & Geese

Accommodations
Mirror Lake Lodge, Box 1346 / 701-567-2571 / $$
Tip Top Motel, Box 707 / 701-567-2437 / $

Campgrounds and RV Parks
Mirror Lake Park, Box 103 / 701-567-4363

Restaurants
Pastime Steakhouse, Box 511 / Open 5pm / Steaks, salads, seafood, pasta, cocktails / 701-567-4627
Peppy's Fast Foods, Box 189 / 701-567-2755
Sidetrack Restaurant and Lounge, Box 1207 / Open 5:30am / Breakfast, lunch and dinner / 701-567-4696

Veterinarians
West River Veterinary Clinic, Box 440 / 701-567-4333

Sporting Goods Stores
Country General, Box 500 / 701-567-2412

Auto Repair
RZ Motors, Box 666 / 701-567-2474
Farmer's Union Oil, Box 1290 / 701-567-4343
Hedahl's Automotive Center, Box 867 / 701-567-4387

AIR SERVICE

Air Dakota Flite Inc., Box 429 / 701-567-2069

MEDICAL

West River Regional Medical Center, Box 125 / 701-567-4561

FOR MORE INFORMATION

Hettinger Area Chamber of Commerce
P.O. Box 1031
Hettinger, ND 58639
701-567-2531

Killdeer and Dunn County

Population–722	Elevation–2,200
County Population–4,005	October Temperature–44°
County Area–1,993 sq. mi.	Acres in CRP–29,388

Killdeer is located in western North Dakota, just south of Little Missouri Bay on Lake Sakakawea. This rustic "Old West" town harbors plenty of amenities and offers easy access to good pheasant, sharptail, Hungarian partridge, and turkey hunting grounds.

UPLAND BIRDS
Pheasant, Sharptail, Gray Partridge, Turkey, Mourning Dove, Sandhill Crane, Snipe

WATERFOWL
Ducks & Geese

Accommodations
Crossroads Motel, South of Killdeer at junction of Highway 22 & 200 / Attached lounge and restaurant / 701-764-5860 / $$

Campgrounds and RV Parks
RV Park, Highway 22 S /

Restaurants
Crossroads, south of Killdeer at junction of Highway 22 & 200 / Open 6am / Breakfast, lunch, dinner 701-764-5927

Roundup Cafe, Roundup Mall / Open 6am / Breakfast, lunch, dinner / 701-764-5600

Buckskin Bar, Central Avenue / 701-764-5321

Stardust Inn, Highway 200 East / 701-764-5092

Veterinarians
Mountain Veterinary Clinic, 701-764-5625

Badlands Vet, 701-764-5022

Sporting Goods Stores
None

Auto Repair
Tony's Repair / 701-764-5558

Air Service
Dunn County Airport/Weydahl Field / 701-764-8909

Typical North Dakota gamebird habitat. (Photo: Blanche Johnson)

MEDICAL

Killdeer Medical Clinic, Roundup Mall / 701-764-5822

FOR MORE INFORMATION

City of Killdeer
Box 270
Killdeer, ND 58640
701-764-5032

Mandan and Morton County

Population–49,256 (with Bismarck)	Elevation–1,700
County Population–1,921	October Temperature–58°
County Area–1,921 sq. mi.	Acres in CRP–52,262

Mandan is located just west of Bismarck on the west side of the Missouri River in Morton County. Mandan and Bismarck offer all the amenities a wingshooter could require, plus it's centrally located, meaning it's a prime spot to hold overnight on your way to other shooting grounds. Check Bismarck's amenities if you can't book a room or find a restaurant in Mandan.

UPLAND BIRDS
Pheasant, Sharptail, Gray Partridge, Turkey, Mourning Dove, Sandhill Crane, Snipe

WATERFOWL
Ducks & Geese

Accommodations

Seven Seas, 2611 Old Red Trail, Exit 152 / 800-597-7327 / Indoor pool, restaurant, lounge, casino / Dogs allowed / $$

Elite Motel, I-94 and exit 155 / 701-663-6497 / 19 rooms, restaurant & lounge next door, HBO / Dogs allowed / $$

River Ridge Inn, I-94 & exit 152 / Dogs allowed / 701-663-0001 / $$

Campgrounds and RV Parks

Fort Lincoln State Park, 4 miles south of Mandan / 701-663-9571 / 56 trailer sites

Restaurants

A & B Pizza, 609 1st Street NE / 701-663-1333

Bonanza Family Restaurant, 1704 East Main Street / 701-663-5858

Settlers Cafe, 406 West Main / Open 6am to 9pm daily / 701-663-6548

Veterinarians

Mandan Veterinary Clinic, 1 mile west of Mandan on Route 4 / 701-663-6805

Midway Veterinary Clinic, 4120 Memorial Highway / 701-663-9841

Sporting Goods Stores

Scheels All Sports (Bismarck), Kirkwood Mall / 701-255-7255

Marv's Own Hardware, 110 Main W / 701-663-9735

K-Mart, 2625 State Street (Bismarck) / 701-223-0074

AUTO REPAIR

Charley's Repair Service & Towing, 800 Main Street West / 701-663-0044
Cenex Auto Repair, 810 Main Street East / 701-663-6401

AIR SERVICE

Mandan Municipal Airport, 4 miles SW of Mandan
Bismarck Municipal Airport / Carriers: United Express, Northwest, Mesaba / 701-222-6502

MEDICAL

Medcenter One, 300 North 7th Street (Bismarck) / 701-224-6000

FOR MORE INFORMATION

Bismarck/Mandan Chamber of Commerce
PO Box 1675
Bismarck, ND 58502
701-223-5660

Medora and Billings County

Population–94	Elevation–2,700
County Population–1,108	October Temperature–48°
County Area–1,152 sq. mi.	Acres in CRP–23,267

Medora is a colorful, historic Western town located in the center of the Little Missouri National Grassland. Just north of town is Theodore Roosevelt National Park and the cabin that was part of Teddy Roosevelt's cattle ranch. A contemporary of Roosevelt's was the Marquis de Mores, a French nobleman who was a cattle rancher in the late 1800s. He built a huge hilltop ranch house that is now a museum. Medora is a fun town with great Western charm and is an ideal place to stay when hunting the grasslands. Pheasant and sharp-tailed grouse are the most popular birds.

UPLAND BIRDS
Pheasant, Sharptail, Gray Partridge, Turkey, Mourning Dove, Snipe

WATERFOWL
Ducks & Geese

ACCOMMODATIONS

Medora Motel, East River Road / 204 rooms, AC, cable TV, outdoor pool / Dogs allowed (must be attended) / 701-623-4444 / $$
Rough Rider Motel, Downtown / 9 rooms, AC cable TV, restaurant / Dogs allowed / 701-623-6721 / $$
Sully Inn, Corner of Broadway and 4th / 19 rooms, AC, cable TV, book store / dogs allowed / 701-623-4455 / $$
America Inn, 75 East River Road South / Indoor pool, continental breakfast / 701-623-4800

CAMPGROUNDS AND RV PARKS

Cottonwood Campground, 5 miles inside Theodore Roosevelt National Park / Tent sites, 66 RV sites / 701-623-4466
The Medora Campground, West side of eastbound Exit 24 / 124 RV sites, 79 electrical sites, showers, sewers / 701-623-4444 / $$

RESTAURANTS

Iron Horse Saloon, Medora / Open 6am to 1pm / Beer, wine, cocktails, breakfast, lunch, dinner, burgers, steaks / 623-9894
Cowboy Cafe, Medora / Open 7am / Breakfast, lunch, dinner 701-623-4343
Rough Rider Hotel / Dinner meals, steaks, seafood, pasta, salad / 701-623-6721

VETERINARIANS

Nearest in Beech:
Beech Veterinary Clinic, East Main / 701-872-4158

SPORTING GOODS STORES

Coyote's Den, Highway 22 North / 701-225-5773

AUTO REPAIR

Medora Auto, south Medora / 701-623-4871

AIR SERVICE

Nearest commercial in Dickinson:
Dickinson Municipal Airport, Carriers: United Express / 701-225-3822

MEDICAL

Nearest in Dickinson:
St. Joseph's Hospital, 30 West 7th Street / 701-225-7200
Dickinson Clinic, 8938 Second Avenue West / 701-225-5183

FOR MORE INFORMATION

Medora Chamber of Commerce
Medora, ND 58645
701-623-4910

Mott and Hettinger County

Population–1,019	Elevation–2,850
County Population–3,445	October Temperature–48°
County Area–1,133 sq. mi.	Acres in CRP–101,652

Hettinger County is in the heart of the best pheasant hunting in North Dakota. Citizens of Mott and Hettinger County have set up a community hunting organization that caters to out-of-state hunters. Area ranchers have made a great deal of their land available for hunting. Contact the Cannonball Company, which runs the hunts.

UPLAND BIRDS
Pheasant, Sharptail, Gray Partridge, Turkey, Mourning Dove, Sandhill Crane, Snipe

WATERFOWL
Ducks & Geese

Accommodations

Mott Motel, Junction Highway 8 and 21 / 20 rooms, AC, Cable TV / Dogs allowed / 701-824-2297 / $$

Dawn to Dusk Bed and Breakfast, Rt. 3 Box 76A / 701-824-2719 / $$-$$$

Campgrounds and RV Parks

American Legion Park, South Mott / Tent sites, 4 RV sites, 4 electric hookups, sewer / 701-824-2163

Restaurants

Pheasant Cafe & Lounge, 206 Brown Avenue / Open 6am / Breakfast, lunch, dinner / Lounge opens 5pm to 1am / 701-824-2851

Veterinarians

Cannonball Veterinary, East of town / 701-824-2950

Sporting Goods Stores

Mott Equity, 509 County Road / 701-824-3296

Auto Repair

Earnie's Repair, South Mott / 701-824-3272

Air Service

Nearest Commercial Service: Hettinger

Blanche Johnson is all smiles with this handsome rooster pheasant. (Photo: Chuck Johnson)

MEDICAL

West River Clinics, 420 Pacific Avenue / 701-824-2391

FOR MORE INFORMATION

Mott Chamber of Commerce
309 East 2nd Street
Mott, ND 58646
701-824-2044

North Dakota Game and Fish
409 Brown Avenue
Mott, ND 58646
701-824-2337

New Town and Mountrail County

Population–1,398	Elevation–1,854
County Population–7,021	January Temp.–10°; July Temp.–80°
County Area–1,837 sq. mi.	Acres in CRP–87,190

New Town is located just off Lake Sakakawea at the north end of Van Hook Arm on the Fort Berthold Indian Reservation. New Town offers plenty of amenities for visiting hunters, whether they are pursuing birds in Mountrail County or on the reservation. The 4 Bears Casino & Lounge, owned by the Three Affiliated Tribes, offers gaming rooms, fine dining, and, of course, a stocked bar.

UPLAND BIRDS
Pheasant, Sharptail, Gray Partridge, Mourning Dove, Sandhill Crane, Snipe

WATERFOWL
Ducks & Geese

ACCOMMODATIONS

The Cottage Inn, West Main Street / 17 rooms / Hunting dogs allowed /Game cleaning stations, freezers, kitchenettes available / 701-627-4217 / $$

West Dakota Inn, East New Town / 701-627-3721 / $$

Four Bears Casino & Lodge, 4 miles west of New Town / 39 rooms / Lounge and restaurant / Breakfast, lunch, dinner / Opens at 6am / Dogs with deposit of $25 / 701-627-4018 / $$-$$$

CAMPGROUNDS AND RV PARKS

Van Hook Bait & Tackle, 6 miles east and 2 miles south / 701-627-3811 / 110 tent sites, 30 electrical sites, shower, sewer

4 Bears Casino & Lodge Camping, 4 miles west of New Town / 701-627-4018 / Full service and primitive camping, water, shower, security, convenience store

RESTAURANTS

Tastee Freez, Main Street / Hamburgers, fries / 701-627-3315

Lucky's Cafe, 4 miles west of New Town / Open 6am / Breakfast , lunch, dinner / 701-627-4018

Scenic 23 Club, 6 miles east of New Town / Lunch, dinner / 701-627-3949

Four Bears Casino and Lodge, 4 miles west of New Town / Open 6am / Breakfast, lunch, dinner, cocktails / 701-627-4018

A classic fall scene: dogs on point and a hunter ready to fire.
(Photo: Blanche Johnson)

VETERINARIANS
Northwest Vet Service (in Stanley), Junction of Highways 2 & 8 / 701-628-2778

SPORTING GOODS STORES
Coast to Coast, Main Street / 701-627-3425
The General, Main Street / 701-627-3939

AUTO REPAIR
Farmer's Union Oil, Main Street / 701-627-3636
Wrensch Chevrolet, Main Street / 701-627-4621

AIR SERVICE
New Town Airport, 1/2 mile south of town / paved runway

MEDICAL
New Town Community Clinic, Main Street / 701-627-2990

FOR MORE INFORMATION
New Town Chamber of Commerce
PO Box 422
New Town, ND 58763
701-627-4812

Stanley and Mountrail County

Population–1,371	Elevation–2,220
County Population–7,021	January Temp.–4°, July Temp.–67°
County Area–1,837 sq. mi.	Acres in CRP–87,190

Stanley is located in northwest North Dakota and serves as the seat of Mountrail County. Lostwood Wildlife Refuge lies 15 miles north of town, while Lake Sakakawea sits 30 miles south. Ample amenities are available for the upland bird or waterfowl hunter.

UPLAND BIRDS
Pheasant, Sharptail, Gray Partridge, Mourning Dove, Sandhill Crane, Snipe

WATERFOWL
Ducks & Geese

Accommodations

The Prairie Host Motel & Lounge, Highway 2 West / 701-628-3500 / 35 units, AC, cable / Dogs allowed for extra $5 a day / $$

Campgrounds and RV Parks

Dakota West RV Park and General Store, Highway 2 / 701-755-3407 / 21 hookups, tent area, showers, laundry

Stanley RV and Tent Park, Highway 8 North / Showers , hookups

Restaurants

Cenex C-Store/Piccadilly Pizza, Highway 2 / 701-628-2921 / Sells bird stamps and hunting licenses

Patten's Post, Highway 2 West / Open 7am to 8pm / Breakfast, lunch, dinner / 701-628-3900

Dairy Queen, 528 South Main Street / 701-628-2635

Veterinarians

Northwest Vet Service, Junction of Highways 2 & 8 / 701-628-2778

Sporting Goods Stores

Dakota Drug, 118 Main / Hunting and fishing supplies and licenses / 701-628-2255

Auto Repair

Alley Auto, Main Street Alley / 701-628-2810

Ken's Tire Service, 4 South Main Street / 701-628-3530

AIR SERVICE

Stanley Airport, Box 892 / 701-628-2110

MEDICAL

Stanley Community Hospital, 502 3rd Street SE / 701-628-2424
Family Care Clinic, Stanley Professional Building / 701-628-3579

FOR MORE INFORMATION

Stanley Commercial Club
Box 974
Stanley, ND 58784

Tioga and Williams County

Population–1,278	Elevation–2,260
County Population–21,129	October Temperature–58°
County Area–2,074 sq. mi.	Acres in CRP–51,875

Tioga is located in northwest North Dakota on the east edge of Williams County. Tioga means "peaceful valley," and this small town lives up to that billing. For the bird hunter, Tioga offers ample amenities and easy access to prime waterfowl and upland bird grounds.

UPLAND BIRDS
Pheasant, Sharptail, Gray Partridge, Turkey, Mourning Dove, Sandhill Crane, Snipe

WATERFOWL
Ducks & Geese

ACCOMMODATIONS

Super 8, 210 2nd Street East / 30 rooms / Dogs allowed for $5 extra a day / morning coffee / Freezer space available / Restaurant and lounge across street / 701-664-3395 / $$

North Fork Lodge, 481 1st Street NE / 701-664-2011 / $$

CAMPGROUNDS AND RV PARKS

Tioga City Park, / 701-664-2563

RESTAURANTS

Sportsman's Cafe, 17 North Main Street / 701-664-2598

Legion Steakhouse, North Main Street / Open 5:30pm / Steaks, salads, seafood / 701-664-2510

Home Style Cafe, 11 1st Street NE / Open 5:30am / Breakfast, lunch and dinner / 701-664-2589

VETERINARIANS

In Stanley, 25 miles away, Northwest Vet Service, Junction of Highways 2 & 8 / 701-628-2778

SPORTING GOODS STORES

Coast to Coast, 23 North Main Street / 701-664-3309

True Value, 108 North Welo Street / 701-664-2950

A grassland swale with tall grass is a sure sign that birds are about. Here, the author walks up to his dog on point. (Photo: Blanche Johnson)

AUTO REPAIR

Tioga Motor Service, / 701-664-2512

AIR SERVICE

Tioga Municipal, 2nd Street NW / 701-664-2343

MEDICAL

Tioga Medical Center / 701-664-3305

FOR MORE INFORMATION

Tioga Chamber Of Commerce
P.O. Box 52
Tioga, ND 58852
701-664-2807

Watford City and McKenzie County

Population–1,784	Elevation–2,105
County Population–6,383	October Temperature–50°
County Area–2,754 sq. mi.	Acres in CRP–35,815

UPLAND BIRDS
Pheasant, Sharptail, Gray Partridge, Turkey, Mourning Dove, Sandhill Crane, Snipe

WATERFOWL
Ducks & Geese

Accommodations
Four Eyes Motel, 125 South Main / 14 rooms, AC, cable TV / Dogs allowed / 701-842-4126

McKenzie Inn, 132 3rd Street SW / 14 rooms, AC, cable TV, coffee, hot tub / Dogs allowed, no fee / 701-842-3980

Watford City Inn, 600 2nd Avenue SW / 50 rooms, AC, cable TV, hot tub, restaurant, lounge, coffee / 1-888-206-0400

Campgrounds and RV Parks
Tobacco Garden, 28 miles north of Watford City / Primitive tent sites, 65 RV sites, 65 electric, shower, sewer, swimming pool / 701-842-6931

Summit Campground, 20 miles south on US 85 / Tent sites, 5 RV sites / 701-842-2393

Squaw Creek Campground, 15 miles South on US 85 / Tent sites, 41 RV sites, sewer, water / 701-842-6508

Restaurants
Carl's Bakery, 221 North Main Street / 701-842-2325

Chuck Wagon Cafe, 108 Park Avenue / Open 6am / Breakfast, lunch, dinner / 701-842-3115

Veterinarians
Watford City Veterinary, 1 mile north of town on Main Street / 701-842-2037

Sporting Goods Stores
Ace Hardware, 140 North Main / 842-3321

Farmer's Union Oil, 101 South Main / 842-3639

AUTO REPAIR

Badlands Auto, Highway 85 and Main / 701-842-3123

AIR SERVICE

Watford City Airport, East edge of town off Highway 85 / Nearest commercial in Williston

MEDICAL

McKenzie Hospital, 508 North Main Street / 701-842-3000

FOR MORE INFORMATION

McKenzie County Tourism Bureau
P.O. Box 699
Watford City, North Dakota 58854
800-701-2804

Williston and Williams County

Population–13,131	Elevation–1,857
County Population–21,129	October Temperature–45°
County Area–2,074 sq. mi.	Acres in CRP–51,875

Williston, located in northwestern North Dakota, lies near the confluence of the Missouri and Yellowstone Rivers. The habitat created by these rivers provides good pheasant hunting, while turkey hunting is also good along the Yellowstone in McKenzie County. The area's agricultural base provides decent numbers of sharptails, Huns, pheasants, and a few mourning doves. Key waterfowl hunting can be found near the two major rivers to the south and east, the prairie potholes to the north, and Lake Sakakawea to the east. Williston offers everything the traveling hunter needs, including a nice selection of motels and restaurants, well stocked sporting goods stores, and a lively night life.

UPLAND BIRDS
Pheasant, Sharptail, Gray Partridge, Mourning Dove, Sandhill Crane, Snipe

WATERFOWL
Ducks & Geese

ACCOMMODATIONS
Super 8 Lodge, 2324 2nd Avenue West / 7901-572-8371 / Dogs allowed with permission, call ahead / $$

Airport International Inn, Highway 2 & 85 / 701-774-0241 / Dogs allowed, case-by-case decision / $$

Select Inn, Highway 2 and 85 North / 60 rooms, AC, cable TV, indoor pool, lounge / Dogs allowed in 12 smoking rooms / 701-572-4242

El Rancho Motor Hotel, 1623 2nd Avenue West / 92 rooms, AC, cable TV, restaurant, breakfast, lunch and dinner, and lounge, casino / Dogs allowed / 701-572-6321

CAMPGROUNDS AND RV PARKS
Buffalo Trails Campground, NE of Williston / 701-572-3206

RESTAURANTS
Dairy Queen, 1620 2nd Avenue / Burgers and fries / 701-572-6474

Fireside Dining and Lounge, 1002 2nd Street West / Steaks, seafood, pasta, chicken, cocktails / 701-572-0677

Kalley's Kitchen, Highway 2 North & 85th / Open 24 hours / Breakfast, lunch, dinner / 701-774-1103

DK's Bar and Grill, 2402 1st Avenue West / Dinner and cocktail lounge, open 5pm, closes 1am / 701-774-3995

VETERINARIANS

Western Veterinary Clinic, Highway 2 & 85 West / 701-572-7878

Williston Veterinary Clinic, 308 West 26 Street / 701-572-9271

SPORTING GOODS STORES

Hunting & Archery Outfitters, Highway 2 West / 701-572-3203

Scenic Sports and Liquor, 1201 Broadway East / 701-572-8696

AUTO REPAIR

Goodyear Auto Service, 1909 2nd Avenue West / 701-572-6167

Westland Auto Repair, 301 26th Street West / 701-774-8341

AIR SERVICE

Sloulin Field International Airport, Highway 2 and 85 North / 701-774-8594

MEDICAL

Mercy Hospital, 1301 15th Avenue West / 701-774-7400

FOR MORE INFORMATION

Williston Chamber of Commerce
PO Box G
Williston, ND 58802
701-572-3767

Williston Convention and Visitors Bureau
10 Main Street
Williston, ND 58802
701-774-9041

Guides and Outfitters

The West Region

NORTH FORK LODGE

Box 481 Tioga, ND 58852 / 701-570-2313
Contact–Dallas and Val Lalim
Land–10,000 acres
Game – Pheasant, sharptail grouse, Huns, ducks, Canada geese, snow geese
Personal Guide – Available
Dogs – Provided or use your own
Extras – Meals, accommodations, kennels

ELKHORN LODGE

HCR 1 Box 70 Fortuna, ND 58844 / 701-834-2374
Contact: Jamie & Cicile Wehrman
Land – 4,000 acres
Game – Pheasant, Huns, sharptail grouse, ducks, geese, swans
Personal Guide – No; hunt on your own
Dogs – Bring your own dog
Extras – Single cabin available (sleeps eight)

CANNONBALL COMPANY

HCR 1, Box 75, Regent, ND 58650 / 701-563-4411
Contact: Brad and Cheryl Nasset
Land–30,000 acres
Game – Pheasant, Huns, sharptail grouse, waterfowl
Personal Guide – Guided hunts only
Dogs – Provided or bring your own
Extras – Bed and breakfast or houses available; meals available also

BADLANDS GUIDE SERVICE

421 1st Street SW Dickinson, ND 58601 / 701-225-6109
Contact:Billy and Betty Freitag
Land – 3,000 acres
Personal Guide – Available or hunt on your own
Game – Huns, wild pheasant, sharptail grouse, turkey
Dogs – Dogs provided or you can hunt with your own
Extras – Motel available

The Lakes and Gardens

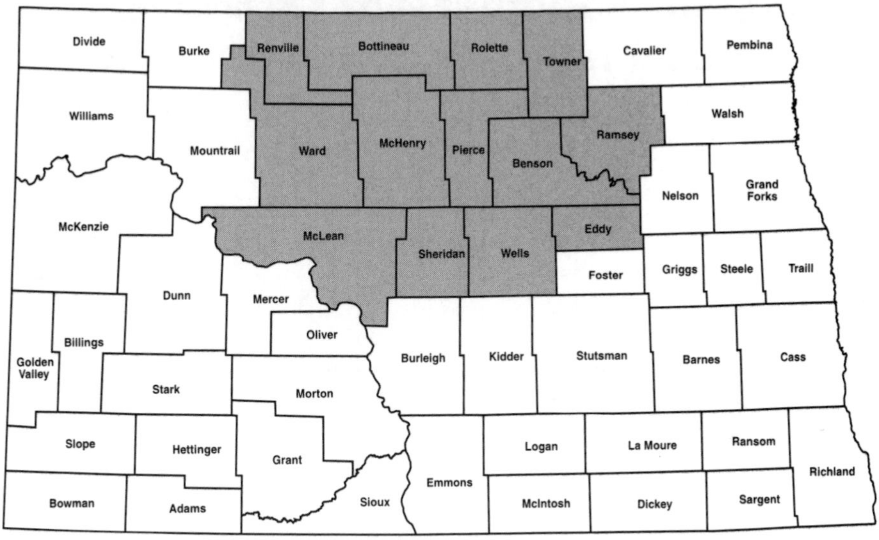

This region is located in north central North Dakota, with its heart being Devil's Lake. The region's west border is formed partially by the Missouri River and Lake Sakakawea. To the north, it borders Canada.

This region is covered with potholes, making it the state's major breeding ground for waterfowl. The potholes also attract huge flights of migrating snow geese, Canada geese, and a variety of ducks. Waterfowl hunting is king here, and shooting can be tremendous throughout fall. However, it is part of Special Waterfowl Zone 1, and licenses for nonresidents are limited (see license information). October is, perhaps, the ideal month to plan a waterfowl hunt in this region.

Upland bird hunting is fair to good in the lakes and gardens region, depending on the year. Pheasants, sharp-tailed grouse, and Hungarian partridge offer a mixed bag in the CRP and grasslands areas. There are also options for woodcock in riparian areas and wild turkey in isolated pockets.

Area outfitters offer guided hunts for upland birds or waterfowl, but you can easily find public hunting areas on your own, if that is your preference.

Ring-necked Pheasant Distribution
The Lakes and Gardens Region

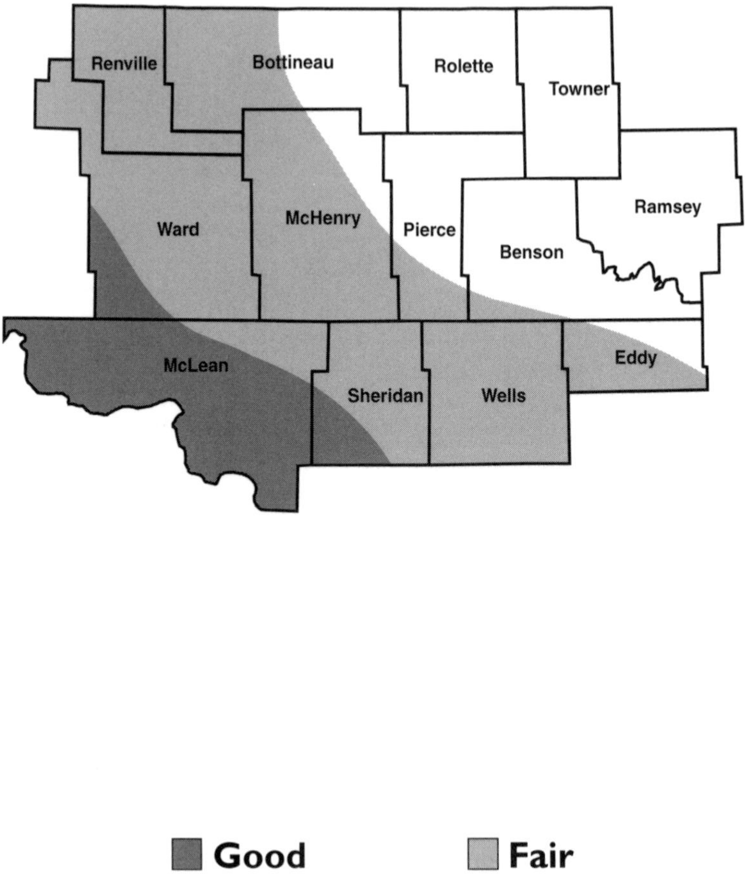

Sharp-tailed Grouse Distribution
The Lakes and Gardens Region

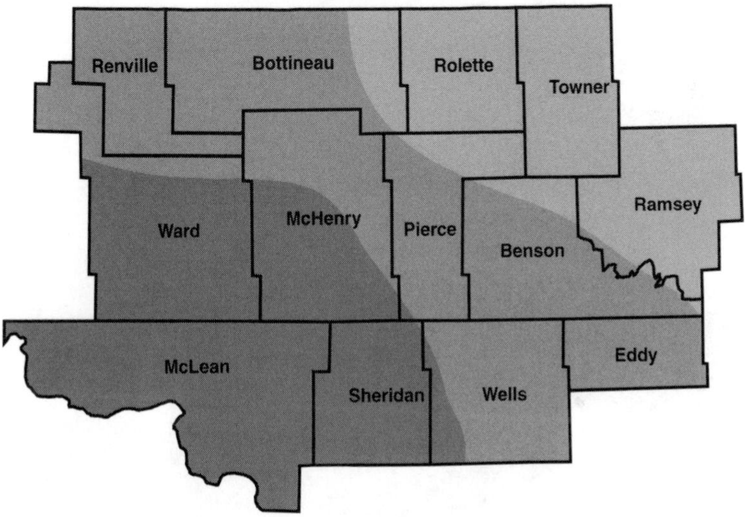

Fair to Good **Fair**

Gray Partridge Distribution
The Lakes and Gardens Region

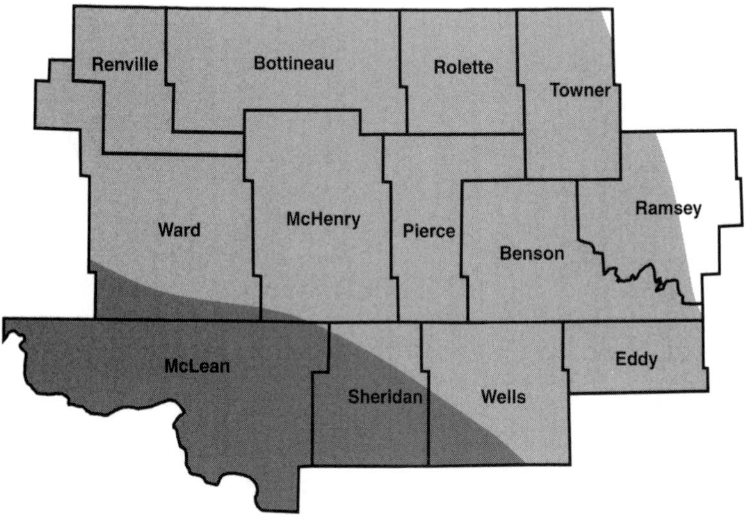

Ruffed Grouse Distribution
The Lakes and Gardens Region

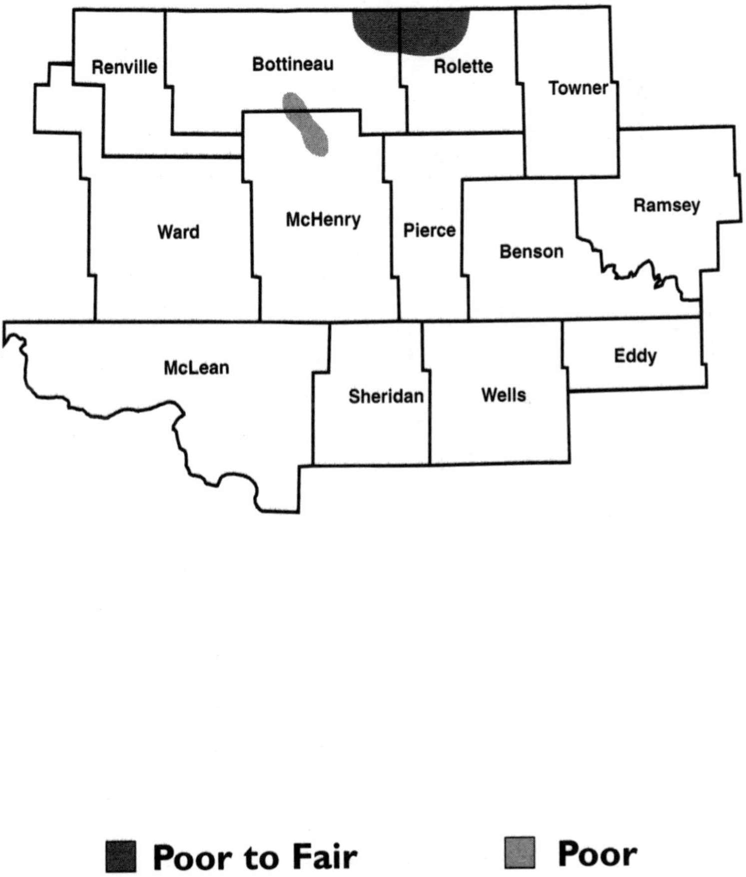

Wild Turkey Distribution
The Lakes and Gardens Region

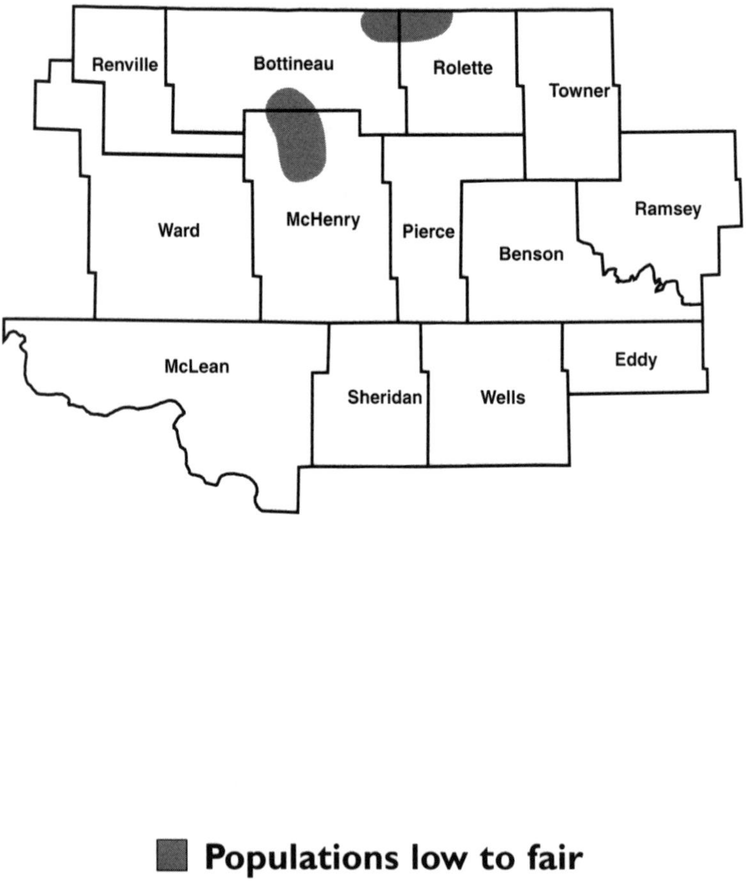

Woodcock Distribution
The Lakes and Gardens Region

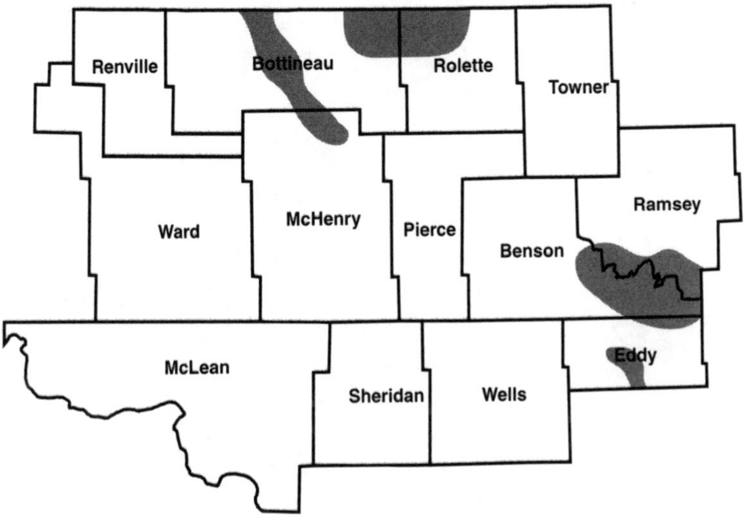

Only found in these drainages

Mourning Dove Distribution
The Lakes and Gardens Region

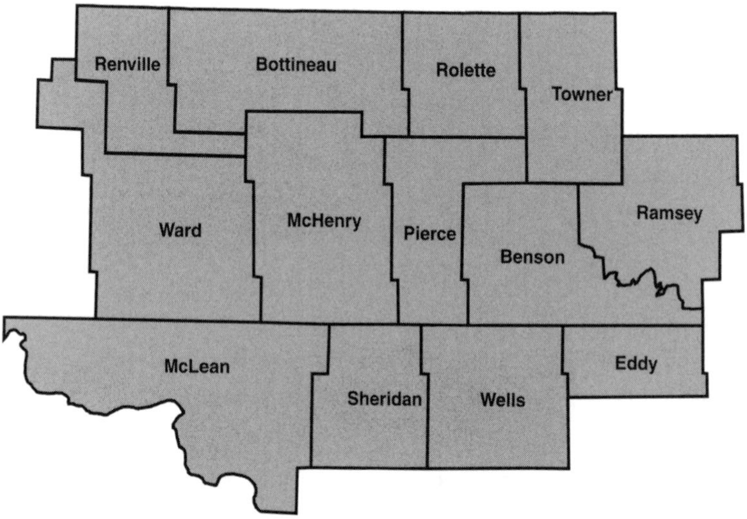

Found throughout region

Common Snipe Distribution
The Lakes and Gardens Region

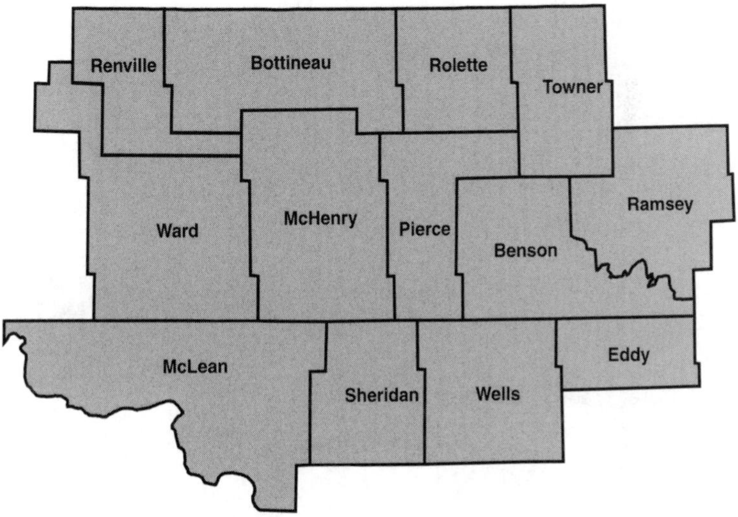

Found throughout region

Sandhill Crane Distribution
The Lakes and Gardens Region

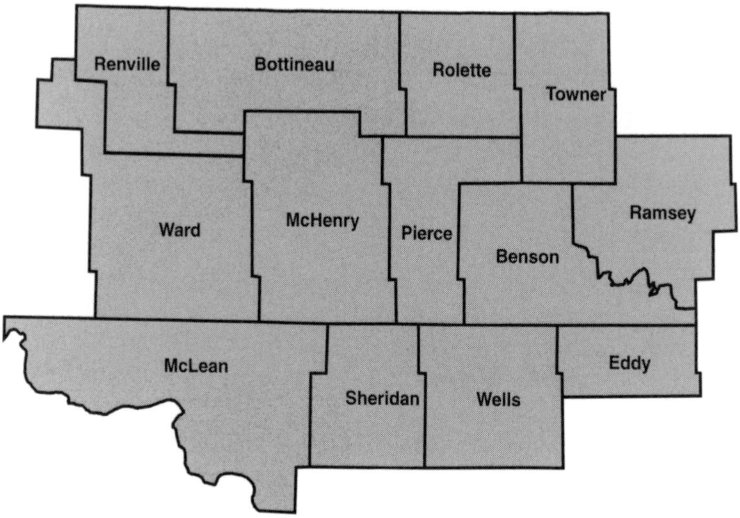

Found throughout region

Bottineau and Bottineau County

Population–2,598	Elevation–1,675
County Population–8,011	January Temp.–2°; July Temp.–68°
County Area–1,668 sq. mi.	Acres in CRP–93,198

Bottineau is located in north central North Dakota, just south of the Canadian border. The town lies west of the Turtle Mountains and directly in the heart of the Central Flyway. Known for its surrounding duck and goose shooting, Bottineau offers excellent accommodations for visiting hunters.

UPLAND BIRDS
Pheasant, Sharptail, Gray Partridge, Ruffed Grouse, Turkey, Mourning Dove, Sandhill Crane, Snipe, Woodcock

WATERFOWL
Ducks & Geese

ACCOMMODATIONS

Loveland Lodge, Highway 5 West / 701-228-2296 / 20 rooms, color cable TV, air conditioning, lounge adjoining / $$

Norway House, Highway 5 East / 701-228-3737 / 46 rooms, lounge, dining room, air conditioning / $$

Turtle Mountain Lodge, Lake Metigoshe / 701-263-4206 / 24 rooms, color TV, air conditioning, lounge, restaurant, indoor pool, hot tub / $$

CAMPGROUNDS AND RV PARKS

Bottineau City Park, East 10th Street / Showers, drinking water, flush toilets, sewage hookup, sewage disposals, electrical hookups, 18 trailer and tent sites / 701-263-5501

Lake Metigoshe State Park, located on Lake Metigoshe, 12 miles north of Bottineau / 90 trailer sites, 47 tent sites, showers, water, flush toilets / 701-263-4651

RESTAURANTS

Family Bakery & Restaurant, 412 Main / Open 6am / Breakfast and dinner / 701-228-2179

Stadium Lounge and Steak Pit, 505 Thompson Street / 701-228-2132

Dairy Queen, Highway 5 West / 701-228-2822

VETERINARIANS

Bottineau Veterinary / 701-228-6990

SPORTING GOODS STORES

Ace Hardware, 510 Main Street / 701-228-2284

Maybe the most stately of all waterfowl, the canvasback is a true trophy for the hunter. (Photo: John Schafer)

AUTO REPAIR

Bee Line Service, 309 Main Street / 701-228-3142
D&B Body Works, Highway 5 East / 701-228-3072

AIR SERVICE

Bottineau Municipal Airport, 9770 13th Avenue NE / 701-228-5265 / Nearest airport with commercial service is in Minot, which is 80 miles away

MEDICAL

Bottineau Clinic, 322 West 4th Street / 701-228-2268
St. Andrews Health Center, 316 Ohmer Street / 701-228-2255

FOR MORE INFORMATION

Bottineau Chamber of Commerce
103 East 11th Street
Bottineau, ND 58318
701-228-3849

Devils Lake and Ramsey County

Population–7,958	Elevation–1,451
County Population–12,681	October Temperature–52°
County Area–1,241 sq. mi.	Acres in CRP–48,485

Devils Lake is located in eastern North Dakota, in Ramsey County, next to the Sully's Hill Game Preserve. Devils Lake offers ample amenities for waterfowl and upland bird hunters. The lake itself provides hunters with numerous duck and goose hunting opportunities; fishermen ply its waters for large walleye, perch, and northern pike.

UPLAND BIRDS
Sharptail, Gray Partridge, Mourning Dove, Sandhill Crane, Snipe, Woodcock

WATERFOWL
Ducks & Geese

ACCOMMODATIONS

Comfort Inn, 215 Highway 2 East / 701-662-6760 / 60 units, continental breakfast, hot tub, indoor pool, FAX and copy machines / Pets allowed, no fee / $$

City Center Motel, 518 5th Street North / 701-662-4918 / 25 rooms, hunter's discount (10 percent for 3 or more day stay) / Dogs allowed, no fee / $

Days Inn, Highway 20 South / 701-662-5381 / 45 rooms, nonsmoking rooms, whirlpool suites / Dogs allowed, no fee / $$

CAMPGROUNDS AND RV PARKS

L&M Bait, Black Tiger Bay, 8 miles east of Devils Lake on Highway 2 / 701-398-3474 / Modern camping $10 a night, primitive $7 a night

Shelver's Grove State Park, Rt 1 Box 165 / 701-766-4015 / 27 modern campsites and 5 primitive sites

Elks Lodge, Old Highway 2 East / 701-662-4915 / water and electrical hook up, restaurant and lounge

RESTAURANTS

Felix's Restaurant, Highway 2 / Opens at 11:30am, closes at 3; dinner from 5pm on / 701-662-4941

Dakota Sioux Casino, 16 miles southeast of Devils Lake / Free shuttle service / food and lounge, blackjack, craps, poker, keno, bingo

Cove Restaurant, Woodland Resort Highway 19 West / 701-662-5966

Dairy Queen, 616 5th Avenue South / burgers / 701-662-4622

Old Main Street Cafe, 416 4th Street / Open 6am / Breakfast, lunch, dinner / 701-662-8814

VETERINARIANS

Lake Region Veterinary Service, Highway 2 East / 701-662-3321

SPORTING GOODS STORES

Home of Economy, Highway 2 / 701-662-5046 / Guns, calls, ammo, waders, boots, clothes
Wal-Mart, 403 US Highway 2 West / 701662-5203
K-Mart, 701 5th Avenue South / 701-662-4621
Gerrells Sports Center, 415 4th Street / 701-662-8133

AUTO REPAIR

Outlaw Automotive, Highway 2 East / 701-662-4973
Big Al's Auto Maintenance, 1004 Highway 2 East / 701-662-2038

AIR SERVICE

Devils Lake Airport, Highway 19 / Carrier: United Express / 701-662-6310

MEDICAL

Mercy Hospital, 1031 7th Street / 701-662-2131

FOR MORE INFORMATION

Community Development Corporation
PO Box 879
Devils Lake, ND 58301
701-662-4933

Devils Lake Chamber of Commerce
Highway 2 East
Devils Lake, ND 58301
701-662-4903

Garrison and McLean County

Population–1,830	Elevation–1,920
County Population–10,457	October Temperature–52°
County Area–2,065 sq. mi.	Acres in CRP–96,611

Garrison is located in central North Dakota's McLean County. The town rests on the north shore of Lake Sakakawea and offers hunters quick access to the lake and surrounding fields.

UPLAND BIRDS
Pheasant, Sharptail, Gray Partridge, Mourning Dove, Sandhill Crane, Snipe

WATERFOWL
Ducks & Geese

ACCOMMODATIONS

Garrison Motel, Highway 37 East / 30 units, air conditioning, cable TV / Dogs allowed in smoking rooms, must be attended / 701-463-2858 / $$

Lakewood Motel, Highway 37 / 6 apartments, 10 rooms, cable TV / Dogs allowed / 701-463-8404 / $

Robins Nest, 101 Central Avenue / Bed and breakfast / 701-463-2281 / $$$

CAMPGROUNDS AND RV PARKS

Sportsman's Centennial Park, 5 miles east, 2 miles south and one mile west of Garrison / 701-337-5377 / RV camping, water, groceries

RESTAURANTS

Stoney End, Frontage Road, 1 mile east of town / Lounge open at 4pm , dinner starts at 5pm / Steaks, chicken, seafood, salad / 701-337-5590

Dairy Queen, 182 North Main / Lunch, dinner / 701-463-2044

Lakeroad Restaurant, Highway 37 and 2nd SW / Open 6:30am to 9 or 10pm / Breakfast, lunch, dinner / 701-463-2569

Totten Trail, Highway 83, 9 miles SE of Garrison / 701-337-5513

VETERINARIANS

Garrison Veterinary, South 109 4th Street SW / 701-463-2222

A big northern Canada goose is an impressive trophy.
(Photo: Blanche Johnson)

SPORTING GOODS STORES

Bill's Sports, 22 North Main / 701-463-7442

AUTO REPAIR

Ron's Auto, #1 Central Avenue NE / 701-463-2210

AIR SERVICE

Garrison Airport, Aero Drive / 701-337-9499

MEDICAL

Garrison Memorial Hospital, 407 3rd Avenue SE / 701-463-2275

FOR MORE INFORMATION

Garrison Chamber of Commerce
PO Box 459
Garrison, ND 58540
800-799-4242

Harvey and Wells County

Population–2,263	Elevation–1,600
County Population–5,864	October Temperature–52°
County Area–1,288 sq. mi.	Acres in CRP–64,613

Harvey, a quaint railroad town, is located in central North Dakota in Wells County. Touted as a friendly, slow-paced community, Harvey offers quick access to waterfowl and upland bird hunting along with ample accommodations.

UPLAND BIRDS
Pheasant, Sharptail, Gray Partridge, Mourning Dove, Sandhill Crane, Snipe

WATERFOWL
Ducks & Geese

ACCOMMODATIONS

R and R Motel, Highway 3 and 52nd / 701-324-2271 / 20 rooms, air conditioning, clean, convenient / Dogs are allowed, bring kennel if possible, please / $$-$

American Motel, 575 East Brewster / 701-324-2293 / 16 rooms, air conditioning / Dogs allowed, no cost / $$

Amigo Hotel, Highway 3 and 52nd / 701-324-2510 / 10 rooms, air conditioning / Dogs allowed / $

CAMPGROUNDS AND RV PARKS

West Side Park, Highway 3 and 52nd / 701-324-4744 / Tent sites, 17 RV sites showers, swimming

Lonetree Wildlife Management Area, 5 miles South and 3 miles west of Harvey / 701-324-2211 / Three primitive campgrounds

RESTAURANTS

Town and Country / Breakfast at 6am / 701-324-2260

Artos Supper Club & Lounge, Highway 52 and 3rd / Steaks, seafood, pasta, hamburger / 701-324-2693

JW's Pizzeria & Family Restaurant, Highway 52 Bypass / Open 5am to 11pm / Breakfast, lunch and dinner / 701-324-4617

Tastee Freez, Highway 52 / 701-324-4423

VETERINARIANS

Mid-Dakota Veterinary Clinic, Highway 52 Bypass / 701-324-2221

Snow geese setting on a prairie pothole. (Photo: Craig Bihrle)

Sporting Goods Stores

Coast to Coast, 110 East 10th Street / 701-324-2319

Auto Repair

Lowell's Auto & Truck Repair, Highway 52 Bypass West / 701-324-4614
Harvey Repair, 115 West 10th Street / 701-324-2896

Air Service

Harvey Municipal Airport, Highway 3 North / Nearest commercial carrier in Minot (75 miles away) / 701-324-9596

Medical

St. Aloisius Medical Center, 325 East Brewster / 701-324-4651

For More Information

Harvey Area Chamber of Commerce
106 East 8th Street
Harvey, ND 58341
701-324-2604

Kenmare and Ward County

Population–1,250	Elevation–1,810
County Population–57,921	October Temperature–52°
County Area–2,041 sq. mi.	Acres in CRP–58,476

UPLAND BIRDS
Pheasant, Sharptail, Gray Partridge, Ruffed Grouse, Mourning Dove, Sandhill Crane, Snipe

WATERFOWL
Ducks & Geese

Accommodations
San Way Motel, 819 North Central / 701-385-4238 / 35 rooms, dogs allowed / $$

Campgrounds and RV Parks
City Campground, NE on Highway 52 / Bathroom and showers, electrical hookup, 20 RV sites, 11 tent sites / 701- 385-4232

Restaurants
Cindy's Cafe / Open 6am to 7pm / Breakfast, lunch, dinner / 7 days a week 701-385-4861

Ying Bin Chinese Restaurant / Lunch and dinner / Open 11am to 9pm / Closed Monday / 701-385-4447

52 North Restaurant and Lounge, Highway 52 / Open 11am to 9pm / 701-385-4313

Veterinarians
Jordahl Animal Hospital, 4825 North Broadway, Minot / 701-852-4744

Sporting Goods Stores
None

Auto Repair
Central Automotive, 216 Central Avenue North / 701-385-3206

Air Service
None

Medical
Kenmare Community Hospital, 307 1st Avenue NW / 701-385-4296

For More Information
City Hall
701-385-4232

Minot and Ward County

Population–34,544	Elevation–1,715
County Population–57,721	October Temperature–56°
County Area–2,041 sq. mi.	Acres in CRP–58,476

Minot is located in western North Dakota just off Route 52 in Ward County. A cultural and shopping hub, Minot offers full amenities for the upland bird or waterfowl hunter.

UPLAND BIRDS
Pheasant, Sharptail, Gray Partridge, Mourning Dove, Sandhill Crane, Snipe

WATERFOWL
Ducks & Geese

Accommodations

Best Western International, 1505 North Broadway / 701-852-3161 / Dogs allowed, no fee / $$

Comfort Inn, 1515 22nd Avenue SW / 701-852-2201 / Dogs allowed, no fee / $$

Casa Motel and Campground, 1900 West 2 & 52 Bypass South / 701-852-2352 / Dogs allowed, no fee / $

Select Inn, 225 22nd Avenue NW / 100 rooms / Dogs allowed, $25 damage deposit / 701-852-3411 / $$

Dakota Inn, 2401 West 2 and 52 Bypass South / 129 rooms / 701-838-2700 / No dogs / $$

Days Inn, 2100 4th Street SW / 81 rooms / Dogs allowed with $20 deposit, leash required, must be attended / 701-852-3646

Campgrounds and RV Parks

Expressway RV Park & Campground, 717 27th Street SE / 701-852-6889

KOA Campground, Highway 52 East / 701-839-7400

Pat's Motel & Campground, 2025 SE 27 (1.5 miles SE of Minot) / 701-838-5800

Restaurants

Bonanza Family Restaurant, 1445 South Broadway / 701-852-4644

Field & Stream Restaurant, Highway 83 North / 701-852-3663

Perkins Family Restaurant, 405 20th Avenue South / 701-838-2024

Veterinarians

Jordahl Animal Hospital, 4825 North Broadway / 701-852-4744, after hours call 701-838-7887

Pinkerton Animal Hospital, 2105 North Broadway / 701-852-3055 for appointments or emergencies

Morning flight. (Photo: Christopher Smith)

SPORTING GOODS STORES

Scheels All Sports, Dakota Square Shopping Center / 701-852-1010
K-Mart, 1 20th Avenue SE / 701-852-4175
Jim's Gunworks, 14 NW 19th / 701-838-0899
Northwest Sporting Goods, 1405 South Broadway / 701-852-4865
Big Bear Sport Center, 3010 South Broadway / 701-838-5958

AUTO REPAIR

Country Auto, Highway 83 North / 701-839-4177

AIR SERVICE

Minot International Airport / Serviced by Northwest / 701 857-4724

MEDICAL

Minot Center for Family Medicine, 123 1st Street SW / 701-858-6700

FOR MORE INFORMATION

Minot Chamber of Commerce
1020 20th Avenue SW
Minot, ND 58702
701-852-6000

Rolla and Rolette County

Population–1,371	Elevation–1,818
County Population–12,772	October Temperature–44°
County Area–914 sq. mi.	Acres in CRP–56,106

Rolla prides itself as a quiet, peaceful little town full of friendly people. Located in north central North Dakota, just south of the Canadian border, on U.S. Highway 281, its central location makes Rolla an ideal base for hunters.

UPLAND BIRDS
Sharptail, Gray Partridge, Ruffed Grouse, Turkey, Woodcock, Mourning Dove, Sandhill Crane, Snipe

WATERFOWL
Ducks & Geese

Accommodations

Bilmar Motel and Smugglers Grill, Highway 5 West / 35 rooms / Dogs allowed / Supper only / Open 5pm to 10pm / Bar and small lounge, cocktails served / 701-477-3157 / $$

Northern Lights Motel, Highway 281 East / 16 rooms / Dogs allowed for $10 extra fee / 701-477-6164 / $$

Campgrounds and RV Parks

Rolla City Park, 4th Street SE / Hookups for trailers and tent sites, bathroom and shower / 701-477-3610

Restaurants

Smugglers Grill and Bar (Bilmar Hotel), Highway 5 West / 701-477-3157

Chicken Hut, Main Avenue East / 701-477-3289

D & B Pizza, 12 SE 2 / 701-477-3739

Veterinarians

Bottineau Veterinary, nearest vet / 701-228-6990

Sporting Goods Stores

Coast To Coast, 102 Main Avenue East / 701-477-3629

St. John Hardware, 10 miles northwest of Rolla in St. John / 701-477-5454

Auto Repair

Bill's Service Station, 19 Main Avenue West / 701-477-3782

Everson Auto Parts, 101 Front Street / 701-477-6161

Neameyer Auto Service, 209 Main Avenue West / 701-477-3421

Don't let the monotony of some of North Dakota's game country fool you. Even the middle of vast expanses of grasslands can hold birds. (Photo: Blanche Johnson)

AIR SERVICE

Airport of Rolla, RR 1 / 701-477-5145

MEDICAL

Presentation Medical Center, 213 NE 3 / 701-477-3161

FOR MORE INFORMATION

Rolla Chamber of Commerce
Box 726
Rolla, ND 58367

Rugby and Pierce County

Population–2,900	Elevation–1,547
County Population–5,052	October Temperature–44°
County Area–1,077 sq. mi.	Acres in CRP–61,544

UPLAND BIRDS
Pheasant, Sharptail, Gray Partridge, Mourning Dove, Sandhill Crane, Snipe

WATERFOWL
Ducks & Geese

Accommodations

Econo Lodge, Highway 2 East / 60 rooms, AC, cable TV, indoor pool, continental breakfast, restaurant and lounge open 11am to 11pm / Dogs allowed / 701-776-5776 / $$

Hub Motel, Junction Highways 2 and 3 / 18 rooms, AC, cable TV, restaurant and lounge open / Open 6am to 11pm / Dogs allowed for $5 a night per dog / 701-776-5833 / $$

Campgrounds and RV Parks

Hillman Inn Campground, 1 block W of Highways 2 and 3 / Tent sites, 47 RV sites, electric, shower, sewer, laundry / 701-776-5272

Restaurants

Bob's Pizza Inn, Highway 2 East / Pizza, pasta, salads / 701-662-5054

Coffee Shop, 110 SE 2nd / Open 7:30am to 5:30pm / Breakfast, lunch, dinner / 701-776-5177

Cornerstone Cafe, Highway 2 and 3 / Open 7am / Breakfast, lunch, dinner / 701-776-6528

Dairy Queen, Highway 2 East / Burgers, fries, shakes / 701-623-5812

Veterinarians

Rugby Veterinary, 107 Industrial Park / 701-776-5726

Sporting Goods Stores

Bucks Sport Shop, 128 South Main Avenue / 701-776-5296

Auto Repair

Central Car Clinic, Highway 3 North / 701-776-2873

AIR SERVICE

Rugby Municipal Airport, North of town

Nearest commercial service in Minot (64 miles away): Carriers Northwest and United

MEDICAL

Heart of America Medical Center, South Main / 701- 776-5261

FOR MORE INFORMATION

Rugby Chamber of Commerce
Junction Highways 2 & 3
Rugby, ND 58368
701-776-5846

Guides and Outfitters

The Lakes and Gardens Region

SHEYENNE VALLEY LODGE

RR 1 Box 27 Goodrich, ND 58444 / 701-884-2432
Contact: The Mertz's
Land–50,000 acres
Game – Geese, ducks, wild pheasant, sharptail grouse, Huns, swans
Personal Guide – Available but you can hunt on your own
Dogs – Dogs and kennels available; can hunt with your own dog
Extras – Lodging and meals, lounge

HILLVIEW HUNTING ACRES

RR 4 Box 171A, Minot, ND 58701 / 800-838-1057
Contact: Bob Saunders
Land – 250 acres
Game – Planted pheasants, chukars
Personal Guide – Available or hunt on your own
Dogs – Available or bring your own
Extras – Smoked pheasants

JIG M UP GUIDE SERVICE

49 4th Ave NW Garrison, ND 58540 / 701-463-2134
Contact: Paul Folden
Land – Less than 1,000 acres
Game – Geese, ducks, sharptail grouse, pheasant, Huns
Personal Guide – Available or hunt on your own after a couple days
Dogs – Bring your own

BONZO'S

Box 323 Garrison, ND 58540 / 701-463-7431
Contact: Jeff Brennan
Game–Canada geese
Personal Guide – Available or hunt on your own
Dogs – Bring your own
Extras – Motel available

The Prairies and Coteaus

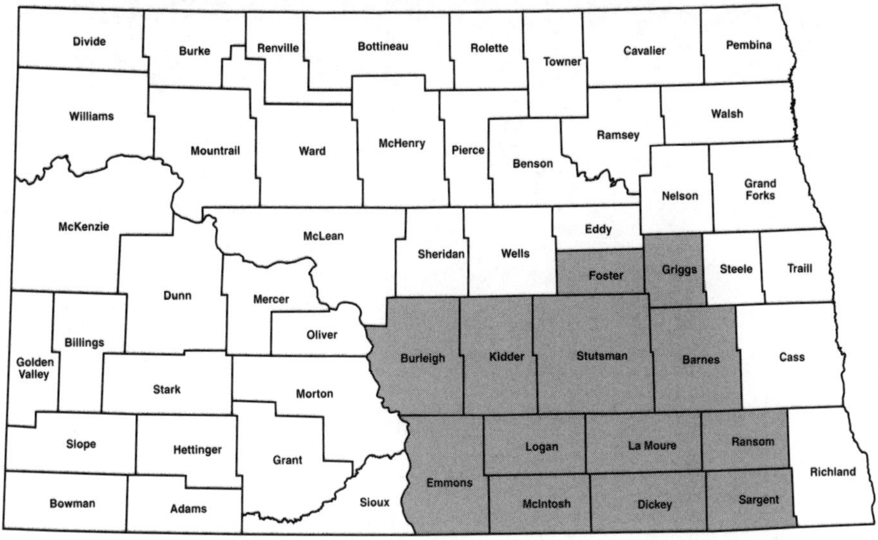

This region also harbors thousands of small ponds and potholes that are extremely attractive to waterfowl and provide excellent duck and goose shooting. National Wildlife Refuges and cultivated croplands draw birds in as well. Typical terrain consists of rolling hills, farm lands, and prairie potholes. If you're looking for a varied hunt, the prairies and coteaus region can offer just that. You can set up for snow and Canada geese, including giant Canada geese to 16 pounds, in the morning, and then hunt ducks in the afternoon. After that, you can hunt pheasants and sharp-tailed grouse, which are fairly abundant, or chase Hungarian partridge, which are present in lesser numbers.

Ring-necked Pheasant Distribution
The Prairies and Coteaus Region

Sharp-tailed Grouse Distribution
The Prairies and Coteaus Region

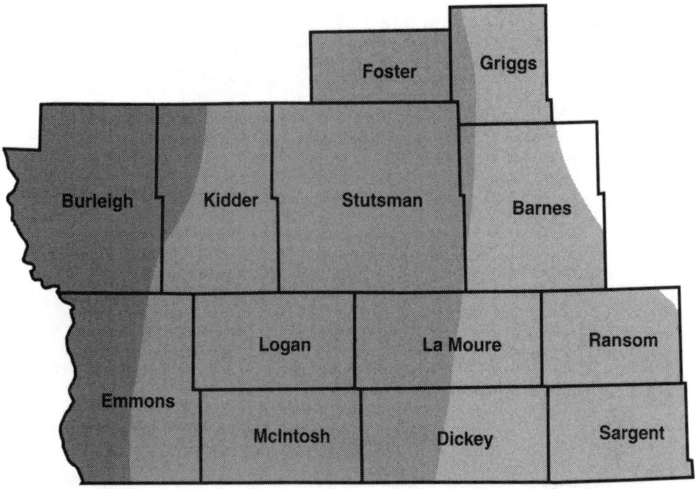

■ **Fair to Good** ■ **Fair**

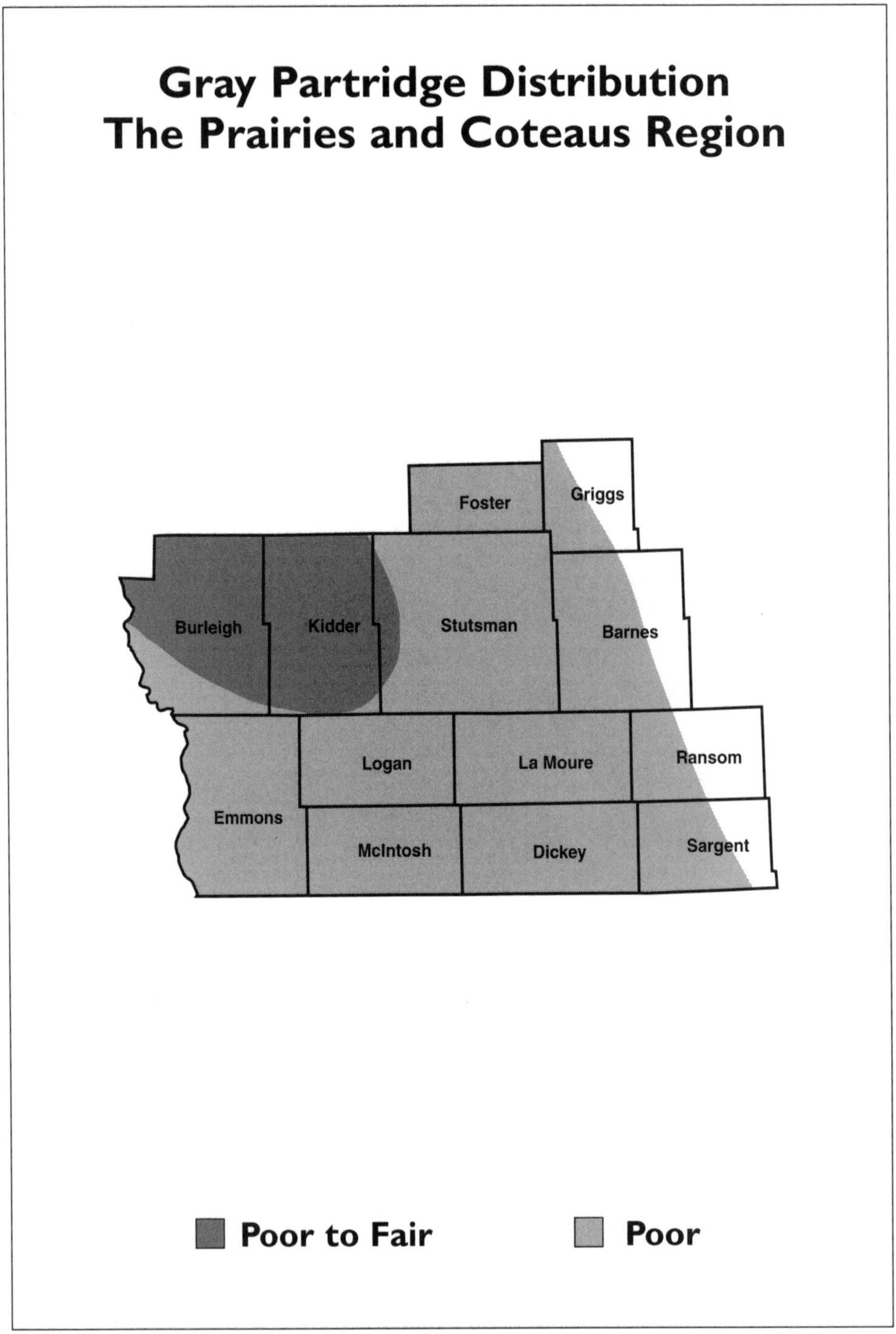
Gray Partridge Distribution
The Prairies and Coteaus Region
Foster
Griggs
Burleigh
Kidder
Stutsman
Barnes
Logan
La Moure
Ransom
Emmons
McIntosh
Dickey
Sargent
Poor to Fair
Poor

Wild Turkey Distribution
The Prairies and Coteaus Region

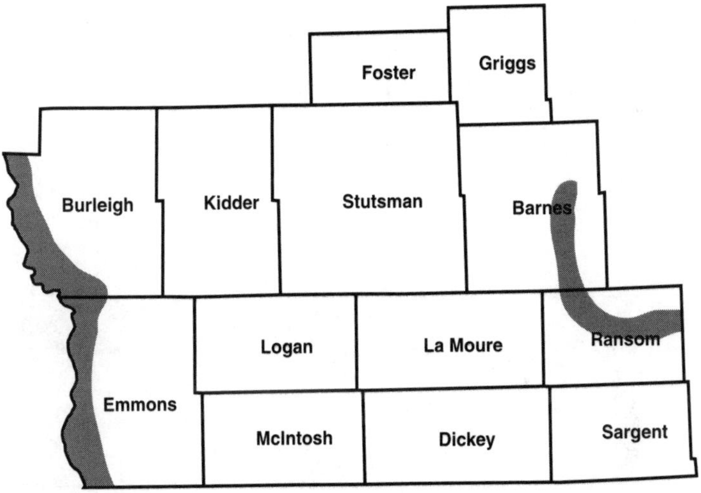

Populations low to fair

Woodcock Distribution
The Prairies and Coteaus Region

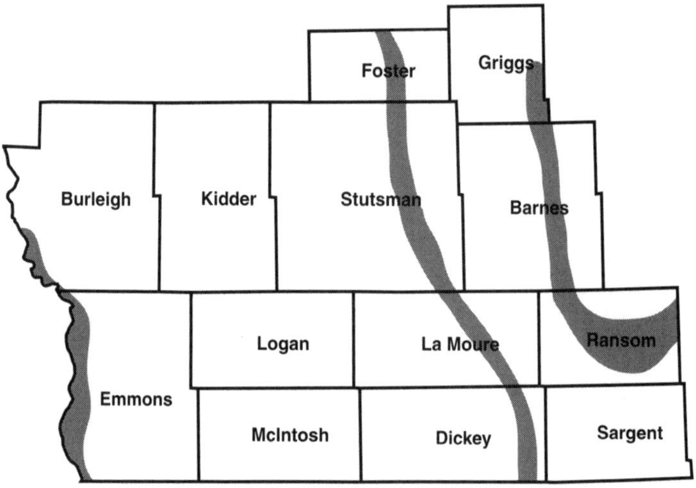

Only found in these drainages

Mourning Dove Distribution
The Prairies and Coteaus Region

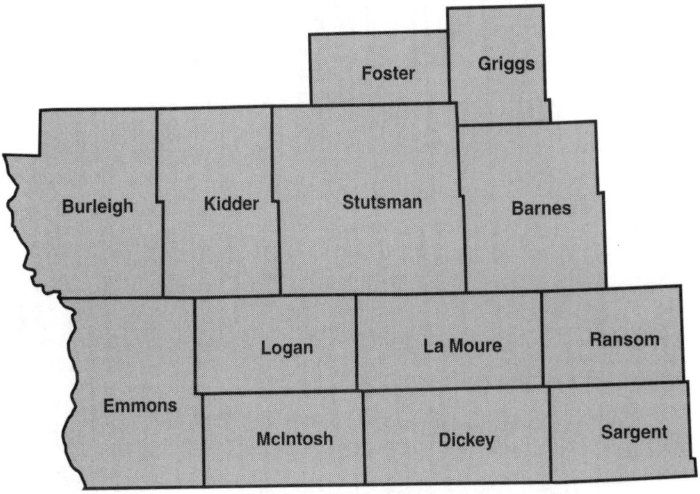

Found throughout region

Common Snipe Distribution
The Prairies and Coteaus Region

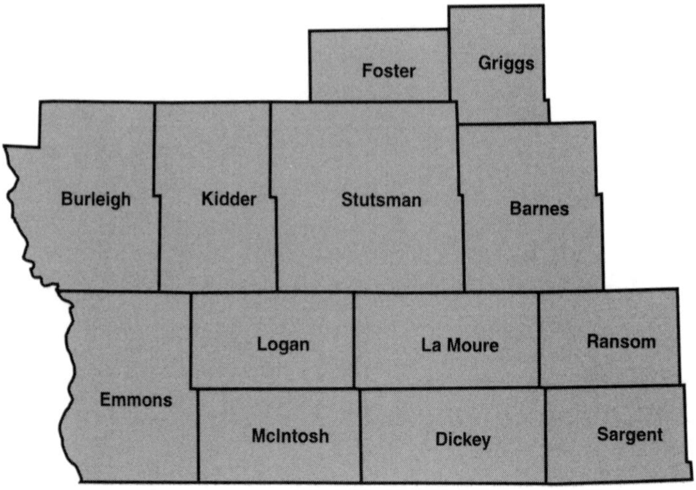

Found throughout region

Sandhill Crane Distribution
The Prairies and Coteaus Region

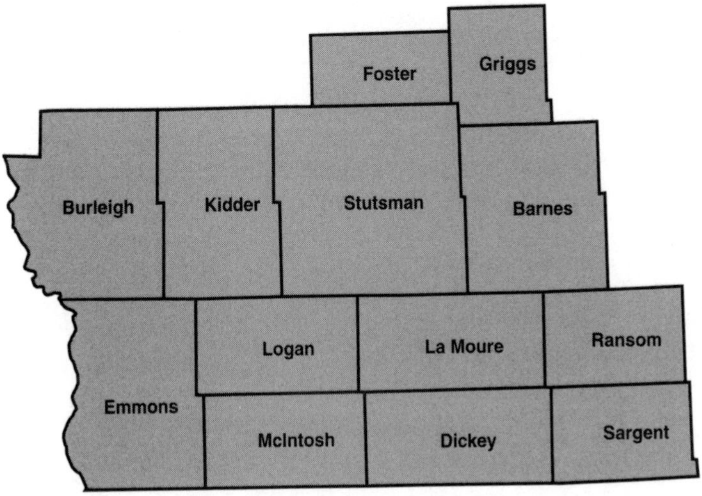

Found throughout

Bismarck and Burleigh County

Population–66,573 (including Mandan)	Elevation–1,700
County Population–60,131	October Temperature–58°
County Area–1,618 sq. mi.	Acres in CRP–99,890

Bismarck is the capital of North Dakota, offering all amenities to visiting bird hunters. Located in south central North Dakota, in Burleigh County, Bismarck is a prime hub for those hunting waterfowl or upland birds throughout the state. It is the state's third largest city. See also Mandan accommodations.

UPLAND BIRDS
Pheasant, Sharptail, Gray Partridge, Turkey, Woodcock, Mourning Dove, Sandhill Crane, Snipe

WATERFOWL
Ducks & Geese

Accommodations

Select Inn, I-94 & US 83 / Dogs allowed / East Forty Restaurant next door / 701-223-8060 / $$

Super 8, 1124 East Capitol Avenue / 701-255-1314 / 61 rooms / Dogs allowed in smoking rooms / $$

Seven Seas Motor Inn, I-94 and Exit 152, 2611 Old Red Trail / 701-663-7401 / Dogs allowed, no fee / $$

Comfort Inn, 1030 East Capitol Avenue / 701-223-1911 / Dogs allowed, no fee / $$

Holiday Inn, 605 East Broadway & 6th Street / 701-255-6000 or 1-800-465-4329 / Dogs allowed, must be attended / $$

Kelly Inn, 1800 North 12th / 701-223-8001 / 101 rooms / Dogs allowed in smoking rooms / $$

Campgrounds and RV Parks

Bismarck KOA, 3720 Centennial Road / 701-222-2662 / 36 tent sites / Two cabins / Full service laundry

Mandan Camping Area, 3rd Avenue & 2nd Street SW / 701-667-3260 / Tent and trailer sites

General Sibley Campground, 4 miles south of Bismarck on Washington Street / 701-222-1844 / 70 tent sites and 126 trailer sites

Restaurants

Bonanza Family Restaurant, Highway 83 North / Breakfast, lunch, dinner / 701-223-1107

Giovanni's Pizza, 1523 East Thayer Avenue / Pizza and pasta / 701-258-0900

Mallards taking off from a grainfield. (Photo: Craig Bihrle)

Red Lobster Restaurant, 1130 East Century / Steaks and seafood / 701-222-2363

Hong Kong Restaurant, 1055 Interstate Avenue / Take out, delivery, sit down / 701-223-2130

Dakota Farms Family Restaurant, 1301 East Main (Bismarck), 1120 East Main (Mandan) / Home-style meals 7 days a week / 701-258-0559 (Bismarck); 701-663-7322 (Mandan)

Denny's, 405 South 7th Street / Open 24 hours for breakfast, lunch, dinner / 701-223-2015

Sergio's Mexican Bar and Grill, 401 East Bismarck Expressway / Dine in or take out / Bar / 701-223-3422

Settlers Cafe, 406 Main Street West (Mandan) / Open 6am to 9pm daily / 701-663-6548

Season's Cafe, 800 South 3rd Street / Seafood, lunch buffet, burgers, steaks / 701-258-7700

VETERINARIANS

All Pets Veterinary, 200 West Sweet Avenue / 701-255-7387

Missouri Valley Veterinary Clinic, 1801 Commerce Drive / 701-222-1912

Sporting Goods Stores

Scheels All Sports, Kirkwood Mall / 701-255-7255
Sioux Sporting Goods, 510 East Broadway Avenue / 701-223-1145 or 1-800-284-9263
Pro Sporting Goods, 7152 Highway 18 / 701-224-9596
K-Mart, 2625 State Street / 701-223-0074

Auto Repair

Sandy's Auto Repair, 6117 7th Street SW / 701-663-4357

Air Service

Bismarck Municipal Airport, Airport Road / Carriers: United Express, Northwest, Mesaba / 701-222-6502

Medical

Medcenter One, 300 North 7th Street / 701-224-6000
St Aloisius Medical Center, 900 East Broadway / 701-224-7000

For More Information

Bismarck Chamber of Commerce
2000 Schafer Street
Bismarck, ND 58502
701-223-5660

Carrington and Foster County

Population–2,500	Elevation–1,550
County Population–3,983	October Temperature–50°
County Area–640 sq. mi.	Acres in CRP–21,958

UPLAND BIRDS
Pheasant, Sharptail, Gray Partridge, Mourning Dove, Sandhill Crane, Snipe

WATERFOWL
Ducks & Geese

ACCOMMODATIONS
Super 8, Highway 281 / Cable TV, restaurant and lounge, continental breakfast, laundry / Dogs allowed / 701-652-3982 / $$-$$$

Chieftain Motel, Highway 281 / 50 rooms, restaurant and lounge, cable TV, car plug-ins, rooms with direct outside access / No dogs / 701-652-3131 / $$

CAMPGROUNDS AND RV PARKS
City Park, Highway 281 Southern / 6 electrical hookups, no tent sites, first-come, first-serve basis, no reservations / 701-652-2597

RESTAURANTS
The Prairie Inn, Junction 200 & Highway 281 / Homemade baked goods / 701-652-3976

Chieftain, Highway 281 / Breakfast, lunch, dinner / 701-652-3982

Ace Cafe/Donna's Diner, 943 Main Street / Open 6am / Breakfast, lunch, dinner / 701-652-1776

VETERINARIANS
Mid-Dakota Veterinary Service, 1525 7th Street South / 701-652-1555

SPORTING GOODS STORES
Dry Dock Bait and Tackle, Highway 281 South / 701-652-2421

VETERINARY
Mid-Dakota Veterinary, 1525 7th Street / 701-652-1555

AUTO REPAIR
NAPA Auto Parts, RR 1 / 701-652-3663

Pintail ducks drawn to a prairie pothole. (Photo: Craig Bihrle)

Clark's Auto & Truck Service, 1209 Main Street West / 701-652-3053

Air Service

Carrington Airport Authority, Highway 200 West / 701-652-9205

Medical

Carrington Health Center, 800 North 4th Street / 701-652-3141

For More Information

Carrington Chamber of Commerce
P.O. Box 138
Carrington, ND 58421
701-652-2524

Ellendale and Dickey County

Population–1,798	Elevation–1,110
County Population–6,107	
County Area–1,139 sq. mi.	Acres in CRP–52,545

UPLAND BIRDS
Pheasant, Sharptail, Gray Partridge, Turkey, Woodcock, Mourning Dove, Sandhill Crane, Snipe

WATERFOWL
Ducks & Geese

ACCOMMODATIONS
Oxenrider Motel and Campground, Highway 281 / AC, cable TV, 14 rooms, 4 electrical sites / Dogs allowed / 701-349-3641 / $-$$

Prairie Winds Motel, Highway 281 and 11 / 30 rooms, AC, cable TV, continental breakfast / Dogs allowed / 701-349-3771 / $$

CAMPGROUNDS AND RV PARKS
Oster Park, North Ellendale / Tent sites, 3 RV sites, 3 electrical showers, sewer / 701-349-3252

RESTAURANTS
Hot-Stuff Pizzeria, 118 Main Street / Pizza to go / 701-349-3910

Ranch Restaurant and Lounge, Highway 281 North / Open 7am / Breakfast, lunch, dinner / 701-349-4479

Nodak Cafe, 95 Main Street / Breakfast, lunch, dinner / 701-349-4529

VETERINARIANS
Dean Christianson, Ashley / 701-872-4979

SPORTING GOODS STORES
Coast to Coast, 139 Main Street / 701-349-3274

AUTO REPAIR
Bob's Repair, 50 1st Street North / 701-349-3280

AIR SERVICE
Ellendale Airport, Highway 11 East / 701-349-9522

MEDICAL
Ellendale Clinic, 141 Main Street / 701-349-3331

Jamestown and Stutsman County

Population–15,571	Elevation–1,498
County Population–22,241	October Temperature–46°
County Area–2,263 sq. mi.	Acres in CRP–159,061

Jamestown is located in eastern North Dakota just off Interstate 94 east of Fargo and Valley City in Stutsman County. Situated near Jim Lake and the James River, Jamestown offers excellent local hunting options or a convenient layover for travelling sportsmen. The town hosts the National Buffalo Museum and the world's largest buffalo—a 46-foot long, 26-foot high, 60-ton concrete monument.

UPLAND BIRDS
Pheasant, Sharptail, Gray Partridge, Woodcock, Mourning Dove, Sandhill Crane, Snipe

WATERFOWL
Ducks & Geese

Accommodations

Select Inn, 111 2nd Street NE, next to Jamestown Mall / Dogs allowed / 701-252-0700 / $$
Dakota Inn, Highway 281 South & I-94 / 701-252-3611 / 120 rooms / $$$
Buffalo Motel, 1530 6th Avenue SW / 701-252-0180 / Dogs allowed, no fee $$
Comfort Inn, 811 20th Street SW / 701-252-7125 / Dogs allowed, no fee $$

Campgrounds and RV Parks

Smokey's Campground, Highway 281 North / 701-252-0659
Jamestown KOA Campground, 1-94 West Exit 256 / 701-252-6262

Restaurants

Bonanza Family Restaurant, Highway 281 South & I-94 / 701-252-184
Chuckwagon Restaurant and Lounge, 204 17th Street SW / 701-252-8469
Arby's, 1801 7th Avenue SW / 701-252-2048
Big Jim's Cafe and Steakhouse, Highway 281 South & I-94, Exit 258 / Steak, pasta, seafood / 701-251-1600
Perkins Family Restaurant, Highway 281 South & I-94, Exit 258 / 24 hours / Breakfast, lunch, dinner / 701-252-1370
Trappers Family Restaurant & Pizza, Highway 281 South & I-94, Exit 258 / 701-252-8263

Veterinarians

Country Acres Veterinarian Clinic, Highway 282 South / 701-252-7133
Southwood Veterinary Clinic, 833 18th Street SW / 701-252-3430

Hunting cultivated farmland in central North Dakota. (Photo: Blanche Johnson)

Sporting Goods Stores

Goodroad Sports, 121 2nd Street SW / 701-252-5671
Gun & Reel Sports Inc., 115 West 1st Street / 701-252-2850

Auto Repair

Auto Clinic, 450 1st Street West / 701-252-2365
Eckman's Auto Service, Park Plaza / 701-252-6341

Air Service

Jamestown Airport, Box 1560, Airport Road NE / Commercial carrier: United Express / 701-252-6466

Medical

Jamestown Hospital, 410 5th NE / 701-252-1050

For More Information

Jamestown Chamber of Commerce
210 10th Street SE
Jamestown, ND 58402
701-252-4830

Linton and Emmons County

Population–1,450	Elevation–1,499
County Population–4,830	October Temperature–44°
County Area–1,499 sq. mi.	Acres in CRP–58,928

Linton is located in south-central North Dakota's Emmons County. The town offers adequate accommodations for upland bird and waterfowl hunters. Due to its location just north of the South Dakota state line, it's an ideal base area for those wingshooters who spend time in both of the Dakotas.

UPLAND BIRDS
Pheasant, Sharptail, Gray Partridge, Turkey, Woodcock, Mourning Dove, Sandhill Crane, Snipe

WATERFOWL
Ducks & Geese

ACCOMMODATIONS

Don's Motel, Highway 83 South / 701-254-5457 / 24 rooms / Dogs allowed, no fee / $

Willows Motel, Highway 83 South / 701-254-4555 / 26 rooms, air conditioning, cable TV, freezers / Dogs allowed, no fee / $$

CAMPGROUNDS AND RV PARKS

Beaver Creek Recreation Area, Lake Oahe / 701-254-9000

RESTAURANTS

Hot Stuff Pizzeria, 116 West Hickory Street / 701-254-9077

Mr. J's, South Broadway / Open 6:30am to 8pm / Breakfast, lunch, dinner / 701-254-4410

Starlight Cafe, 127 South Broadway / Open 6:30am / Breakfast, lunch, dinner / 701-254-4651

VETERINARIANS

Linton Vet Service, South of Linton / 701-254-4483

SPORTING GOODS STORES

Coast to Coast, 119 Broadway / 701-254-4980

Ed's Hardware & Fur, 121 North Broadway / 701-254-5344

On a cold, clear day, a hunter and his Chesapeake Bay retriever wait for a flight of divers. (Photo: Blanche Johnson)

AUTO REPAIR

Bob's Auto Repair, 104 South St. Paul Road / 701-254-5398
Jim's Car Care, 309 North Broadway / 701-254-4743
Leo's Repair Shop, North of Linton / 701-254-4847

AIR SERVICE

Linton Memorial Airport, 3/4 mile south of Linton / 701-254-5449

MEDICAL

Linton Hospital, 518 North Broadway / 701-254-4511
Linton Medical Center, 518 North Broadway / 701-254-4521

FOR MORE INFORMATION

Linton Chamber of Commerce
101 NE 1st Street
Linton, ND 58552
701-254-4267

Lisbon and Ransom County

Population–2,117	Elevation–1,250
County Population–5,921	October Temperature–48°
County Area–862 sq. mi.	Acres in CRP–46,694

UPLAND BIRDS
Pheasant, Sharptail, Gray Partridge, Turkey, Woodcock, Mourning Dove, Sandhill Crane, Snipe

WATERFOWL
Ducks & Geese

Accommodations

Island Park Motel, 1 mile South on Highway 32 / 35 rooms, AC, cable TV, restaurant, lounge adjacent / 701-683-4114 / $$

Campgrounds and RV Parks

Dead Colt Creek Recreation Area, 5 miles South, 1.5 miles East / 10 RV sites, 10 electric / 701-683-5555

Sandager Park, NW Lisbon / 20 RV sites, 16 electric, showers / 701-683-4221

Restaurants

Lisbon Cafe, 222 Main Street / Open 6am / Breakfast, lunch, dinner / 701-683-5919

Pit Stop Bar and Grill, 100 Main Street / Open 5pm / Steaks, burgers, salad, cocktails, beer / 701-683-5507

Veterinarians

Hovland Veterinary, West Highway 27 / 701-683-4686

Sporting Goods Stores

Coast to Coast, 406 Main Street / 701-683-4642

Trustworthy Hardware, 414 Main Street / 701-683-4511

Auto Repair

Ford Sales and Service, 309 12th Avenue West / 701-683-4195

Air Service

Nearest in Wahpeton: Harry Stern Airport, / 701-642-5777

Medical

Dakota Clinic, 819 Main Street / 701-683-4134

Valley City and Barnes County

Population–7,163	Elevation–1,225
County Population–12,545	October Temperature–53°
County Area–1,498 sq. mi.	Acres in CRP–41,784

Valley City, the gateway to the Sheyenne Valley, is located in eastern North Dakota, just off I-84, an equal distance between Jamestown and West Fargo. Resting in Barnes County, Valley City offers quick access to excellent waterfowl and upland bird hunting in the nearby croplands.

UPLAND BIRDS
Pheasant, Sharptail, Gray Partridge, Turkey, Woodcock, Mourning Dove, Sandhill Crane, Snipe

WATERFOWL
Ducks & Geese

ACCOMMODATIONS

Super 8, I-94 & Exit 292 / 701-845-1140 / Dogs allowed (with kennel, no fee) $$
Valley City Motel, 1139 Main Street West / 701-845-2208 / No dogs / $
Bel-Air Motel, 2315 West Main / 701-845-3620 / Dogs allowed, no fee / $
Red Cedar Motel, 410 6th Avenue / 701-646-6260 / No dogs $$
Wagon Wheel Inn, 455 Winter Show Road / 701-845-5333 / Dogs allowed, need to be attended / $$

CAMPGROUNDS AND RV PARKS

Tourist Park, East Valley City / 10 full hookups, sewer, water, electric, shower, restrooms

RESTAURANTS

Subway, 1240 West Main / 701-845-5489
Hilltop Cafe, Exit 292 off I-94 / Breakfast, lunch, dinner / 701-845-3257
Roby's Family Restaurant, 1066 West Main / Breakfast, lunch, dinner / 701-845-4284
Kenny's Family Restaurant, Exit 290, West Main Street / Breakfast, lunch, dinner 701-845-4442
Elks, 161 West Main / 701-845-1110 / Steaks, seafood, pasta

VETERINARIANS

VC Vet Hospital, 1068 SW 4 / 701-845-3662

SPORTING GOODS STORES

Northwestern Industries, 416 West Main / 701-845-1031

AUTO REPAIR

Berger Repair, 145 12th Avenue SW / 701-845-4989
Good Year, 250 NW 2 Valley City / 701-845-2233

AIR SERVICE

Valley City Municipal Airport

MEDICAL

MeritCare Clinic, 520 Chautauqua / 701-845-6139

FOR MORE INFORMATION

Valley City Area Chamber of Commerce
205 NE 2nd Street
Valley City, ND 58072
701-845-1891

Guides and Outfitters

The Prairies and Coteaus Region

NORTHLAND OUTFITTERS

RR 1, PO Box 101, Medina, ND 58467 / 701-486-3456
Contact: Jim Kleven or Scott Moser
Land–5,000 acres
Game – Ducks, geese, sharp-tailed grouse, pheasants
Personal Guide – Must hunt with a guide
Dogs – Available or bring your own
Extras – Lodging available; meals provided; decoys provided

DAKOTA FINS, FEATHERS & TAILS GUIDE SERVICE

1312 Westwood, Bismarck, ND 58504 / 701-222-1620
Contact: Jim Nagel
Land–14,000+ acres
Game – Sharp-tailed grouse, pheasant, ducks, geese
Personal Guide – Available or hunt on your own
Dogs – Available to use or hunt with your own
Extras – Motel available; lunches available

DAKOTA OUTFITTERS UNLIMITED

829 East View Drive, Bismarck, ND 58501 / 701-224-0494
Contact: Larry Brooks
Land – 30,000 acres private; unlimited acreage public
Game – Wild pheasant, sharp-tailed grouse, Huns, mourning doves, ducks and geese
Personal Guide – Must hunt with a guide
Dogs – Dogs available or hunt with your own
Extras – Field lunches, motel booking service; various hunting areas include Cannonball River, Heart River, prairie potholes, Turtle Mountains

SENIOR GOSLINGS GOOSE LODGE

614 South 12th Street, Bismarck, ND 58504 / 701-255-1695
Contact: Pete Ressler
Game – Ducks and geese
Personal Guide – Available; can not hunt on your own
Dogs – Available or bring your own
Extras – Motel available and meals provided

CLUB NORDAK

344 Dakota Street N, Streeter, ND 58483 / 800-677-3793
Contact: Jason Brown
Game – Ducks, geese, pheasant, sharptails
Personal Guide – Available
Dogs – Available

Hunting Prairie Potholes

by Christopher S. and Jason A. Smith

Most waterfowl hunters look with great anticipation at the projected fall flight of ducks, crossing their fingers every year that this may be the one in which we achieve the North American Waterfowl Management Plan's goal of 100 million birds.

The basis for these projections come from breeding-duck surveys in the heartland of waterfowling: the Great Plains of the U.S. and the Prairie regions of southern Manitoba and Saskatchewan. This "duck factory" is responsible for producing almost half of the entire continent's flight of ducks.

For this reason, hunting the prairie potholes of the Dakotas, Iowa, Nebraska, and the Canadian provinces is popular and productive. These potholes, the remnants of glacial activity, occur mostly in agricultural areas, so permission will more than likely be needed before you can plop down alongside one. Some potholes are ringed with tall weeds or cattails in which you can stand and become almost invisible. But due to intensive farming, other potholes may not have much cover. Then, a pop-up blind will usually provide

Canada geese resting on a prairie pothole. (Photo: John Schafer)

The Duck Factory of North America—the Prairie Potholes. Almost half of the continent's breeding population of ducks is found in places such as this. (Photo: Christopher Smith)

enough concealment, or simply hunkering down on the ground against a hillside can also do the trick. On these denuded ponds, proper camouflage and holding still are of extreme importance.

Prairie pothole hunting can be difficult at times for one simple reason: the potholes are scattered throughout the countryside, and if the ducks are moved off one pothole—or are shot at—they'll simply drop over onto another one, one that isn't being hunted, and sit tight. With nothing to move them around, you might only get shooting at one or two flocks. This is one time when a little pressure from other hunters is welcome. In most cases, though, there are shooting opportunities constantly presenting themselves, and some of the best puddle duck shooting occurs over these small bodies of water.

Another way to hunt these potholes, other than just setting up in the middle or along the edge, is to forget decoys and simply park yourself under the flight lanes between potholes. Pass-shooting buzzing puddlers is a humbling way to spend an afternoon. Just hold way out in front, keep swinging, and don't count your empties.

For those times when you're not waiting in pass-shooting ambush, decoys figure prominently, especially on larger potholes. Most of the time, decoys can simply be scattered about, but be sure to leave empty water in shotgun range so that you're presented with killing shots as the birds attempt to land. Not many decoys may be needed, but in larger potholes, a rig of a couple dozen placed in some ducky-looking spots is a sure-fire way to get some shooting.

Calling is as important here as it always is in puddle duck hunting, and dogs can mean the difference between taking your limit home or not finding a downed bird. These potholes are often quite deep in the middle, and if you don't have a dog, a belly-boat or small canoe is a must in order to retrieve most of your birds. If pass-shooting, a dog keeps you from having to get up and retrieve your own birds—pure laziness here. With Fido, your faithful picker-up, the whole thing can become a sort of driven-duck shoot.

One of the nicest things about prairie pothole hunting is the variety of ducks you'll encounter. One time in North Dakota, we identified just about every variety of puddlers on the continent, and we took seven different species of dabblers during a three-day hunt, plus canvasbacks, redheads, a bluebill or two, and a few geese. Most of these birds will respond to a mallard call, but it might be useful to have a pintail or wigeon whistle on your lanyard as well.

This wigeon and blue-winged teal were taken minutes apart. Gadwall, mallards, pintails, shovelers, and assorted divers are all possible during a day on a prairie pothole. (Photo: Christopher Smith)

The Valley

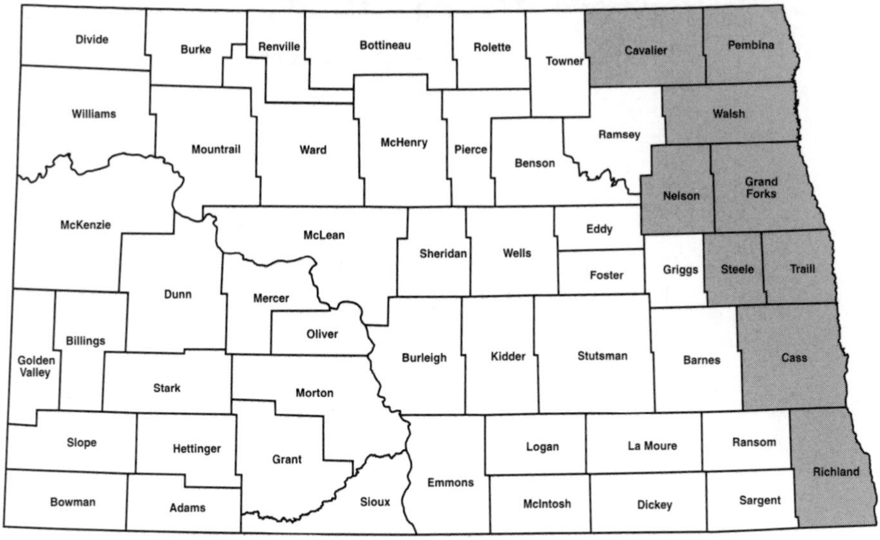

This region stretches north to south along North Dakota's eastern border. The best hunting options lie in the southeast corner of the region, near Lisbon, where good pheasant populations are strong. Woodcock are also present in decent numbers along the river bottom riparian strips. There is also fair hunting for ruffed grouse in the region's northern sections. North Dakota's greatest population center, Fargo, offers all the amenities that a traveling hunter needs.

Ring-necked Pheasant Distribution
The Valley Region

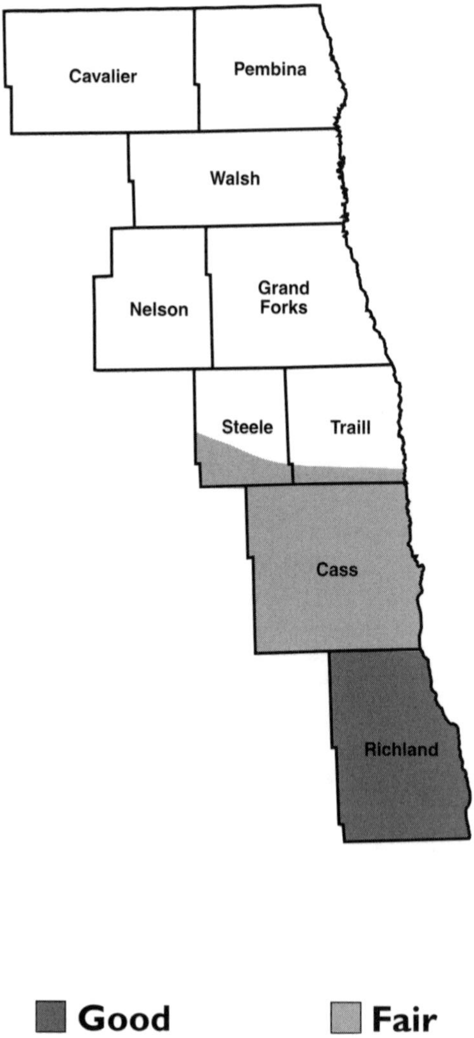

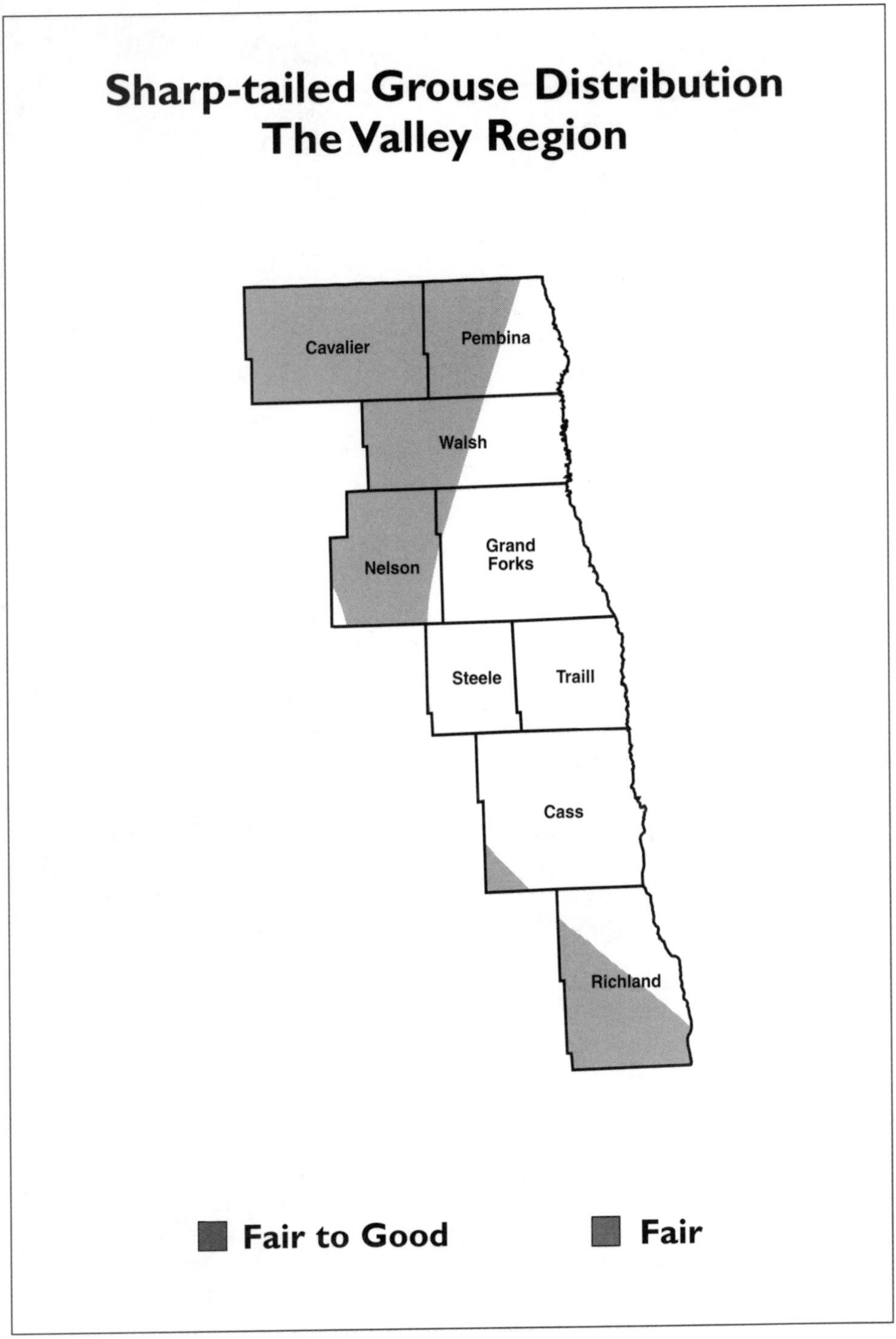
Sharp-tailed Grouse Distribution
The Valley Region
Cavalier
Pembina
Walsh
Nelson
Grand Forks
Steele
Traill
Cass
Richland
Fair to Good
Fair

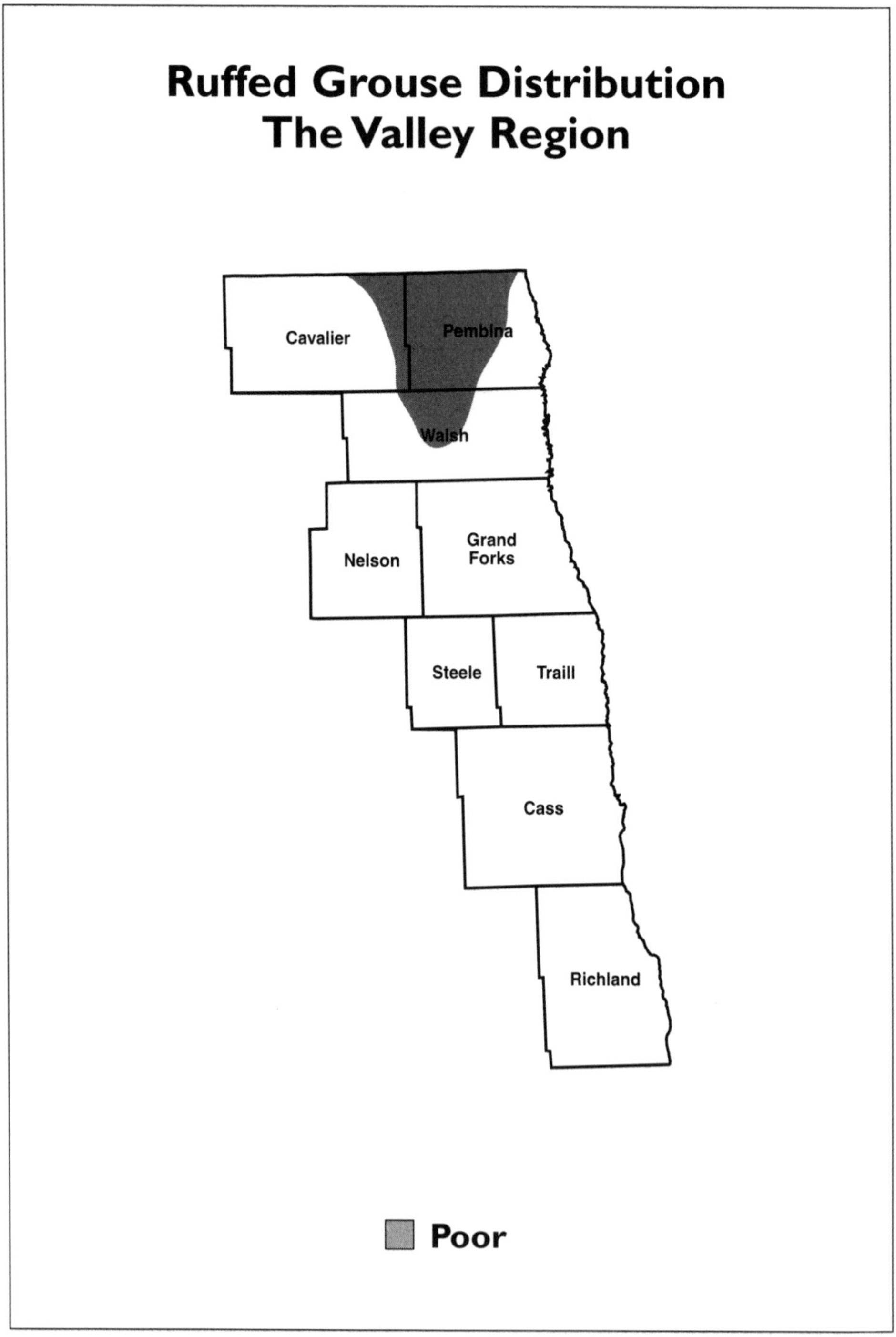
Ruffed Grouse Distribution
The Valley Region
Cavalier
Pembina
Walsh
Nelson
Grand Forks
Steele
Traill
Cass
Richland
Poor

Wild Turkey Distribution
The Valley Region

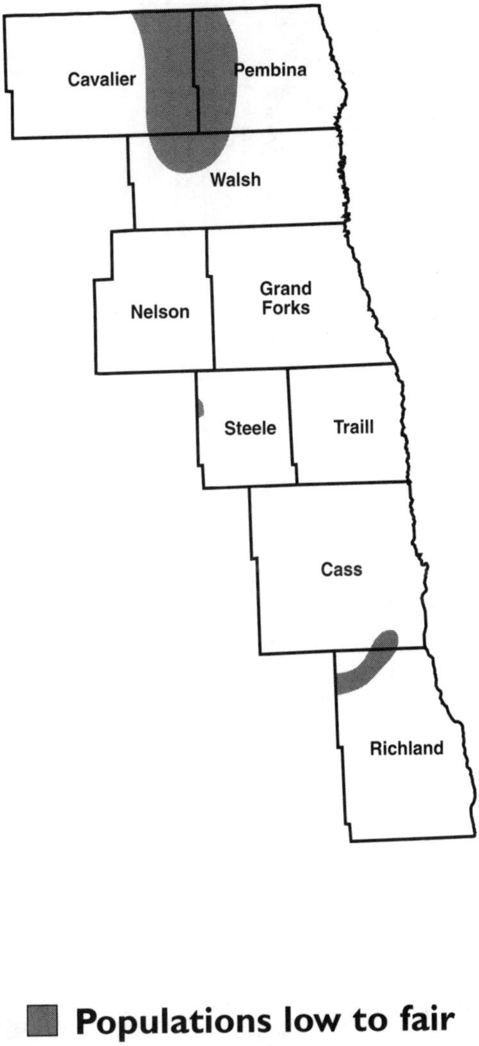

Woodcock Distribution
The Valley Region

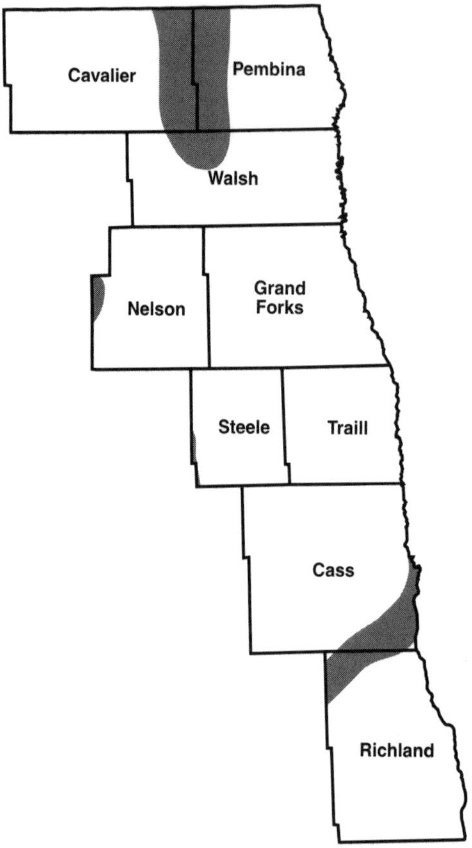

Only found in these drainages

Mourning Dove Distribution
The Valley Region

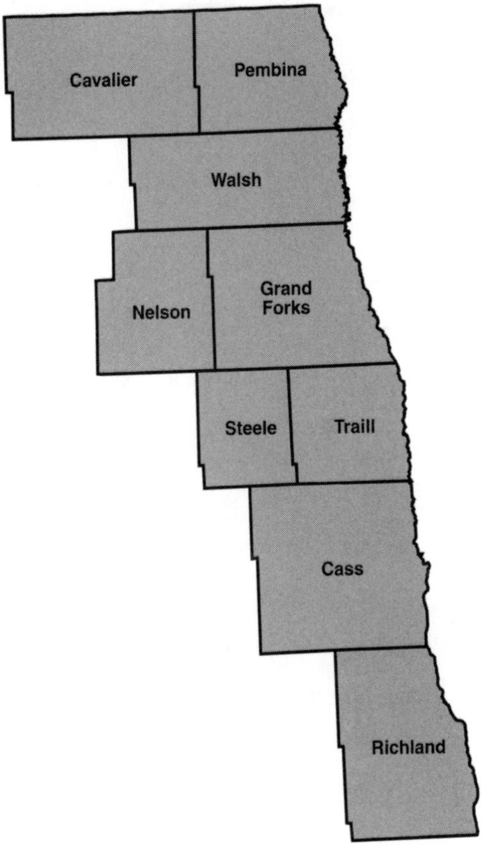

Found throughout region

Common Snipe Distribution
The Valley Region

Found throughout region

Sandhill Crane Distribution
The Valley Region

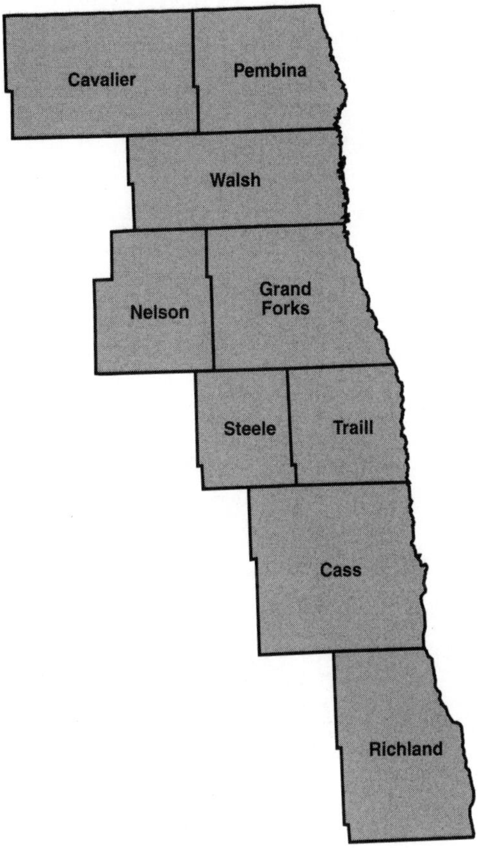

Found throughout but denser populations in western part of region

Drayton and Pembina County

Population–900	Elevation–790
County Population–9,238	October Temperature–52°
County Area–1,120 sq. mi.	Acres in CRP–28,937

UPLAND BIRDS
Sharptail, Ruffed Grouse, Turkey, Woodcock, Mourning Dove, Snipe

WATERFOWL
Ducks & Geese

ACCOMMODATIONS
Motel 66, I-29 & Highway 66 / 24 rooms / Dogs allowed / 701-454-6464 / $$
Sweet Dreams Inn, 602 Melbourn Street / 701-454-3437 / $
Red River Resort, 602 Melbourn Street / 10 rooms / Dogs allowed if attended / 701-454-6184 / $$

CAMPGROUNDS AND RV PARKS
Catfish Haven Resort & Campground, East Drayton / 701-455-3838
Red River Resort, 602 Melbourn Street / 701-454-6184

RESTAURANTS
Curnal's Dakota Fried Chicken / Chicken and jo-jo's / 701-454-6116
Hastings Landing Restaurant & Lounge, Main Street / Breakfast starts at 8am, lunch, dinner / Lounge opens at 5pm / 701-454-6434

VETERINARIANS
Park River Veterinary Clinic (nearest), Park River Highway 17 West Park River / 701-284-6514

SPORTING GOODS STORES
Cenex, 806 Main / 701-454-6531

AUTO REPAIR
Harold's Body Shop, Main Street / 701-454-3977

A young hunter with a pair of beautiful wood ducks. (Photo: John Schafer)

AIR SERVICE

Drayton Municipal Airport, two miles north of town

MEDICAL

Drayton Clinic, 809 Main / 701-454-3311

FOR MORE INFORMATION

Drayton Chamber of Commerce
P.O. Box 265
Drayton, ND 58225

Grafton and Walsh County

Population–5,084	Elevation–630
County Population–13,840	October Temperature–56°
County Area–1,290 sq. mi.	Acres in CRP–66,598

Grafton is located in east-central Walsh County in the northeast corner of the state. Agriculture is the area's principal industry and provides hunters with excellent upland bird and waterfowl hunting opportunities. Hunters basing out of Grafton will find ample amenities. The average temperature in December is 7.6 degrees; 81 degrees during summer

UPLAND BIRDS
Sharptail, Ruffed Grouse, Turkey, Woodcock, Mourning Dove, Sandhill Crane, Snipe

WATERFOWL
Ducks & Geese

Accommodations

Super 8, 948 West 12th / 32 rooms / No dogs / 701-352-0888 / $$
Midtown Motel, 728 Manvel Avenue / Dogs allowed / 701-352-0231 / $$
Leonard Motel, Highway 17 West / Dogs allowed / 701-352-1730 / $$

Campgrounds and RV Parks

Listow Park Campground, West 5th Street / 701-352-1842 / Hookups, sewer water

Restaurants

Hardee's, Highway 17 East / Burgers / 701-352-3104
Trails West Cafe, 413 Hill Avenue / Open 7am / Breakfast, lunch, dinner / 701-352-1785
Pizza Hut, 755 West 12th Street / pizza, salad / 701-352-1093
Extra End Sports Bar, 15 East 5th Street / Food, drink, blackjack, pool, TV / 701-352-3072

Veterinarians

Park River Veterinary Clinic, RR1, Box 54, Park River / 701-284-6514

Sporting Goods Stores

Ace Hardware, 85 East 4th Street / 701-352-1750
True Value, 532 Hill Avenue / 701-352-1633

Thick cover with nearby water offers ideal habitat for upland birds. (Photo: Blanche Johnson)

Auto Repair

Heritage Inc., 413 Griggs Avenue / 701-352-2992

Air Service

Grafton Municipal Airport, RR 3 / 701-352-0271

Medical

Unity Medical Center, 164 13th Street West / 701-352-1620
Grafton Family Clinic, 155 West 14th Street / 701-352-2000

For More Information

Grafton Chamber of Commerce
Corner of 5th Street and Hill Avenue
Grafton, ND 58237
701-352-0781

Fargo and Cass County

Population–80,441	Elevation–898
County Population–102,875	October Temperature–50°
County Area–1,767 sq. mi.	Acres in CRP–12,159

Fargo, located in the Red River Valley, is North Dakota's largest city. It offers everything a bird hunter could ask for and serves as an ideal hub for those hunting waterfowl or uplands in the southeast portion of the state. Fargo is remembered best for three notorious tidbits: in 1893 most of the business district burned to the ground; in 1885 disgruntled spouses flocked from eastern cities to Fargo due to the ease at which divorces were attained. In 1996 the movie *Fargo* put the city on the map.

UPLAND BIRDS
Pheasant, Sharptail, Woodcock, Mourning Dove, Sandhill Crane, Snipe

WATERFOWL
Ducks & Geese

ACCOMMODATIONS

Best Western Doublewood, 3333 13th Avenue SW / 701-235-3333 / Dogs allowed with $50 deposit / $$

Best Western Kelly Inn, 3800 Main Avenue / 701-282-2193 / Dogs allowed, no deposit required / $$

Motel 6, 1202 36th Street South / 701-232-9251 / Dogs allowed, no deposit required / $$

Select Inn, I-19 & 13th Avenue South / 701-282-6300 / Dogs allowed / Speedway restaurant next door / $$

CAMPGROUNDS AND RV PARKS

Ashby Resort & Campground, Highway 82 & Pelican Lake (in Minnesota) / Water turned off in mid-October / 9-unit motel year-round (dogs allowed) / 8 tent sites / 8 RV sites / 800-332-9209

Red River Valley Fairgrounds, 1201 West Main, West Fargo / Over 80 RV hookup sites / unlimited tent sites / 701-282-2200

RESTAURANTS

Embers Restaurant, 3838 Main Avenue / 701-282-6330

Bonanza Family Restaurant, 2515 South University / 701-232-3137

The Oven Door, 1338 3rd Avenue North / 701-232-3207

Sports Bar and Grill, 619 NP Avenue North / Lunch, dinner, cocktails / Open 7 days / 11am–11pm / 701-293-2085

Great Northern Restaurant and Brewery, 425 Broadway / Wood baked pizzas, pasta, microbrews / 701-235-9707

Veterinarians

A-1 Pet Care, 1230 Coulee Road / 701-223-7115

Animal Health Clinic, 1441 South University / 701-222-8255

Sporting Goods Stores

Custom Gun Works, 401 North University / 701-232-8525

Scheels, 13th Avenue South / 701-298-2918

Valley Gun and Pawn, South 209 / 701-280-0981

Auto Repair

Midas, 3041 Main Avenue / 701-298-8224

Air Service

Hector International Airport, / 701-241-8168 / Carriers: Northwest, United Express

Medical

Merit Care Clinic, 1220 Sheyenne Street / 701-282-4446

For More Information

Fargo Chamber of Commerce
321 4th Street North
Fargo, ND 58102
701-237-5678

Grand Forks and Grand Forks County

Population–49,425	Elevation–848
County Population–70,683	October Temperature–53°
County Area–1,440 sq. mi.	Acres in CRP–69,729

Grand Forks is located at the junction of the Red and Red Lake Rivers in far eastern North Dakota's Grand Forks County. Combined with East Grand Forks in Minnesota, the Grand Forks area supports over 100,000 people. For the bird hunter, either hub provides plenty of amenities and quick access to local hunting grounds.

UPLAND BIRDS
Sharptail, Mourning Dove, Sandhill Crane, Snipe

WATERFOWL
Ducks & Geese

ACCOMMODATIONS

Select Inn, I-29 & US 2 / Dogs allowed / Speedway restaurant next door / 701-775-0555 / $$

Econo Lodge, 900 North 43rd Street / 701-746-6666 / Dogs allowed, no fee / $$

Holiday Inn, Jct. I-29 & Highway 2 West, Exit 141 / 701-772-7131 / $$

Comfort Inn, 3251 30th Avenue South / 701-775-7503 / 67 rooms, indoor pool / Dogs allowed, no fee / $$

Best Western Town House, 710 1st Avenue North / 701-746-5411 / 113 rooms, indoor pool, restaurant, lounge, casino / No dogs / $$

CAMPGROUNDS AND RV PARKS

Grand Forks Campground, RR 1 / 701-772-6108 / Full service sites, laundry

River's Edge Campground, East Grand Forks / 218-773-7481 / 25 sites, some electrical hookups, showers

Wagon Train RV Park, Rt. 1 / 17 sites with water, electricity and dump station / 701-775-7722

RESTAURANTS

Wendy's, 1503 South Washington / Burgers / $

Jeannie's Restaurant, 1106 South Washington / Open 24 hours for breakfast, lunch, and dinner 701-772-6966 / $$

GF Goodribs Steakhouse, 4223 12th Avenue North / 701-746-7115 / $$-$$$

Italian Moon, 810 South Washington / Pizza, Mexican, ribs, chicken, 25 pasta dinners / 701-772-7277 / $-$$

Red Lobster, 32nd Avenue North / Seafood, steaks / 701-772-8770 / $$

VETERINARIANS

Kindness Animal Hospital, 701-772-7289

Red River Small Animal Clinic, 701-746-0011

SPORTING GOODS STORES

Scheels, 13755 South Columbia / 701-780-9424

AUTO REPAIR

Danny B's General Repair, 2205 Gateway Drive / 701-772-1375

AIR SERVICE

Grand Forks International Airport, 2787 Airport Drive / Carriers: Northwest, United Express, Northwest Airlink / 701-795-6981

MEDICAL

United Hospital, 1200 South Columbia Road / 701-780-5000

FOR MORE INFORMATION

Grand Forks Convention and Visitor Center
4251 Gateway Drive
Grand Forks, ND 58203
701-746-0444

Wahpeton and Richland County

Population–9,135	Elevation–960
County Population–18,148	October Temperature–49°
County Area–1,436 sq. mi.	Acres in CRP–29,669

Wahpeton is located in extreme southeast North Dakota in the Red River Valley of Richland County, where wheat and other cash crops reign. The upland bird hunter should find many options when based in Wahpeton. Upland birds and waterfowl are abundant. There are plenty of amenities for the visiting hunter.

UPLAND BIRDS
Pheasant, Sharptail, Turkey, Woodcock, Mourning Dove, Sandhill Crane, Snipe

WATERFOWL
Ducks & Geese

ACCOMMODATIONS

Comfort Inn, 209 13th Street South / 701-642-1115 / Air conditioning, cable TV, indoor pool, whirlpool, sauna / Dogs allowed / $$

Super 8, 995 21st Avenue North / 701-642-8731 / Cable TV with free HBO, in-room whirlpools, indoor swimming pool, laundry, restaurant, lounge / Dogs allowed / $$

Starlite Motel, 1005 4th Avenue South / 701-642-6627 / Dogs allowed / $

CAMPGROUNDS AND RV PARKS

Chahinkapa Campground, 1004 RJ Hughes Drive, 16 RV sites with electrical hookup, unlimited tent sites, showers, 7-day limit / 701-642-2811

RESTAURANTS

Buffingtons, 995 21st Avenue North / Open 6am for breakfast, lunch, dinner / 701-642-6300

Dairy Queen, 90 Dakota Avenue / Burgers, ice cream / 701-642-2212

Tomacelli's Pizza, 118 North 6th Street / Pizzas, pasta / 701-642-3940

VETERINARIANS

Dakota Veterinary, Old Highway 13 / 701-642-9277

SPORTING GOODS STORES

Action Reaction Sports, 419 Dakota Avenue / 701-642-8611

Setting out the dekes for a morning duck hunt. (Photo: Blanche Johnson)

AUTO REPAIR

Goodyear Tire and Repair Center, 715 Dakota Avenue / 701-642-5515

AIR SERVICE

Harry Stern Airport, / 701-642-5777

MEDICAL

Dakota Clinic, 275 11th Street South / 701-642-2000
Meritcare Clinic, 332 2nd Avenue North / 701-642-7000

FOR MORE INFORMATION

Wahpeton Chamber of Commerce
118 6th Street North
Wahpeton, ND 58075
701-642-8744

West Fargo and Cass County

Population–13,800	Elevation–900
County Population–102,875	October Temperature–50°
County Area–1,767 sq. mi.	Acres in CRP–12,159

UPLAND BIRDS
Pheasant, Sharptail, Woodcock, Mourning Dove, Sandhill Crane, Snipe

WATERFOWL
Ducks & Geese

ACCOMMODATIONS

Days Inn, 525 East Main Avenue / 61 rooms, cable TV, indoor pool, continental breakfast / 701-281-0000 / Dogs allowed with $15 deposit / $$

Super 8, 825 Main Avenue East / 42 units, nonsmoking rooms, morning coffee and pastries, cable TV / Dogs allowed / 701-282-7121 / $$

High 10 Motel, 1402 West Main / 75 rooms, cable TV, outside plug-ins, laundry facility, nonsmoking rooms / Dogs allowed / 701-282-6491 / $$

Sunset Motel, 731 West Main / Smoking & nonsmoking rooms, kitchenettes, water slide and pool / Dogs allowed / 701-282-3266

CAMPGROUNDS AND RV PARKS

Red River Valley Fairgrounds, 1201 West Main, West Fargo / Over 80 RV hookup sites / Unlimited tent sites / 701-282-2200

RESTAURANTS

Smokey's Steakhouse, Lounge & Casino, Highway 10 West / 710-281-1648

Jiggs Homestyle Restaurant, Westgo Square, 10 Morrison / 710-281-9750

Randy's Restaurant, 807 Main Avenue West / 701-277-1968

VETERINARIANS

West Fargo Animal Hospital, 730 13 Avenue East / 701-282-2898

SPORTING GOODS STORES

Scheels All Sports, 3202 13th Avenue South (Fargo) / 701-298-2918

Twin City Army Store, 1623 38th Street SW (Fargo) / 701-282-0832

AUTO REPAIR

All City Repair, 100 Main Avenue West / 701-281-9460

Dino's Road Service and Repair, 225 Main Avenue East / 701-282-2440

Author hunting the grasslands with his German wirehair. In typical grassland country, a hunter might bag a pheasant, sharptail, or Hun—part of the variety offered in grasslands. (Photo: Blanche Johnson)

AIR SERVICE

Hector Airport, Municipal Airport Information Center / Northwest and United Express / 701-241-8168

MEDICAL

West Fargo Clinic, 550 13th Avenue East / 701-282-2770

FOR MORE INFORMATION

West Fargo Chamber of Commerce
101 Sheyenne Street
West Fargo, ND 58078
701-282-4444

Guides and Outfitters

The Valley Region

DAKOTA HUNTING CLUB & KENNELS

PO Box 13623, Grand Forks, ND 58208 / 701-772-2010
Contact: George Newton
Land–640 acres
Game–Planted pheasant, chukar, quail
Personal Guide–Available or hunt on your own
Dogs–Available or hunt with your own

Hunting the Indian Reservations in North Dakota

North Dakota has four Indian reservations, three of which provide excellent hunting for upland birds, waterfowl, and big game. Inclusive, they offer a substantial 1,650,000 underhunted acres.

Each reservation has its own fish and game department and license fees. You will need a tribal license when you hunt on the Indian reservations, and a federal duck stamp is required for waterfowl. However, you do not need a North Dakota state license.

Most of the reservations have hunting guides, often referred to as "hunting partners," available. You can obtain a list of hunting partners from tribal fish and game departments.

If you are a first-timer to the reservations, I recommend a guide for at least the first day. A good guide will show you the most productive areas to hunt, which makes future hunting trips much easier to plan. Many of the reservations have full-scale casinos, hotels, and restaurants for relaxing after hours. If you like to gamble, you can combine a hunting trip with some gambling fun.

While the Indian reservations offer some prime wingshooting opportunities, some problems can arise. Check with tribal fish and game departments and get a complete copy of all of the rules, regulations, and bag limits before you arrive. If you encounter any problems, report them to the tribal game warden. Despite occasional problems, Indian reservations are a great place to hunt. You will generally find few hunters in the field and excellent habitat, along with plenty of game birds.

Standing Rock Indian Reservation

One million acres
Yanktonai, Hunkpapa Tribes, Sioux Nation
Standing Rock Fish &Wildlife
P.O. Box D
Fort Yates, ND 58538
701-854-7236

This huge reservation covers portions of two states, South and North Dakota. A tribal hunting license allows access to the entire reservation in both states. Standing Rock's east border is the Missouri River, which offers excellent hunting for ducks and geese. Pheasants, sharp-tailed grouse, and Hungarian partridge are also plentiful. Hunters may also encounter doves, and there are spring and fall seasons for wild turkey.

Standing Rock owns the Prairie Knights Casino and Lodge, located in Fort Yates, south of Bismarck, right on the Missouri River's banks. For more information on the casino and motel, call 1-800-425-8277.

North Dakota Indian Reservations

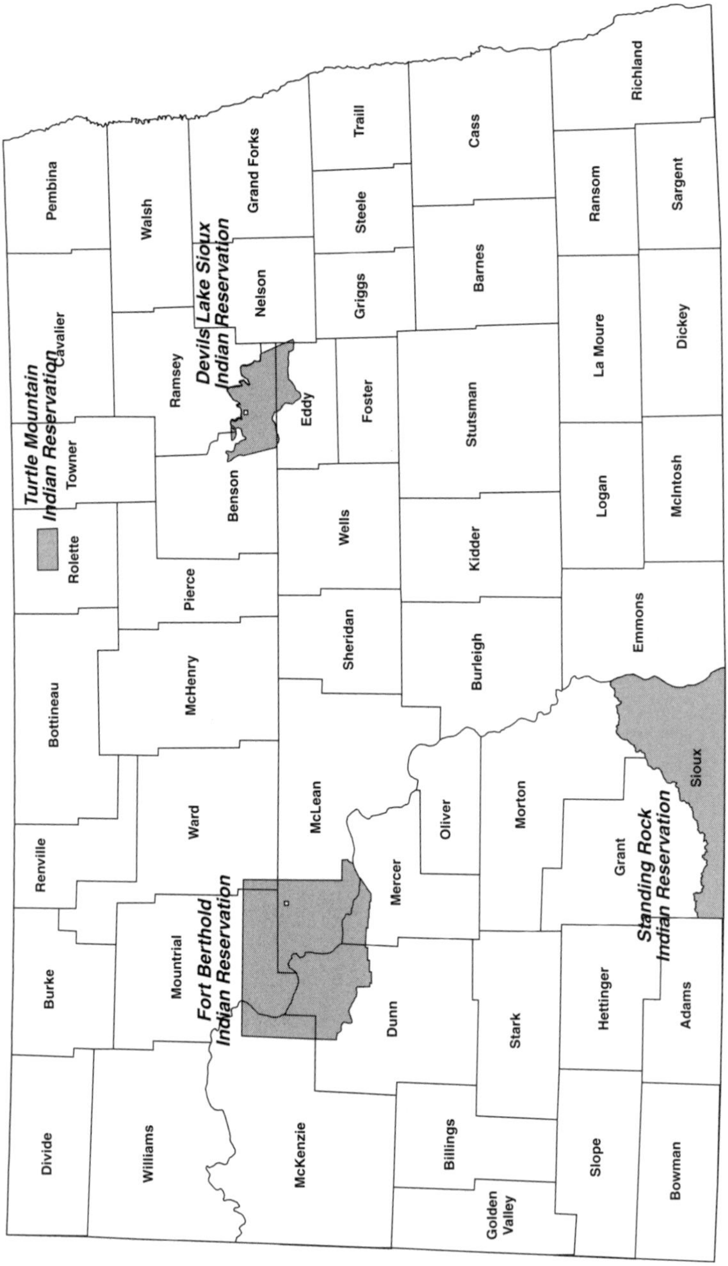

Duck hunting on the Missouri River. (Photo: Craig Bihrle)

Fort Berthold Indian Reservation

400,000 acres
Three Affiliated Tribes
Natural Resources Department Game and Fish Division
HC-3, Box 2
New Town, ND 58763
701-627-4760

Fort Berthold Indian Reservation is located in north central North Dakota, with tribal lands bordering both sides of Lake Sakakawea. Lake Sakakawea is an enormous Missouri River impoundment cutting through a good portion of west-central North Dakota. Located in the heart of the Central Flyway, its tantalizing waters draw hoards of migrating snow and Canada geese each fall. There is also excellent hunting for puddle ducks and diving ducks around the impoundment. Pheasants, sharp-tailed grouse, Hungarian partridge, doves, and sandhill cranes are also available in decent numbers. Due to this variety of birds, the reservation lends itself nicely to those who are interested in a mixed-bag, upland bird and waterfowl hunting trip. Visiting hunters can find excellent accommodations and services at New Town, located in the northern section of the reservation, Watford City to the west, and Garrison to the east.

Devils Lake Sioux Indian Reservation

Spirit Lake Dakotah Nation
250,000 acres

Devils Lake Indian Reservation is located in northeast North Dakota, bumped up against the southern shores of Devils Lake. Because it sits in the center of the prairie pothole region, hunting for ducks and geese on the reservation is outstanding. The reservation also offers seasons on upland birds, with pheasants and sharptails being the most abundant species. The town of Devil's Lake, located in the northern part of the reservation, provides excellent motels and restaurants for visiting hunters.

Turtle Mountain Indian Reservation

No hunting for nontribal members.

National Grasslands

North Dakota is part of the mixed grass prairie region, and at one time the state was covered with prairie grasses. Today, there are two national grasslands in the state with over one million combined acres. These grasslands are managed for multiple use one of them, of course, being hunting. Hunting can be quite good in the grasslands; they provide excellent food and cover for birds and big game animals.

History of the Grasslands

These lands were once home to many Indian tribes, including Kiowa, Cheyenne, Crow, and Sioux, as well as huge buffalo herds that were their main source of food and clothing. By the end of the 1870s, Indians had lost their use of the lands. Late in the 19th century, under the Homestead Act of 1862, settlers, primarily farmers and cattlemen, made their homes on the grasslands. However, due to low amounts of rainfall, less than 20" a year, the land was not well suited to farming. The drought and dust bowl of the 1930s saw thousands of homesteaders leave the area and abandon their farms.

From 1933 to 1943, nearly 10 million acres of drought-stricken land were purchased by the federal government. During this period, hundreds of thousands of acres were reclaimed, shelter belts were planted and erosion controls installed. By 1945 the lands were once again supporting soil-stabilizing grasses.

On June 23, 1960, nearly 4 million acres of Land Utilization Projects, located in the Great Plains region, became national grasslands to be managed by the National Forest Service as part of the National Forest system. These lands, unsuitable for cultivation, were now managed for wildlife, habitat, forage, prairie woodlands, water and outdoor recreation to the benefit of both land and people. Hunting is one of the primary purposes and uses of the grasslands.

Habitat Types in the National Grasslands

Trees: Cottonwoods, green ash, boxelder, elm, and juniper are located in woody draws, riparian areas, and shelter belts.

Upland Shrubs: Silver sagebrush, big sagebrush, and yucca

Other Shrubs: Buffaloberry, chokecherry, plum, and willow are found primarily in woody draws, riparian areas, and shelter belts.

Short Grass: Primarily buffalograss and bluegrass.

Mid and Tall Grasses: Mid grasses include western wheatgrass and needle grasses. Tall grasses include prairie sandreed, prairie cordgrass, and big bluestem.

Aquatic Habitats: open water, including streams, stock ponds and reservoirs.

All of the grasslands are a mixture of public and private land. It is important that you obtain a map of the grassland that you intend to hunt so that you can identify the public land. Make sure you have permission to hunt on private land that is posted.

North Dakota National Grasslands

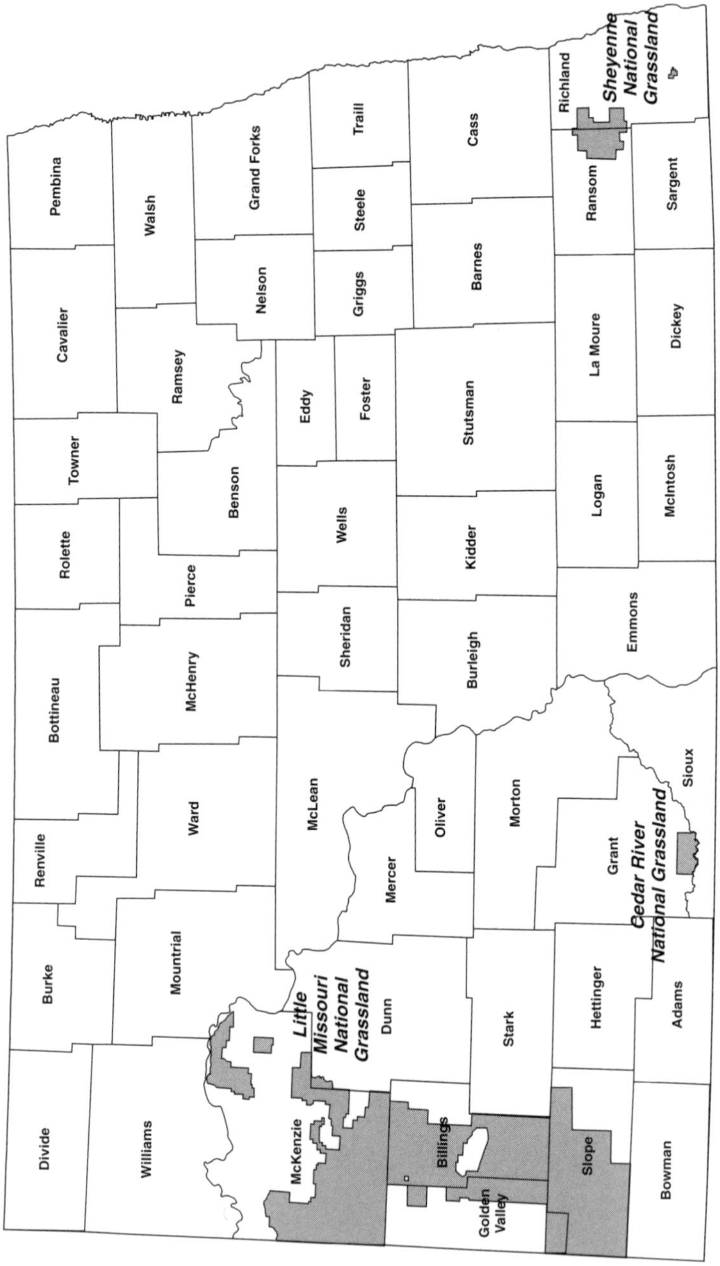

Little Missouri National Grasslands

One million acres
The West Region
Species Available: Sharp-tailed grouse, pheasants, sage grouse, and Huns

The Little Missouri National Grassland is one of my favorite places to hunt. Located on the western edge of North Dakota and stretching 150 miles long, it is the largest of the 19 national grasslands. State Highway 94 divides the Little Missouri Grasslands, and just north of I-94 is Theodore Roosevelt National Park. The park encompasses two ranches that President Roosevelt owned and operated in the late 1800s and offers a very interesting museum and visitor center to visit between hunts.

Medora, a great old Western town, sits just south of I-94 and is a good place for a hunter to stay with over 350 rooms and a number of fine restaurants in town. Located on a bluff overlooking town is the elegant Chateau de Mores 26-room mansion, which is open to visitors. The Chateau was home of the Marquis de Mores and his wife, Medora, neighbors of Roosevelt and owners of a large cattle and horse ranch.

One of the Little Missouri's best attributes is its excellent upland bird hunting. These grasslands have received very little pressure, and hunters can choose between two generous units: the North Unit, north of I-94, and the South Unit, south of I-94.

The North Unit is more rugged, but both are characterized by miles of rolling prairie, mixed with that challenging badlands terrain. Some of the property is privately owned, but most of it is public. In the North Unit, you might see bighorn sheep and elk, while both units offer abundant populations of whitetail and mule deer. If big game hunting interests you, the Little Missouri Grassland is an ideal choice for a combination deer and upland bird hunt.

Accommodations are a little sparse in the grasslands, but there are two primitive campgrounds in the South Unit and three in the North Unit. I recommend staying in Watford City if you plan to hunt the North Unit. If you want to hunt both units you can stay in Medora or Dickinson, which are located just 40 miles east on I-94. If you are hunting the southern part of the South Unit, the closest town is Bowman. For information on either unit, write or call:

South Unit, Medora Ranger District
161 21st Street West
Dickinson, ND 58601
701 225-5152

North Unit, McKenzie Ranger District
HCO 2, Box 8
Watford City, ND 58854
701-842-2393

Sheyenne National Grasslands

70,000 acres
The Prairies and Coteaus Region
Species Available: Pheasants and sharp-tailed grouse

Sheyenne National Grasslands is located in southeastern North Dakota in Sargent County. Wahpeton is located east of the grasslands, and Lisbon is located just north. Both provide ample accommodations for hunters. There are also primitive camping facilities available. For more information and maps contact:

Sheyenne Ranger District
Box 946, 701 Main
Lisbon, ND 58054
701-683-4342

Cedar River National Grasslands

6,700 acres
The West Region
Species Available: Pheasants and sharp-tailed grouse

Most of this grasslands is located in South Dakota, and to hunt that section you must have a South Dakota hunting license. The closest town is Hettinger, which is located in southwest North Dakota in Adams County. Adams County is considered the state's premier pheasant region. For more information and maps contact:

Grand River/Cedar River Ranger District
Box 390, 1005 5th Avenue West
Lemmon, SD 57638
605-374-3592

National Grassland Hunting Regulations and Seasons

National grasslands hunting seasons are the same as North Dakota's hunting seasons. You will need a state small game hunting license and other applicable licenses and tags. Maps and Information for all of the national grasslands can be obtained at:

National Grasslands Visitor Center
708 Main Street
P.O. Box 425
Wall, SD 57790
605-279-2125

Hunting the Grasslands

My wife, Blanche, and I enjoy hunting the West's vast grasslands—public lands that provide ideal habitat for upland game birds. We were able to hunt the Little Missouri Grasslands in western North Dakota for two days during fall 1996. With over a million acres, these grasslands have excellent hunting for pheasants and sharp-tailed grouse.

We had all five of our German wirehaired pointers with us: Duke, Annie, and three of Annie's six-month-old puppies. The first morning we drove just south of Medora, North Dakota. Pulling off on a dirt road that went down into a long, deep coulee, we parked at the bottom and started hunting.

The area was a mixture of short, ankle-deep prairie grass and small scrub trees. We worked several of the side coulees without any success. All of the dogs were in the bottom of a coulee in thick cover, when Duke went on point. Two sharptails cackled as they flew up, and my snap shot missed them. The puppies

And they're off! Author and his German wirehair pointers set out to work the grasslands. (Photo: Blanche Johnson)

Hunting in the grasslands can be a hot proposition. Here, the author lets his dogs cool down in a snow patch. (Photo: Blanche Johnson)

jumped into the birds at the shot, and then the air was filled with flying sharptails. Blanche brought one down, but I missed both my chances. There had been at least 30 birds in the coulee. We watched as they sailed over the top of the coulee and out of sight. Duke picked up Blanche's bird, and we gave the dogs a short rest to calm them down before moving on.

For the next two hours we covered the surrounding area, and the dogs found four small groups of sharptails. We had nice points on all four groups, with the pups backing Duke and Annie. My shooting improved and I managed to kill two birds. Blanche shot another bird in the last group. It was now 3 p.m., and we had to be in Medina that night for a goose hunt the next day, so we loaded the dogs up and headed out.

On the way home to Montana after a week of hunting central North Dakota for waterfowl and upland birds, we stopped at the grasslands for a final day of hunting. We went to the same area that we had hunted the week before and found no signs that anyone had been hunting there since then. In fact, we saw no signs of hunters on either of the days that we hunted the grasslands.

We put all five dogs down to hunt the coulees. For the first hour we came up empty-handed. Since we had a long ride home, we decided to load up the dogs and leave. I had loaded the puppies and Duke and called Annie, who normally comes when called. However, she did not respond to my call and we couldn't see her. Blanche said that she last saw Annie going back through the barbed wire gate and into a side coulee.

I went to the gate and saw Annie on point at the side of the dirt road. While I was running back to the truck for my gun, Blanche let the dogs out and unpacked her camera. We crossed the fence and found Annie still on point. I went in ahead of her to flush the bird. The other dogs were now backing Annie's point. After kicking the brush in front of Annie, no birds flew up, so I released Annie. The pups, Belle, Hershey, and Sprig, backed their mother, who had relocated the birds about 30 yards ahead. When I walked in beside Annie, the brush exploded with two cock pheasants. In my haste, I shot too fast and missed both birds. Annie looked disgusted with me; she had held the birds for over 10 minutes while we were getting ready.

We watched the birds fly over the top of the coulee and headed that way. At the top of the coulee, we saw a thick group of willows in the bottom of the next coulee with a small creek running through it. Annie and Hershey ran down to

Typical North Dakota grassland hunting. (Photo: Blanche Johnson)

the middle of the thicket and slammed on point, one on each side of the creek. Hurrying down to the creek, we got within 40 yards of the dogs when both cock pheasants flew out. Fortunately, one of them flew right at me. After taking the bird with an incoming shot, Annie retrieved the pheasant and looked pleased. At least I had redeemed myself with my dogs. The rest of the afternoon we found three more cock pheasants, but we couldn't get a shot. While they would hold for my dogs' points, they flushed when they heard us approach.

As the sun set we loaded the dogs and headed for Montana. We had had a wonderful day with plenty of birds, wide open spaces, and no hunting pressure. It doesn't get any better than this.

Note: Since the Little Missouri Grasslands is interspersed with private lands, it is helpful to have a map of the area. There are numerous roads throughout the area that make travel easy. However, most of the roads are dirt or gravel and some may become impassible when wet.

National Wildlife Refuges and Waterfowl Production Areas

North Dakota has 700,000 acres of refuges and production areas, with 16 major refuges and waterfowl management areas.

North Dakota's thousands of prairie potholes were formed when the ice that covered the land receded. The potholes filled with water and attracted the eye of breeding waterfowl. The birds still think it looks good today. That's why North Dakota has more National Wildlife Refuges and Waterfowl Production Areas than any other state. These areas are managed by the U.S. Department of the Interior and provide outstanding opportunities for waterfowl and upland bird hunting.

National Wildlife Refuges

National Wildlife Refuges, established for the conservation of migratory birds, are public lands that typically comprise a large body of water with additional prime habitat located on adjacent lands. Each wildlife refuge also manages a number of smaller public areas called Waterfowl Production Areas that can provide excellent hunting opportunities. You cannot hunt waterfowl on the refuges themselves, but most do offer areas to hunt upland birds. A popular tactic for waterfowl hunters is to work the edge of the refuges and pass shoot waterfowl as they move to and from feeding areas.

Wetland Management Districts and Waterfowl Production Areas

There are several Wetland Management Districts in North Dakota, and each manages some WPAs. All of the Wetland Management Districts and WPAs are considered public land and are open to both waterfowl and upland bird hunting.

North Dakota Wildlife Refuges and Waterfowl Production Areas

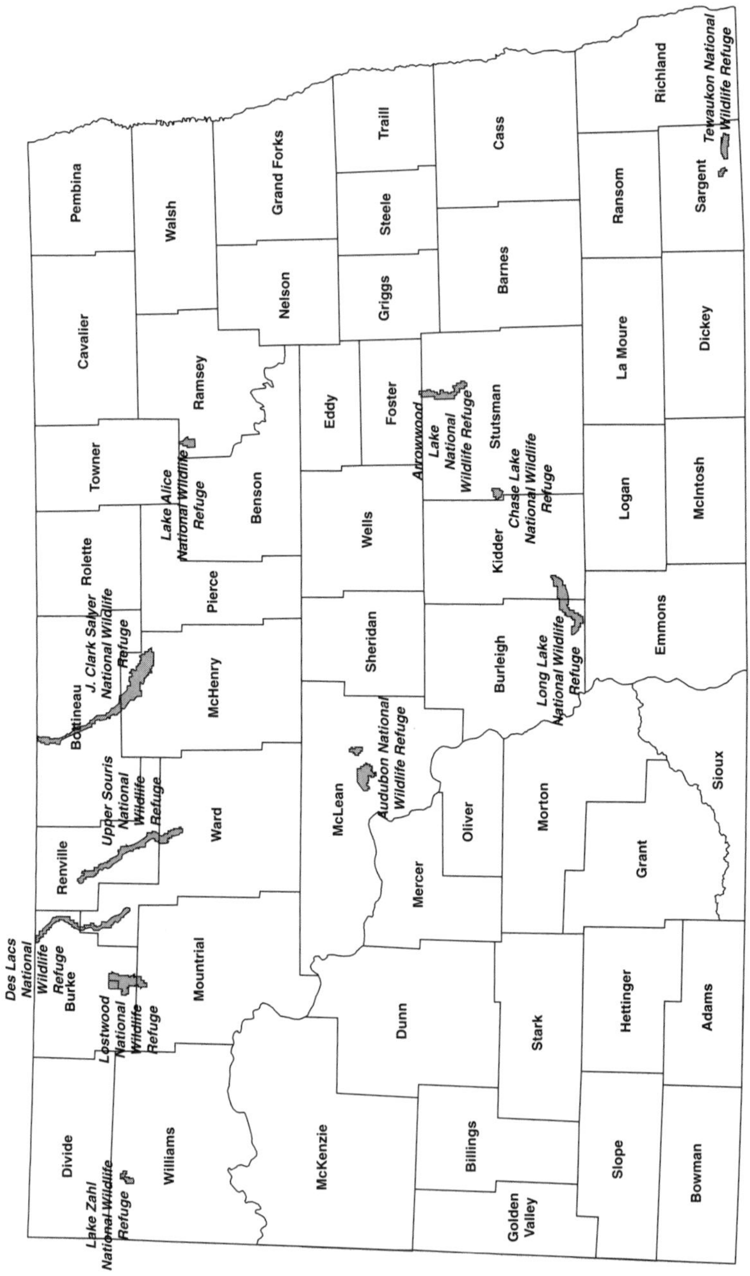

Waterfowl Production Areas

North Dakota's 2,000 areas offer more than 247,000 acres for hunting. Waterfowl Production Areas are smaller than wildlife refuges and range in size from just over 640 acres to a paltry one acre. They provide ideal nesting habitat for waterfowl and good cover for upland birds. WPAs are typically small potholes, but any of them can draw in good numbers of ducks and geese. Hunters will also find great upland bird shooting, mostly on lands bordering the WPAs. There are over 2,000 WPAs in North Dakota, and you can find maps and lists of existing WPAs from their district headquarters. Hunters will also recognize WPAs by the distinctive green sign that is posted on the border of each. The refuges and Wetland Management Districts have maps and a list of the WPAs in their district.

Arrowwood National Wildlife Refuge Complex

73,000 acres
Arrowwood National Wildlife Refuge
Route 1
Pingree, ND 58476
701-285-3341

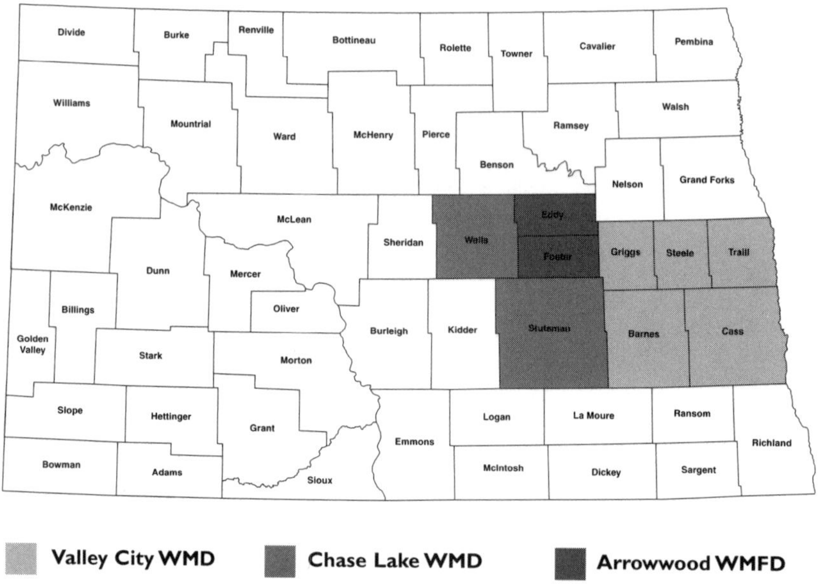

This complex, including the Arrowwood Wetland Management District, Chase Lake Wetland Management District, and Valley City Wetland Management District, encompasses nine counties in east central North Dakota. Hunting is allowed on the refuge for upland birds, with the main gamebirds being pheasants and sharptails. The numerous wildlife production areas provide great waterfowl hunting as well as sandhill cranes. The Chase district has 40 WPAs, Stutsman County has 95 WPAs, and the Arrowwood district has 27 WPAs. An excellent map showing the locations of all the WPAs in the complex is available.

Audubon National Wildlife Refuge

Audubon National Wildlife Refuge
Route 1, Box 16
Coleharbor, ND 58531
701-442-5474

This refuge provides upland bird hunting for pheasants, sharptails, and Huns from December 1 to the end of the state season.

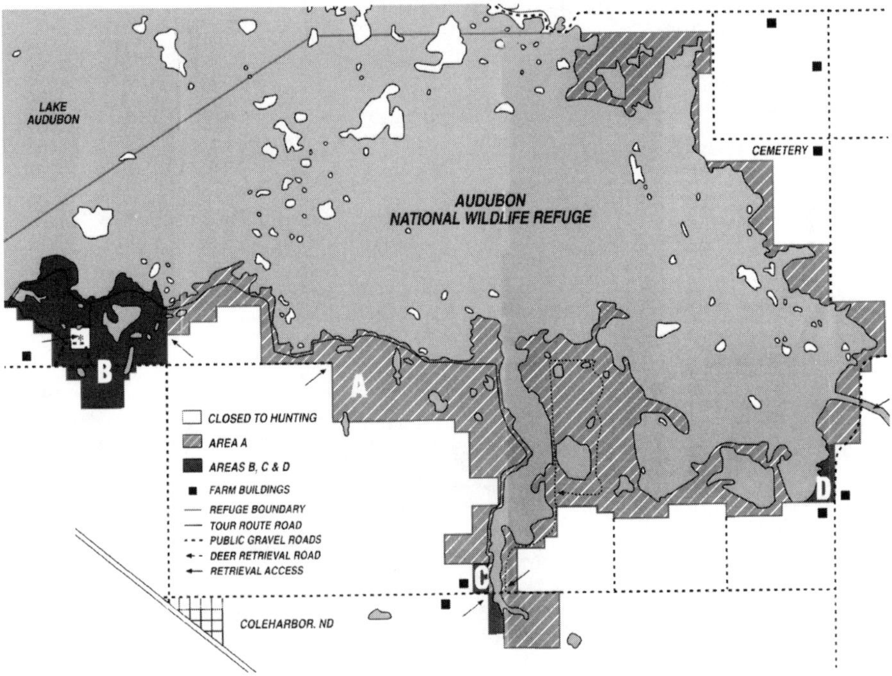

CROSBY WETLAND MANAGEMENT DISTRICT

17,000 acres of WPA; 66,000 acres wetland easements
Crosby Wetland Management District
P.O. Box 148
Crosby, ND 58730-0148
701-965-6488

This district also includes Lake Zahl National Wildlife Refuge as well as numerous WPAs. Dominant duck species are mallard, gadwall, and blue-winged teal, and giant Canada geese are also found here. Sandhill cranes migrate through here, and sharp-tailed grouse gather on "dancing grounds" on the WPAs.

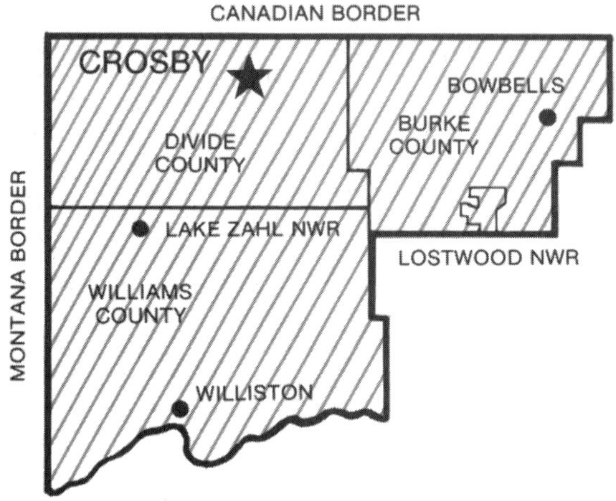

DES LACS NATIONAL WILDLIFE REFUGE COMPLEX

19,544 total acres; 13,600 acres upland; 5,800 acres water and marsh
Des Lacs National Wildlife Refuge
Box 578
Kenmare, ND 58746
701-385-4046

Located in north central North Dakota, this long, narrow riverine refuge extends 26 miles from the Canadian border to 8 miles south of Kenmare. During the fall migration, this refuge has 200,000 snow geese and 50,000 ducks. Geese and ducks feed daily outside the refuge on nearby grainfields. The entire refuge is open to upland bird hunting from December 1 to the end of the state season. Steel shot is required. No waterfowl hunting is allowed on the refuge, however, the areas adjacent to the refuge provide outstanding hunting for waterfowl.

GARRISON DIVERSION UNIT, LONETREE WILDLIFE MANAGEMENT AREA

32,000 acres
North Dakota Game & Fish Department
RR 2, Box 32
Harvey, ND 58341
701-324-2211

The Garrison Unit is located in the central part of the state and is approximately 25 miles long and two to three miles wide. It is managed by the North Dakota Game and Fish Department. There are 24,000 acres of grasslands and 5,000 acres of wetlands. Good upland bird hunting for sharptails, pheasants, and Hungarian partridge can be found here, along with the excellent waterfowl hunting. Each fall thousands of ducks and geese pass through this area.

KULM WETLAND MANAGEMENT DISTRICT

42,000 acres federal land plus 97,000 acres of easement
Kulm Wetland Management District
P.O. Box E
Kulm, ND 58456
701-647-2866

Over 150 waterfowl production areas are located within this district, providing excellent hunting for ducks, pheasants, and sharptails.

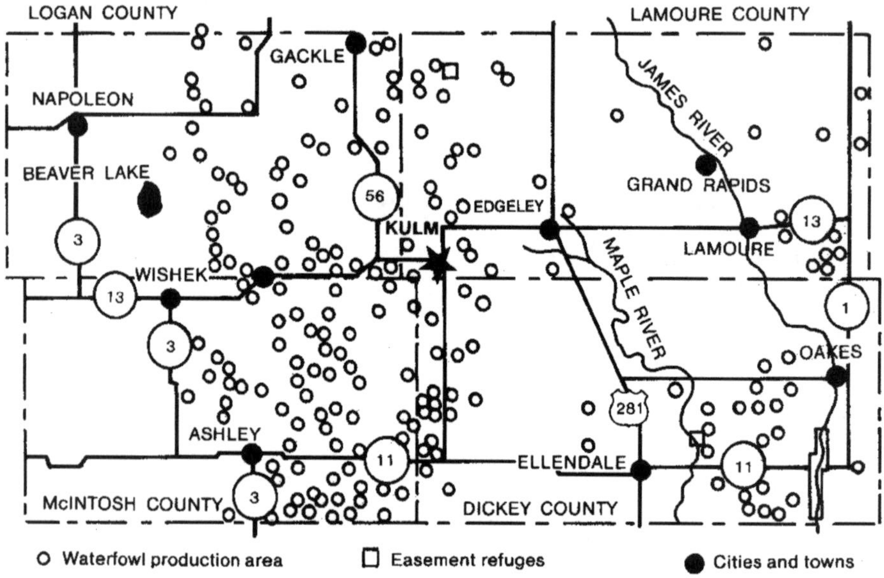

LAKE ALICE NATIONAL WILDLIFE REFUGE

11,500 acres
Lake Alice National Wildlife Refuge
P.O. Box 908
Devils Lake, ND 58301
701-662-8611

Lake Alice serves as a major waterfowl point during the fall migration. Thousands of Canada geese, snow geese, sandhill cranes, and ducks use the lake and surrounding lands each fall. Hunting for both waterfowl and upland birds is permitted on various portions of the refuge. Good hunting for pheasants and sharptails can be found on the upland areas of the refuge.

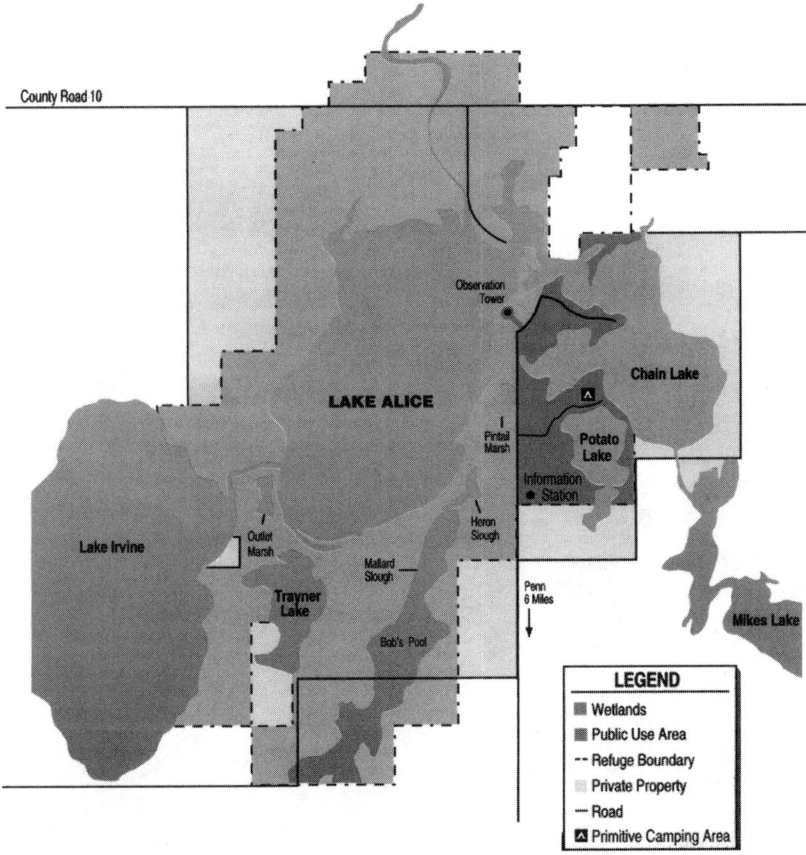

Lake Zahl National Wildlife Refuge

17,000 acres WPA; 66,000 acres wetlands easement
Lake Zahl National Wildlife Refuge
Box 148
Crosby, ND 58730
701-965-6488

Located in Divide, Burke, and Williams Counties in northwest North Dakota, this refuges comprises a total of 92 WPAs ranging in size from the 12-acre Olsen Unit in Divide County to the 2,270-acre Big Meadow Unit in Williams County. Excellent waterfowl hunting for ducks (mallards, gadwall, blue-winged teal) and giant Canada geese. Pheasants, sharp-tailed grouse, and Hungarian partridge are the main upland bird species.

Sandhill cranes. (Photo: Craig Bihrle)

LONG LAKE NATIONAL WILDLIFE REFUGE AND WETLAND MANAGEMENT DISTRICT

23,000 acres
Long Lake Complex
RR 1, Box 23
Moffit, ND 58560
701-387-4397

Located in the counties of Burleigh, Kidder, and Emmons in south central North Dakota, this district encompasses several refuges as well as a number of WPAs. Excellent hunting for waterfowl and upland gamebirds can be found on the WPAs. Pheasants and sharptails are the major upland birds.

Lostwood National Wildlife Refuge

Lostwood National Wildlife Refuge
Route 2, Box 98
Kenmare, ND 58746
701-848-2722

This refuge lies in the highly productive prairie pothole region that produces more ducks than any other region in the lower 48 states. Rolling hills of shortgrass and mixed grass prairie interspersed with numerous wetlands are the dominant features of this area. Waterfowl species include blue-winged teal, mallard, gadwall, wigeon, lesser scaup, and giant Canada geese. The main upland bird found here is sharp-tailed grouse.

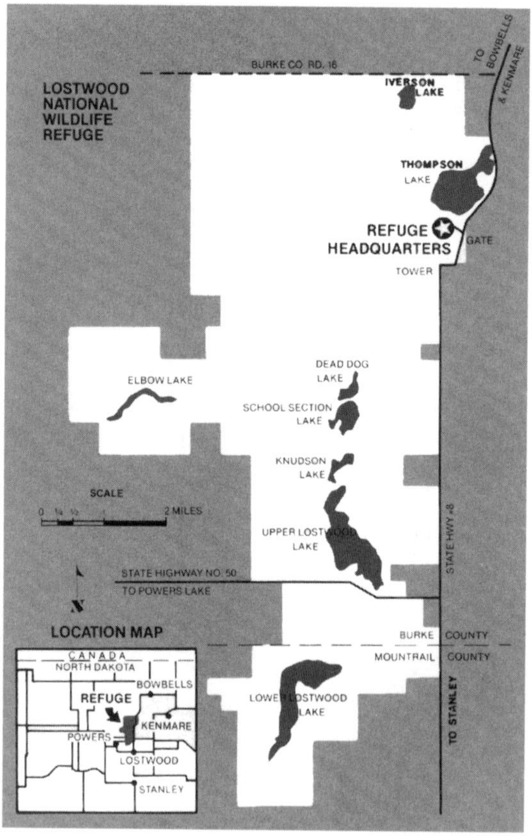

J. CLARK SALYER NATIONAL WILDLIFE REFUGE

59,383 acres
J. Clark Salyer National Wildlife Refuge
Upham, ND 58789
701-768-2548

Located in the north central part of the state within an hour's drive from Minot, this refuge holds excellent waterfowl hunting on the numerous WPAs. Good upland bird hunting for pheasants and sharptails can also be found here.

Setting up decoys on a clear North Dakota day. (Photo: Blanche Johnson)

TEWAUKON NATIONAL WILDLIFE REFUGE

8,444 acres
Tewaukon National Wildlife Refuge
RR 1, Box 75
Cayuga, ND 58013-9763
701-724-3598

This refuge is located on the eastern edge of the central flyway in southeastern North Dakota. The area includes 125 potholes that provide habitat for the dabbling ducks found here. Hunting is allowed on the WPAs. Mallards are the main waterfowl, with pheasants and Huns being the main upland bird species.

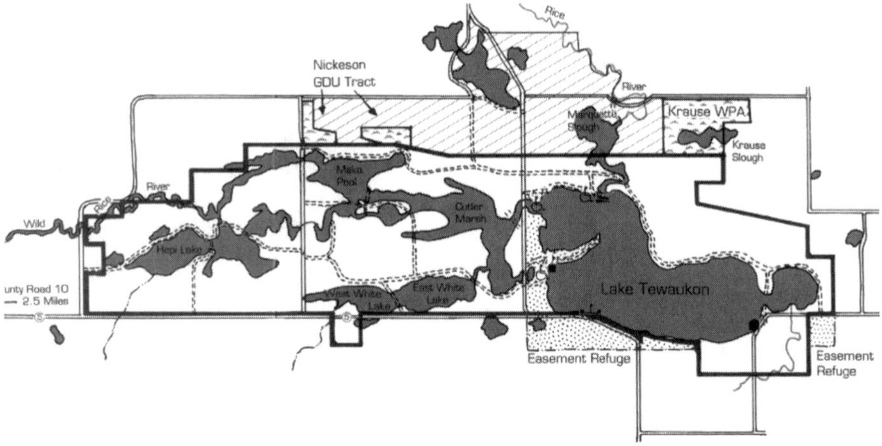

UPPER SOURIS NATIONAL WILDLIFE REFUGE

Upper Souris National Wildlife Refuge
Route 1
Foxholm, ND 58738
701-468-5467

Located north of Minot in the north central part of the state, this refuge is open for hunting upland birds, with pheasants, sharptails, and Huns being the main species. WPAs included here are open for both waterfowl and upland bird hunting.

Hunters can obtain information on all of the North Dakota National Wildlife Refuges and Waterfowl Production Areas by contacting:

US Fish & Wildlife Service
1500 East Capitol Avenue
Bismarck, ND 58501
701-250-4418

Part of the fun of a good hunt: a happy retriever. (Photo: Blanche Johnson)

State Wildlife Management Areas and Other State Lands

The North Dakota Game and Fish Department manages 190,000 acres in State Wildlife Areas. These wildlife areas are scattered throughout the state and vary in size from just hundreds to several thousand acres. Hunting is permitted on all of these areas, and you can obtain a list of management areas, by county, from the North Dakota Game and Fish Department. Ask for their North Dakota Hunting and Fishing Guide.

North Dakota Game and Fish Department Headquarters
100 North Bismarck Expressway
Bismarck, ND 58501-5095
701-328-6300 Fax 701-328-6352
E mail ccmail.ndgf@ranch.state.nd.us

Devils Lake Office
Route 5, Box 281B
Devils Lake, ND 58301
701-662-3617

Dickinson Office
225 30th Avenue SW
Dickinson, ND 58601
701-227-2343

Lisbon Office
Route 2, Box 295
Lisbon, ND 58054
701-683-4900

Lonetree Wildlife Management Area Office
Route 2, Box 32
Harvey, ND 58341
701-324-2211

Mott Office
409 Brown Avenue
Mott, ND 58646
701-824-2337

Oakes Office
P.O. Box 7
Oakes, ND 58474
701-742-2271

Riverdale Office
P.O. Box 506
Riverdale, ND 58565
701-654-7475

Spiritwood Lake Office
Route 1, Box 224
Jamestown, ND 58401
701-252-4634

Williston Office
P.O. Box 2476
Williston, ND 58802
701-774-4320

State School Land

North Dakota has 700,000 acres of state school land, much of which is open for public hunting. State School Lands are managed by the State Land Department.

North Dakota State Land Department
Box 5523
Bismarck, ND 58506-5523
701-328-2800

APPENDIX I
The Hunting Rig

A dependable hunting vehicle, well equipped and in good condition, is an essential part of your equipment for a successful hunt. North Dakota's prairies contain many gravel and dirt roads that can puncture tires or turn to impassable mud gumbo when even briefly besieged by rain or wet snow. And if your vehicle should break down, distances between towns that have auto service can be quite long. That's something you don't want, especially when one of North Dakota's infamous blizzards blasts down out of Canada. Being stranded in your vehicle and a long way from help can simply ruin a hunt. It can also be very dangerous during extreme heat or cold.

Before the start of the hunting season it's a good idea to have a complete vehicle checkup. Change the oil and filters and have all the belts and hoses checked. Make sure that your tires have plenty of tread. If you intend to do a lot of off-road travel, use an all-terrain, mud and snow tire.

My hunting rig is a four-wheel drive, long-bed pickup. Since I carry four or five hunting dogs at a time, I have a fiberglass dog unit mounted on top of the bed. This topper has three dog compartments on each side, and the back opens up for extra

A well stocked hunting rig is a necessity when hunting in wide open country, many miles from the nearest amenities. (Photo: Blanche Johnson)

storage. You can easily use a Suburban, Explorer, or similar type vehicle for your hunting rig.

When I first started hunting the West, I used a two-wheel drive van. While a two-wheel drive will work, you have to be a little more careful where you drive. A four-wheel drive is a definite plus.

As mentioned, North Dakota has tremendous weather variation. Temperatures can drop rapidly, and a major snowstorm can develop in hours. The flat prairies and high winds can create conditions that make roads impassable. There is a real danger that you and your dogs can be stranded out on the road miles from services during a fall storm. Always carry emergency supplies, because failure to do so could cost you your life. Load your rig with all of the equipment and supplies you will need on each trip at the start of the season. After each trip, replenish any supplies that have been used. Here is a check-list to use for your hunting rig. You can use it to supplement your own list if you want.

Hunting Rig Check List

_____ Tool Kit

_____ Ax and Shovel

_____ Flares

_____ Jumper cables

_____ Tow rope

_____ Heavy duty jack and tire iron

_____ Spare tire

_____ Matches

_____ Magnifying glass

_____ Road maps

_____ Air gauge

_____ Flashlight

_____ Spare key

_____ Duct tape

_____ Chains

_____ Fuses

_____ Extra fuel

_____ Blankets

_____ Emergency food

_____ 2 quarts drinking water

APPENDIX II
Hunting Dog Conditioning

Like a professional athlete, your dog requires year-round conditioning to stay in shape. Remember, if you are going to hunt the prairie country of western North Dakota, each day you and your dog will cover about four to five times the area that you would normally hunt in a day back east for grouse or woodcock. I estimate that my dogs run 50 or 60 miles a day when hunting the prairies. If not in good condition, your dog will be worn out long before you're ready to quit hunting for the day.

I take my dogs for a two-mile run every day of the year. With that exercise, dogs maintain their condition and I also get the exercise I need to stay in shape. I try to take my dogs on a longer run at least once a week. Starting in July, I increase our workout to a two or three-hour run at least twice a week. When September arrives we are in good shape for the hunting season.

Always a potential problem, porcupine quills can put a quick end to a hunt if you are not prepared. Always bring pliers on a Western bird hunt. Here, the author extricates quills from one of his wirehairs. (Photo: Brent Phelps)

Before the season begins, I also make sure that all of my dogs have a complete checkup. Throughout the year I feed my dogs Purina Pro Plan adult formula. However, if I am going to hunt the dogs hard for four or five days in a row, I change to the Pro Plan performance feed.

Many people feed their dogs in the morning before a hunt. If this is what you prefer, make sure the dog is fed at least an hour before the hunt to give them time to digest their food—how would you feel with a pile of hash browns, a half dozen eggs, and several slices of toast roiling in your belly before the hunt? For midday snacks, I give my dogs moist burgers, such as Gaines, or Milk Bones. I also carry packets of honey that I can give to the dogs for quick energy.

Heat prostration can be a real problem for a hunting dog during the early hunting season when it can be extremely warm, so carry at least two quarts of water with you in the field. A collapsible canvas water bowl is handy to keep with you–it folds flat and can be carried easily in a hunting coat or vest. It pops open and will hold a pint of water.

At times dogs can run so hard that they lose their electrolytes. Keeping a bottle of Pedialyte with you can help alleviate this problem. Mix some in with the drinking water when you suspect a problem is occurring. This product can be found in most drugstores and is most often used to restore electrolytes in infants.

Carry at least five gallons of water and a complete dog first aid kit in your hunting rig. At the end of the day or during a midday break, it's nice for a dog and hunter to drink their fill.

Last, but not least, carry a hemostat for removing porcupine quills and cactus spines from your dogs. A copy of *Field Guide to Dog First Aid* is always packed along in the pocket of my hunting vest.

Dog Equipment Check List

In the Field

_____ Water

_____ Collapsible water bowl

_____ Honey

_____ Hemostat

_____ *Field Guide to Dog First Aid*

In the Truck

_____ Dog food

_____ Dog bowls

_____ Dog leads

_____ Check cords

_____ First Aid Kit

_____ Dog boots, pad toughener

_____ Training dummies

_____ Beeper Collars

_____ Extra dog whistle

_____ Extra dog collars

_____ Five gallons of water

APPENDIX III
Hunter Conditioning and Equipment

Hunting the western prairies is dramatically different than hunting your favorite grouse or woodcock cover back east. You can drive for miles between ranches and towns without spotting any evidence of civilization. Prairies are characterized by dry, open spaces. Water is scarce.

A normal hunt for Huns, sharptails, and sage grouse starts in early morning when the temperature will be in the 20s. Early in the season (September-October), the temperature may climb into the 60s or even as high as the 90s by noon. Coveys of birds, while numerous, are spread over great distances. I usually leave the truck quite early and return in the late afternoon or evening. In the course of the day I cover 10-16 miles of open prairie. In order to enjoy your hunt, you need to be well conditioned and properly equipped.

Conditioning

I recommend that you start a walking or running program at least four months before you plan to hunt. You should be able to walk about three miles an hour on level ground. Try walking with a weighted pack. Remember, you will be walking with a shotgun, vest, and shells when hunting. Walk in the boots you intend to wear hunting. You don't have to be a marathon runner to have a productive hunt, however, if you are in good shape you can cover more ground.

Clothes

I wear lightweight ankle-high hunting boots. Unless you are hunting for waterfowl or are near a high stream, waterproof boots are not necessary. I wear two pairs of socks—an inner polypropylene sock to wick away moisture and a heavy wool outer sock for support.

I like to wear a light pair of canvas pants during the early part of the season and double-faced pants during the late season.

It is important to layer clothing on your upper body because of the wide range of temperatures you might encounter. Wear two or more layers of lightweight clothing that can be easily removed as temperatures climb, such as a polypropylene undershirt and a canvas or wool overshirt.

Sunburn is a common problem in the West. Always wear sunscreen and a billed hat while hunting. A bandana provides protection from the sun and can be used as a tourniquet for emergency purposes.

Use a hunting shell bag in the early season and a hunting vest during the late season. If the weather is cold and snowy, wear an oilcloth coat and a vest big enough to fit over all your outer garments.

It's also a good idea to carry a pair of light leather shooting gloves. Finally, take a good pair of shooting glasses for sun and eye protection and earplugs to protect your hearing.

Equipment

I carry a small folding knife in a sheath on my belt, along with a 24-inch dog lead. I also have a wristwatch that has a compass on the band and carry a whistle and a hemostat around my neck (it's great for picking out cactus needles). I always carry at least one quart of water for my dogs. When it is especially hot and water is scarce, I carry several quarts because I have come close to losing dogs to heat prostration. I normally wear a small fanny pack that holds water, lunch, camera, and other miscellaneous items. Finally, I carry a small amount of honey for my dogs, which can rejuvenate an exhausted dog.

Following is an equipment list for clothes, dogs, and supplies. Make copies and use it as a checklist when packing for your trip.

APPENDIX IV
Equipment Checklist

CLOTHING

_____ Polypropylene underwear
_____ Inner socks
_____ Wool socks
_____ Long sleeve canvas/chamois shirts
_____ Pants, double-faced
_____ Hunting boots
_____ Billed hat
_____ Bandana
_____ Shooting gloves
_____ Shooting glasses
_____ Ear protectors
_____ Hunting vest/coat
_____ Down vest/coat
_____ Raingear
_____ Hip boots/waders for waterfowl hunting
_____ Chaps

DOG SUPPLIES

_____ Food, bowls
_____ Beeper collar
_____ Lead
_____ Dog boots, pad toughener
_____ Hemostat
_____ Whistle
_____ Water bottles
_____ *Field Guide to Dog 1st Aid*
_____ Dog first aid kit
_____ Record of dog vaccinations
_____ Scissors
_____ Toenail clippers

HUNTING SUPPLIES

_____ *Wingshooter's Guide to ND*
_____ Shotgun/shells
_____ Cleaning kit
_____ Maps
_____ Knife
_____ Fanny pack
_____ Water bottle
_____ Camera, film
_____ Binoculars
_____ Game shears
_____ Ice chest
_____ Notebook, pen
_____ License
_____ Matches
_____ Axe, shovel
_____ Sunscreen
_____ Twine
_____ Decoys, decoy anchor
_____ Compass
_____ Flashlight
_____ Bird calls
_____ Spare choke tubes
_____ Magnifying glass for maps

APPENDIX V
Preparing a Bird for Mounting in the Field

by Web Parton, Taxidermist

The art of taxidermy has made considerable advances in recent years. This is especially true in the realm of bird taxidermy. How you take care of your birds in the field determines the finished quality of your mounts. This crucial step is out of the control of the taxidermist. However, with a modicum of preparation, you can proceed confidently when you are holding a freshly taken bird destined for the book shelf.

Start by putting together a small kit to be carried with you in the field. Use a small plastic container, such as a plastic traveler's soap box. Throw in some cotton balls, a few wooden toothpicks, a dozen or so folded sheets of toilet paper, and a pair of panty hose.

After shooting a bird, examine it closely. First, look for pin feathers. If there are any present, you will notice them on the head directly behind the beak or bill and on the main side coverts below the bird's wing. If there are even a few pinfeathers, the specimen may not be worth mounting. By all means, save it and let your taxidermist make the decision. However, it wouldn't hurt to examine additional birds to find one with better plumage. The taxidermist can always use extra birds for spare parts.

The next step is to check for any bleeding wounds in order to prevent the taxidermist from having to wash the bird before mounting. Plug any visible wounds with cotton. Use a toothpick as a probe to push the cotton into the holes. Now pack the mouth and nostrils, remembering that the body is a reservoir of fluids that can drain down the neck. Make a note or take a photo of any brightly colored soft tissue parts (unfeathered areas) for the taxidermist's reference later. Fold several sheets of toilet paper and lay them between the wings and the body. Should the body bleed, this will protect the undersides of the wings from being soiled. Slide the bird head first into the nylon stocking. Remember that the feathers lay like shingles: they slide forward into the stocking smoothly, but will ruffle if you pull the bird back out the same end. The taxidermist will remove it by cutting a hole in the material at the toe and sliding the bird forward. When the specimen is all the way down, knot the nylon behind its tail. Now you are ready to slide the next one in behind it.

Place the wrapped bird in an empty game vest pocket, allow it to cool, and protect it from getting wet. When you return to your vehicle, place the bird in a cool spot. At home, put it in a plastic bag to prevent freezer burn, and freeze it solid. You can safely wait several months before dropping it off at the taxidermist.

For the traveling hunter, there is the option of next-day air shipping. Provided that you can find a place to freeze the birds overnight, even a hunter on the other side of the nation can get birds to his taxidermist in good shape. Wrap the frozen birds, nylons and all, in disposable diapers. Line a shipping box with wadded newspapers. Place the birds in the middle with dry ice. Dry ice is available in some major supermarkets. Call your taxidermist to be sure someone will be there, and then ship the parcel next-day air. Be sure to contact them the next day so that a search can be instituted in the event that the parcel did not arrive.

Mounted birds are a beautiful memory of your days in the field. With just a little bit of advance preparation, you can be assured of a top-quality mount.

APPENDIX VI
Field Preparation of Game Birds for the Table

The two most important tools for preparing birds in the field for the table are game sheers and a knife with a gut hook.

During early season, when temperatures are in the 70° to 90° range, I draw my birds immediately or shortly after I leave the field. You can draw your birds by several methods.

I make a cut with my sheers at the end of the breast, making a small entry hole into the body cavity. I then take my gut hook, insert it into the cavity and pull out the intestines and other body parts.

The other method I use is to take my sheers and cut up the center of the bird's back, splitting the bird in two. Then you can use your gut hook and knife to clean out the intestines and other body parts.

I like to place my birds in a cooler during the hot early season. When the temperatures are cooler (below 55°), I store my birds in either a burlap or net bag. This type of bag allows air to circulate around the birds.

I like to hang my birds before cleaning and freezing. I hang my birds in a room where the temperature is less than 60° F. I have found that two to three days hanging time is best for the smaller birds (i.e., huns, grouse, woodcock). I hang my larger birds (pheasants, ducks) from four to five days. Hanging birds is a matter of individual preference. My friend, Datus Proper, hangs his birds for a much longer period of time than I do. I suggest that you experiment and then pick a hanging time that suits your tastes.

When the temperature is over 60°F, I clean my birds and freeze them immediately. We wrap our birds in cling wrap, place them in a ziplock bag, and then mark the bag with the type of bird and the date.

APPENDIX VII North Dakota Information Sources

Map Sources

Dakota Fishing Maps
P.O. Box 2448
Bismarck, ND 58502
1-800-762-0367

Northwest Mapping Company
P.O. Box 1234
Bismarck, ND 58502
701-223-1952

North Dakota State Highway Department
c/o Map Sales
608 East Boulevard
Bismarck, ND 58505
701-328-2500

North Dakota State Geological Survey
600 East Boulevard
Bismarck, ND 58505
701-328-4109
North Dakota topographic maps

North Dakota Game and Fish Department
100 North Bismarck Expressway
Bismarck, ND 58501
701-328-6300
Guide to state wildlife management areas

USDA, Medora Ranger District
Route #6, Box 131B
Dickinson, ND 58601
701-225-5151
National grasslands public domain map

US Army Corps of Engineers
District Office
Riverdale, ND 58565
Aerial maps
701-225-0015

US Fish & Wildlife Service
1500 East Capitol Avenue
Bismarck, ND 58501
701-250-4418
National Wildlife Refuge maps

More Information Sources

North Dakota Tourism
Liberty Memorial Building
604 East Boulevard
Bismarck, ND 58505
1-800-HELLO ND

U.S. Fish and Wildlife Service
1500 East Capitol Avenue
Bismarck, ND 58501
701-250-4418

North Dakota Forest Service
307 1st Street East
Bottineau, ND
701-228-5422

State Historical Society
612 East Boulevard
Bismarck, ND 58505
701-328-2666

North Dakota Guides and Outfitters
Contact: North Dakota Game and Fish Department
100 North Bismarck Expressway
Bismarck, ND 58501
701-328-6300
Ask for a list of registered guides and outfitters

APPENDIX VIII
Recommended Product Sources

Listed below are products and suppliers that I use and recommend:

Clothes

Orvis
Historic Route 7A
Manchester, VT 05254
1-800-548-9548

Patagonia
8550 White Fir Street
Reno, Nevada 89533
1-800-638-6464

Simms
101 Evergreen Drive
Bozeman, MT 59772
1-406-585-3557

Patagonia makes a heavy duty pant, called "stand-up pant," that is my favorite late fall and winter hunting pant. I also use their fleece outer garments and their Capilene underwear. Simms makes an outstanding raincoat. They sell only through dealers; check with your local fly shop.

Eyewear

Sporting Optical Specialties
964 Reni Road
Fond du Lac, WI 54935
1-800-521-2239

Sporting Optical Specialties carries Ranger and Costa del Mar glasses. The owners, Jim McConnell and Rob Post, are opticians and can provide you with specialized service for your prescription lenses.

Dog Supplies

Purina Pro Club
P.O. Box 1004
Mascoutah, IL 62224
1-800-851-3148

The Pointing Dog Journal
The Retriever Journal
P.O. Box 968
Traverse City, MI 49685
1-800-272-3246

Purina makes healthful and dependable food for dogs. They have an excellent research lab and make products especially for the hunting dog. I've used Purina's Pro Plan food for 15 years. My dogs love it and perform well with this food. Purina supports hunters and have a special discount plan. *The Pointing Dog Journal* and *The Retriever Journal* are, in my opinion, the two best magazines for sporting dog enthusiasts. Their writers provide the latest news and tips on training and wingshooting.

Recommended Reading

- *American Game Birds of Field and Forest.* Frank C. Edminster. New York: Castle Books, 1954.
- *American Wildlife & Plants: A Guide to Wildlife Food Habits.* Alexander C. Martin, Herbert S. Zim, Arnold L. Nelson. New York: Dover Publishing, Inc., 1951.
- *Autumn Passages: A Ducks Unlimited Treasury of Waterfowling Classics.* Ducks Unlimited & Willow Creek Press, 1995. $27.50
- *Best Way to Train Your Gun Dog: The Delmar Smith Method.* Bill Tarrant. New York: David McKay Company, Inc., 1977. $20.00
- *Bill Tarrant's Gun Dog Book: A Treasury of Happy Tails.* Bill Tarrant. Honolulu: Sun Trails Publishing, 1980. A great collection of fireside dog stories. $25.00
- *Ducks, Geese & Swans of North America.* Frank C. Bellrose. Harrisburg, PA: Stackpole Books, 1976. $49.95
- *A Field Guide to Dog First Aid.* Randy Acker, D.V.M., and Jim Fergus. Bozeman, MT: Wilderness Adventures Press, 1994. An indispensible pocket guide. It could save your dog's life. $15.00
- *Fool Hen Blues: Retrievers, Shotguns, & the American West.* E. Donnall Thomas, Jr. Bozeman, MT: Wilderness Adventures Press, 1995. Don hunts sharptails, Huns, sage grouse, mountain grouse, pheasants, and waterfowl against the wild Montana sky. $29.00
- *Game Birds of North America.* Leonard Lee Rue, III. New York: Harper & Row, 1973.
- *Game Management.* Aldo Leopold. Madison, WI: University of Wisconsin Press, 1933.
- *Good Guns Again.* Steve Bodio. Bozeman, MT: Wilderness Adventures Press, 1994. A survey of fine shotguns by an avid gun collector and trader. $29.00
- *Grasslands.* Lauren Brown. New York: Alfred A. Knopf, 1985.
- *Grouse and Quails of North America.* Paul A. Johnsgard. Lincoln, NE: University of Nebraska Press, 1973.
- *Gun Dogs and Bird Guns: A Charlie Waterman Reader.* Charles F. Waterman. South Hamilton, MA: Gray's Sporting Journal Press, 1986.
- *Hey Pup, Fetch It Up: The Complete Retriever Training Book.* Bill Tarrant. Mechanicsburg, PA: Stackpole Books, 1979. $25.00
- *How to Hunt Birds with Gun Dogs.* Bill Tarrant, Mechanicsburg, PA: Stackpole Books, 1994. Bill covers all the birds, what dogs to use and how to hunt each game bird. $21.00
- *A Hunter's Road.* Jim Fergus. New York: Henry Holt and Co., 1992. A joyous journey with gun and dog across the American Uplands. A hunter's *Travels with Charlie.* $25.00
- *Hunting Upland Birds.* Charles F. Waterman. New York: Winchester Press, 1972.
- *Kicking Up Trouble.* John Holt. Bozeman, MT: Wilderness Adventures Press, 1994. John takes you on a delightful bird hunting trip through Montana. $29.00

•*Life Histories of North American Gallinaceous Birds.* Arthur Cleveland Bent. New York: Dover Publishing, Inc. 1963.

•*Meditations on Hunting.* José Ortega y Gasset. Bozeman, MT: Wilderness Adventures Press, 1995. The classic book on hunting. Special edition. $60.00

•*Peterson Field Guides: Western Birds.* Roger Tory Peterson. Boston: Houghton Mifflin, 1990.

•*Pheasants of the Mind.* Datus C. Proper. Bozeman, MT: Wilderness Adventures Press, 1994. Simply the best book ever written on pheasants. $25.00

•*Problem Gun Dogs.* Bill Tarrant. Mechanicsburg, PA: Stackpole Books, 1995. $20.00

Prairie Ducks. Lyle K. Sowls. Lincoln, NE: University of Nebraska Press, 1978.

•*A Sand County Almanac.* Aldo Leopold. New York: Oxford University Press, 1949.

•*Training the Versatile Retriever to Hunt Upland Birds.* Bill Tarrant. Bozeman, MT: Wilderness Adventures Press, 1996. $29.95

•*Waterfowl: An Identification Guide to the Ducks, Geese and Swans of the World.* Houghton Mifflin Co. $29.95

•*Waterfowling Horizons: Shooting Ducks and Geese in the 21st Century.* Christopher S. and Jason A. Smith. Wilderness Adventures Press, September 1997. $39.95

Western Forests. Stephen Whitney. New York: Alfred K. Knopf, 1985.

•Available from Wilderness Adventures

Index

E

F

G

H

N

O

P

R

NOTES

NOTES

NOTES

NOTES

NOTES

NOTES